DIGITIZING FAULKNER

DIGITIZING FAULKNER
Yoknapatawpha in the Twenty-First Century

Edited by Theresa M. Towner

University of Virginia Press • *Charlottesville and London*

University of Virginia Press
© 2022 by the Rector and Visitors of the University of Virginia
All rights reserved
Printed in the United States of America on acid-free paper

First published 2022

9 8 7 6 5 4 3 2 1

Library of Congress Cataloging-in-Publication Data

Names: Towner, Theresa M., editor.
Title: Digitizing Faulkner : Yoknapatawpha in the twenty-first century / edited by Theresa M. Towner.
Description: Charlottesville : University of Virginia Press, 2022. | Includes bibliographical references and index.
Identifiers: LCCN 2022002140 (print) | LCCN 2022002141 (ebook) | ISBN 9780813948294 (hardcover ; acid-free paper) | ISBN 9780813948300 (paperback ; acid-free paper) | ISBN 9780813948317 (ebook)
Subjects: LCSH: Faulkner, William, 1897–1962—Databases. | Digital Yoknapatawpha (Online database) | Yoknapatawpha County (Imaginary place)—Databases. | LCGFT: Essays. | Literary criticism.
Classification: LCC PS3511.A86 Z78194 2022 (print) | LCC PS3511.A86 (ebook) | DDC 813/.52—dc23/eng/20220218
LC record available at https://lccn.loc.gov/2022002140
LC ebook record available at https://lccn.loc.gov/2022002141

Cover art: Faulkner in the 1950s. (Library of Congress, Prints & Photographs Division, Carl Van Vechten Collection, LC-USZ62–117954)

This book is dedicated to
James B. Carothers
—teacher, mentor, scholar, friend—

CONTENTS

Introduction: From Yoknapatawpha to the Virtual World   1

Faulkner from 30,000 Feet: Locations, Characters, and Events in Digital Yoknapatawpha   9
JOHANNES BURGERS

Locations, Ownership, and Information Flow   34
JENNIE JOINER

"Around a Hundred and at Least Triplets": Exploring Characters in Digital Yoknapatawpha   51
CHRISTOPHER RIEGER

Events in Digital Yoknapatawpha: Making Faulkner's World Move   69
LORIE WATKINS

Visualizing Narrative Modes: The Narratological Mapping of Trauma in Faulkner's *Sanctuary*   84
BEN ROBBINS

Reading the *Portable Faulkner* through Digital Yoknapatawpha: Recovering the "Problems" and "Difficulties" of "Appendix Compson 1699–1945"   104
ERIN PENNER

Faulkner's Human Hive: Complex Systems in *The Hamlet*   125
JOHN MICHAEL CORRIGAN

Digital *Yaakni Patafa*: Plotting Indigenous Space and Race   151
MELANIE BENSON TAYLOR

Digital Yoknapatawpha: Pedagogical Practices and the Politics of Digital Humanities in the Twenty-First-Century Classroom   171
REN DENTON

Work in Progress 193
STEPHEN RAILTON

Notes on Contributors 213

Index 217

DIGITIZING FAULKNER

INTRODUCTION
From Yoknapatawpha to the Virtual World

IN A LATER part of William Faulkner's novel *The Town*, Gavin Stevens observes Yoknapatawpha County from the vantage point of "a mild unhurried farm road presently mounting to cross the ridge and on to join the main highway leading from Jefferson to the world. And now, looking back and down, you see all Yoknapatawpha in the dying last of the day beneath you":

> First is Jefferson, the center, radiating weakly its puny glow into space; beyond it, enclosing it, spreads the County, tied by the diverging roads to that center as is the rim to the hub by its spokes. . . . the rich alluvial river-bottom land of old Issetibbeha, the wild Chickasaw king with his Negro slaves and his sister's son called Doom who murdered his way to the throne . . . the same fat black rich plantation earth still synonymous of the proud fading white plantation names . . . Sutpen and Sartoris and Compson and Edmonds and McCaslin and Beauchamp and Grenier and Habersham and Holston and Stevens and De Spain. . . . Then the roadless, almost pathless perpendicular hill country of McCallum and Gowrie and Frazier and Muir . . . then and last on to where Frenchman's Bend lay beyond the south-eastern horizon, cradle of Varners and antheap for the north-east crawl of Snopes. (330, 331–32)

For over eighty years, Faulkner criticism has attempted to "see all Yoknapatawpha," in one way or another. One of the most ambitious of these is the ongoing Digital Yoknapatawpha (DY), housed at the University of Virginia and supported by grants from the National Endowment for the Humanities. The present volume is a collection of essays inspired by the contributors' involvement with that project. DY is encoding the texts set in Faulkner's mythical county into a complex database with sophisticated front-end visualizations in order to see what the nascent field of digital humanities can show us about that world and the people who inhabit it; it is a twenty-first-century research tool brought to bear upon not only twentieth- but also nineteenth-century sensibilities, ideologies, behaviors, and material cultures. These essays from the editors who have now spent extensive time and energy thinking about how to bring Faulkner and the digital world together contribute to scholarship by asking the corollary questions of how (or even whether) such efforts modify our understanding of Faulkner's texts.

The volume begins with four essays that derive from the four basic components that make up DY: visualizations, locations, characters, and events. Johannes Burgers opens the collection; his work "contends that DY's approach to encoding common narrative entities like locations, characters, and events is portable, scalable, and reproduceable for other digital interventions." He provides compelling explanations of how the visualizations in DY work and what kinds of things they show, and he offers commentary on how "consolidating the data and projecting it back onto Faulkner's own map provides provocative insight into how Faulkner viewed the demography of his county." He concludes that "the character distributions across time and space throw into question the traditional teleology of Faulkner's career as of one linear development. Instead, it may be more productive to think of Faulkner's interests with Yoknapatawpha as concurrent, multifarious, and conceived through different spatial contexts." Jennie Joiner then turns our attention to locations in DY, beginning with an insight into Faulkner's own cartographic efforts: "Faulkner's map is surprisingly devoid of icons of any sort. Instead, he relies on words, short snippets of text that tell us what happens in the space rather than anything about the location itself, other than where it is located geographically." In this way, we may begin thinking about Faulkner's proprietorship in the legend of his *Absalom, Absalom!* map as ownership of information flow—a commercial enterprise that, for readers of the map to access or understand, they must read his other novels: "His map thus becomes an amalgamation of *his* understanding of Yoknapatawpha and the stories and novels he had written to that point in his career." She argues, "Ownership as a thematic concept runs throughout Faulkner's Yoknapatawpha fiction. Ownership for some characters reflects independence; for others, a choice to assume responsibility. Faulkner, in laying his claim of ownership to Yoknapatawpha, clearly communicates both." Christopher Rieger takes up the many, many characters who inhabit Faulkner's pages and our project: "Because many characters appear in multiple works, the DY database can provide insights into a single character as he or she changes and develops across Faulkner's fictional universe." He notes several of the ways that DY notes and explains inconsistencies among Faulkner's fictions, like Burgers concluding that "DY allows these inconsistencies and evolutions to be captured, whereas in the print guides of the past, definitive and sometimes contradictory choices were made; for example, Volpe includes Elnora in the Sartoris family tree, but Brooks does not. The DY genealogy allows you to see both versions almost instantaneously. This lack of limitation, in fact, is perhaps the chief advantage that a database like DY has over printed volumes." Lorie Watkins's essay on how DY represents events begins with the observation, "All readers of William Faulkner have experienced at least one moment (and probably many more) when they suddenly realize that they have absolutely no idea what just happened in a text." Consequently, she explains, "by entering textual events into the database, scholars contributing to the project seek to outline what actually happens in a text. Those of us teaching Faulkner and working on the database realize that readers and students are going to seek help somewhere, and we want them to turn to Digital Yoknapatawpha for that guidance. That said, we are very committed to making the site a supplement to the text, not a replacement for it"—a principle articulated by many of these contributors.

The next three essays explore theoretical and thematic implications of our mapping efforts by looking at specific texts. Ben Robbins points to a particular feature of DY and its usefulness in examining *Sanctuary*: "DY's MapIt feature allows users to plot the different events in a given text according to their narrative status under five categories: narrated, told, remembered, hypothesized, and narrated-plus-consciousness." "Using Faulkner's 1931 novel *Sanctuary* as a case study, a novel that contains each of the five 'narrative statuses' under which we categorize events," he shows "how the MapIt function reveals the relationship between authorial choice of narrative mode and the representation of a traumatized consciousness." He uses "a close reading of *Sanctuary*'s events" to "demonstrate how tropes of the traumatized narrative structure Temple's memory, consciousness, and discourse through omission, indirection, and repetition. Additionally, the DY maps show how these patterns are manifested in the text's overall spatial and temporal organization." He concludes that DY "speculatively visualizes modernist narratives, offering new insights into the spatial and temporal boundaries of narrative modes." Erin Penner turns her attention to the production as well as the content of the infrequently studied "Appendix Compson 1699–1945," beginning with Malcolm Cowley's role as editor of the *Portable Faulkner*. In details as small as production correspondence, "his repeated failure to recall Faulkner's preference—much less the author's exact wording—exposes the cost of his desire to unify and therefore simplify Faulkner's Yoknapatawpha County for the *Portable Faulkner*." DY can serve as a corrective to that impulse, she explains: "Consistency is, of course, what Cowley asked of Faulkner, but DY equips users to call consistency into question. Rather than follow Cowley's lead in assembling a 'whole' from Faulkner's work that could be extended to the South more generally, DY invites Faulkner readers to identify precise relationships among his fictions. The digital project offers a third way: not Cowley's insistence that discrepancies be resolved, nor Faulkner's refusal to return to earlier work to integrate the worlds he has created. Instead, the data of DY is grounded in particular texts, but it also facilitates comparisons across Faulkner's body of work." Drawing our attention to an overlooked character in this overlooked text, Penner finds that "Faulkner's insistence on the crowd of bodies, and the influence of such bodies on [Melissa] Meek's story, is a reminder of the many bodies needed to account for the Yoknapatawpha he created. In a character catalog like the one the 'Appendix' purports to be, or a map of land that is carved up into plantations, these figures would recede from view. But DY's insistence on accounting for all those drawn by Faulkner enables readers to see that background movement and the press of bodies." John Michael Corrigan takes a model from computer science in order to analyze the complex social systems in *The Hamlet*. After explaining the model, he notes, "If one employs these characteristics in an analysis of Faulkner's representation of Yoknapatawpha, it becomes clear that the writer's fictional world is not just complex in the general literary usage of the term, including such features as multiple levels of meaning, nonlinear structure, and intertextuality. Faulkner also presents Frenchman's Bend as a dynamic network of social space in which distributed patterns of human movement spontaneously produce emergent and adaptive behavior." He then takes up close readings of key scenes in the novel, ending with "what is perhaps Faulkner's most complicated narrative sequence, the horse auction, in which systems complexity involves the simultaneous emergence of hierarchy and its destabilization in the chaotic, but still coherent, pattern of the social body of Frenchman's Bend." In this context, "Digital Yoknapatawpha immediately presents its users with such a network visualization of Faulkner's narratives, permitting the user to see the broader contours of Faulkner's county with its interlinking networks—families, farms, plantations, hamlets, and towns—as they dynamically form complex assemblages of modernity."

Taking us to even less-explored critical territory, Melanie Benson Taylor analyzes the roles of Native Americans in Faulkner's texts, focusing on how mapping those texts reveals Faulkner's evolving imagination of the people who first inhabited his county. She begins with a caveat regarding some of the limits of DY: "The goals of the Digital Yoknapatawpha Project seem to contradict nearly every tenet of indigenous wisdom and practice." "And yet," she continues, "while all of these choices may prompt conceptual and ethical challenges for scholars of indigenous cultures, they may nonetheless have uncanny and compelling pertinence for Faulkner's post-plantation, U.S. southern context in particular. DY is, in fact, uniquely poised to force uncomfortable but necessary conversations about the complexities of indigenous identity as *both* a phenomenon inextricable (if extirpated) from land and territory *and* a racial conceit spawned by the very settlement of that land—twin disgraces elided permanently in the American narrative, which Faulkner captured with unmatched nuance and horror." She concludes with the provocative suggestion that "perhaps the most compelling way to conceive of Faulkner's Indians, ultimately, is in the form of a meticulously presenced absence—a potent paradox that captures, in all its contortions, the ambivalence, repression, and horror of a region structured on concentric removals and appropriations. The power of DY is its capacity to lay bare these patterns."

The final two essays in this volume take up DY's roles in pedagogy and classroom practice. Beginning from the premise that "pedagogy is political," Ren Denton "examines DY's functioning within institutions where there is increasing public pressure to shift from foundational knowledge pedagogies to pedagogies that induce activity-centered learning. . . . DY's resources offer pedagogical versatility that blends both." She offers practical examples from her own experience as well as theoretical models for thinking about teaching. Discussing *Absalom, Absalom!* (always a tough sell in the classroom), she notes, "When students visually see [Sutpen's] store as a shared space, the activities that take place in that shared space take on numerous metaphors ready for exploration and interpretation. Through careful analysis of the text and DY visual cues, students are guided into a research area that builds a solid foundation on which to build an interdisciplinary knowledge of sociology, psychology, and Faulkner's literary representations of America's darker secrets associated with the plantation's model of economics that continues to govern our brand of capitalism." She ends with an encouraging observation: "As I intentionally focused my students' concentration on specific themes, I witnessed how Digital Yoknapatawpha provides students opportunities to examine physical spaces while making abstract ideas more accessible."

As the creator and director of Digital Yoknapatawpha, Stephen Railton has the final word in this volume. Noting that "one of the best and worst things about any digital project is that there's no place in virtual reality to write 'The End,'" Railton explains his own involvement in the digital humanities since the days of the Apple II: "Part of my original attraction to DH . . . was the opportunity it offered to connect with a larger audience than I'd been able to reach in my published work as a scholar—the 'world wide' part of 'www' is very seductive—but at the start I was mainly thinking about the students in my own classrooms." He offers a telling example of one among many things that DY can do: "Our maps include timelines that display the narratives in time as well as space. As part of a text's animation sequence, this added temporal dimension reveals one of Faulkner's most characteristic artistic signatures, the way his stories so often move backward as well as forward, continually returning to the 'past'—earlier events in the characters' lives or the region's history. Such repeated temporal recursions are a very effective way to dramatize how the present is saturated by the past, how as Faulkner memorably puts it, 'The past is never dead.'" Not only that, "It is not really about 'the past,' but rather about its presence." To conclude, he articulates the great hope that inspires all of our work on this project and in this book: "For me, however, DH is always a means rather than an end; books remain the destination." "Beyond just grabbing our students' attention, it might be a way to engage their curiosity and intelligence. It might be a way to lead them back to the experience of reading, with an enhanced ability to explore and appreciate what they will find when they open the books we believe in as fundamental parts of their education and our evolving culture."

Producing a volume of essays originating in our digital work is one way we hope to bring traditional scholarship into dialogue with emerging fields in digital humanities—and to do so for professional scholars, teachers, and general readers alike. Many from such audiences have attended our annual sessions about Digital Yoknapatawpha during the University of Mississippi's Faulkner conference and expressed great interest and enthusiasm for the whole undertaking, and our presentations at scholarly conferences in the United States and abroad have met with similar responses. In describing our work, we are always careful to point out that DY is not a substitute for reading Faulkner's work; nor is it a sort of high-tech CliffsNotes. We intend for readers to supplement their reading of Faulkner, to dig deeper into their own thinking about how texts make meaning, and we hope that readers of our essays in this volume will see new possibilities for acquiring knowledge. Each of the contributors has found new ways of seeing Yoknapatawpha by virtue of looking digitally, and now that all of the Yoknapatawpha fictions have been entered into the database, we would like to share with our readers what we are still learning about Faulkner's county. It is an honor to acknowledge the crucial contributions of the project's technologists—especially Worthy Martin, Robbie Bingler, and the rest of the staff of the Institute for Advanced Technology in the Humanities at the University of Virginia, and Rafael Alvarado, now at Virginia's Data Science Institute; the other individuals and centers credited in Railton's essay; and the collaborators whose names appear in the DY Credits. They have not only given this digital project life in the world; they have brought new life to Faulkner's Yoknapatawpha.

Work Cited

Faulkner, William. *The Town*. 1957. Vintage International, 2011.

Faulkner from 30,000 Feet

LOCATIONS, CHARACTERS, AND EVENTS IN
DIGITAL YOKNAPATAWPHA

Johannes Burgers

With over 250,000 data points distributed across roughly 2,000 locations, 5,000 characters, and over 8,000 events, Digital Yoknapatawpha (DY) represents one of the most comprehensive and robust databases available for any single author's corpus.[1] Compared to "Big Data," though, DY is tiny and about the size of a set of student records at a small college. The data is therefore simultaneously big by humanities standards, and small by data science standards. What the data lacks in scale, however, it makes up for in precision. Generated by more than thirty different scholars over many years, the data was systematically and rigorously acquired. There is now more empirical knowledge about Faulkner and Yoknapatawpha than there was before, but the full implications of this knowledge and what it means remain to be seen. This essay provides a broad overview of the data and, informed by insights from the fields of literary cartography and narratology, delimits what this data can and cannot tell scholars about Faulkner's mythical county. As such, it functions as a kind of data-side introduction to the more scoped analyses that compose this volume.

Yet rather than provide reams of statistics, which is neither interesting nor useful, here the data is leveraged to paint a demographic picture of Faulkner's Yoknapatawpha fiction. From this portrait, we can draw three related conclusions. First, somewhat unsurprisingly, the Yoknapatawpha fictions predominantly focus on the lives of upper-class white males. Second, by using techniques common in ecology, it is possible to show that there are several separate and unequal social groups. Third, mapping social spaces reveals that the likelihood of interactions between races increases when characters move farther away from the town of Jefferson and the hamlet of Frenchman's Bend.

Beyond providing an overview of what is possible with the DY data, this essay also stakes out a larger claim for DY in the field of digital humanities. In particular, it contends that DY's approach to encoding common narrative entities like locations, characters, and events is portable, scalable, and reproduceable for other digital interventions. While it is tempting to suggest that the robust and flexible data model was a consequence of prescient theoretical forethought, it has more often been the result of a team of very dedicated scholars trying to thread some of the most complex works of the twentieth century through the very unforgiving eye of a twenty-first-century digital needle. Naturally, the DY team encountered exceptions to the classification schema throughout the encoding process. While it is not productive to detail all of these, it is instructive to highlight some of the more significant edge cases that necessitated revisions to the data model and, consequently, required updating many, many individual records. This iterative revision process has allowed the database to evolve as an extension of Faulkner's work, rather than an external imposition on it. Though Faulknerian in origin, these lessons and standards for data creation are also useful for other digital projects because they strike a productive balance between ease of implementation and iterability on the back end, and multidimensional scholarship on the front end.

While the data-encoding process is highlighted in other parts of this volume, a short overview is helpful for understanding some of the more advanced data manipulations later in this essay. The data was created by populating three different tables: locations, characters, and events. Primarily, locations are places inside or outside Yoknapatawpha where events occur, and, secondarily, locations are also places that play a significant role in the narrative even if no action occurs there. Characters are those human entities that are either present or mentioned at locations. An event is a textual unit that demarcates one continuous action by one or more characters at one location for a discrete period of time. The three tables are keyed to each other in a relational database that enables the data to be viewed from the perspective of locations, characters, events, a combination of the three, or all three simultaneously, as with the main interface. Their full power lies not so much in the individual tables, but in the complex queries that are possible between and among them. There are about fifty different variables spread across three tables, and there are 2^{50}, or roughly 1 quadrillion, ways to combine this data. This is a very large number, though data size should not be confused with utility (Lane 111). For the foreseeable future, the many ways in which the data can be represented, recombined, and recontextualized will not be exhausted. This does not mean that all representations are equally faithful to the data. Any visualization or query necessarily needs to be limited by an understanding of the data creation process in the locations, characters, and events tables.

In theory, the data entry for the tables is a sequential process; in reality this is far messier, and editors often find themselves updating and revising all three tables simultaneously. Still, for simplicity's sake it is useful to treat them one by one. To best understand the underlying data for the demographic overview that closes this essay, it is most logical to proceed from events and then move onto locations and characters. The data in events divides the corpus into meaningful textual units. These provide a measure of prominence of locations and characters through their frequency distributions. Locations, in turn, provide the contours of Yoknapatawpha's different population centers by virtue of their relative density on the map. Finally, characters pass and repass through different population centers throughout the course of the text, and the data available makes it possible to provide an overview of what kinds of characters appear in what areas.

Events

Events create connections between characters and between characters and locations, and can only be entered once all of the characters and locations have been established. Conceptually, events are a more meaningful way to divide the corpus into smaller units of narrative than an arbitrary measure such as chapter, page, or paragraph number. The idea of dividing a narrative into smaller units is not new, and there is still an active debate between narratologists as to what constitutes a narrative event (for an excellent overview, see Baroni and Revaz), or whether such a division is even possible (Phelan 4). In order to make sure events are consistently defined across the databases, the editors went through a strict norming process and relentless peer-review. Despite these efforts, it would be a mistake to assume that all events are equal measures of the same phenomenon. In part this is due to the nature of collaboration and the sheer complexity of Faulkner's fiction, but it is also intrinsic to decomposing a narrative more generally.

While some of this is will be discussed later in this volume, possible variance in event boundaries can have a distorting effect on corpus-wide overviews. For example, demographic analysis relies on inferences based on frequency patterns in the events, but it is impossible to calculate how the variance between events might weight individual counts. Put more simply, it is the same effect as measuring a room using paces. This method provides a good overview, but is not detailed enough to build a house.

One way event boundaries are inconsistent is in their measure of discourse time—the time it takes to read the passage (Chatman 62). For various reasons, this project used the Vintage paperback editions of the texts and delimited events by page number and order on the page. Since the different texts have different word counts per page, an event that is two pages long in one text might only equal one page in another. A more complex problem occurs when multiple events are on the same page. In such cases, the length of the events is not known. In the event sequence 10.1—10.4, for example, it does not necessarily follow that 10.1 is one quarter of the length of 10.2 or 10.4. It could very well be that event 10.1 is only a couple of words long, and event 10.4 is most of the page. This problem is compounded when a text has a large number of short events. For example, in *The Sound and the Fury*, Quentin is one of the most present characters in the text based on the event count, but this is only because during his perambulations across Boston, he is continuously slipping in and out of memories, each of which is counted as a separate action. The only way to accurately measure how long Quentin or any other character is actually present on the page throughout as text is by using word count. The data has been structured so that events can be linked to word count in the future.

Relatedly, events also do not consistently measure story-time, or the duration of the event in the narrative (Chatman 62). An event might recall something over the course of several years and only take up part of a page, while an event spanning several pages might center on a fleeting experience or emotion. Editors do enter probable dates for each event, but these are usually given as a range for when an event occurred, because quite often the exact date is unknown. Not knowing the duration of an event in story-time distorts the perception of how integral a character may be to the overall arc of the text. For example, in *The Sound and the Fury,* Quentin and the unnamed Italian girl, with whom he walks for part of his fateful day, occur together in twenty-three events. Meanwhile, he and other major characters appear together less frequently—Benjy in twenty-two, Jason fourteen, and Dilsey seven. Obviously, though, Quentin has spent more time with those characters than he has with the Italian girl.

Finally, there is no way to measure how central a character is to an event. The data simply is not that granular, and likely never will be. Characters may be present at an event, but may not meaningfully contribute to the plot. For example, the "men of Frenchman's Bend" in *The Hamlet* are present in a little under 17 percent of all events, but they only provide side commentary. They are not, in any traditional sense, major characters. Complicating matters even further is that being present or absent at an event does not necessarily measure how important a character is to the overall plot. For instance, in *Go Down, Moses,* Lucius Quintus Carothers McCaslin is long dead and therefore never present in any of the events, yet he is mentioned frequently because his legacy is extremely consequential to the narrative.

These different qualifications all complicate the insights provided by a frequency distribution. It could be that one character, *A*, appears in two multi-page events in one text, while another character, *B*, appears in four events across four texts each less than a page long. There is no way to measure which of the two characters is present for a longer period of time, plays a more active role, or makes a more significant contribution to the history of Yoknapatawpha. In short, character *B* will be counted more often than character *A*, and, thereby, will be given more importance, even if he or she is relatively inconsequential from the perspective of the reader. Arguably, since demographic overviews are done at scale and individual characters are grouped by their attributes, the discrepancies between events might even out in the long run, but beyond wishful thinking, there is no compelling reason to believe this. Frequency counts are therefore at best suggestive of patterns and relative distributions.

This extensive list of limits of what is knowable through events should not overshadow the tremendous accomplishment they represent. A corpus of nearly six thousand pages has been systematically and intelligently split across 8,000 text-units that in turn contain characters and locations. Not only do events contain the text order, they also store, with a high degree of accuracy, the chronological order and narrative style, and, with less certainty, where the event fits in the broader Yoknapatawpha timeline. Thus, while events are at best a blunt instrument for measuring character and location distributions, the counts paint a compelling if incomplete picture of the demographics of Yoknapatawpha.

Locations

Narratives, by their very nature, have a spatial component (Bodenhamer, "Narrating Space and Place" 13). Literary cartography attempts to represent spatial relationships in narrative, and in this endeavor has profited from the rise of widely available geographic information systems (GIS) and the emergence of digital humanities methodologies (Piatti 89). At the heart of this field resides a central contradiction: A significant share of fiction cannot be mapped by traditional cartographic means. This is not a technological limitation but a fundamentally linguistic one. Textual descriptions of places represent a host of complications for geographers, even when the description is of a known place in the real world (Brindley 2–3; Guo 1073–80; Vasardani 2525–27). Nevertheless, when fictional texts give an account of a place in the real world, these can still be rendered, but doing so requires significant intervention (Reuschel and Hurni 294–95). Accordingly, some of the most rewarding literary spatial projects are those where georeferencing is an option, either because it treats known places like London (Evans and Wilkins) or known topographies like the Lake District (Murrieta-Flores). Of course, not all fictional spaces have a real-world analog. For readers and narrative scholars alike, such worlds are not inherently problematic (Ryan 25); but for literary cartographers, fictional worlds consisting of "fuzzy evidence, conceptual space, and relative time" present a significant conceptual problem for traditional mapping methods (Bodenhamer, "Making the Invisible Visible" 212). Without real-world referents that anchor the text to a specific time and place, all points on a map are situated around an arbitrary center. Faulkner has met readers and the DY editors halfway by creating maps of his fictions that provide the position, orientation, and relative distance for some key stories. He created the first map in 1936 and included it with *Absalom, Absalom!* and then provided a second map with the *Portable Faulkner* in 1945.[2] These maps have served as a baseline for organizing space and time in Yoknapatawpha.

As Jennie Joiner's essay in this volume documents, the locations devil is in the Faulknerian details, or the lack thereof. Because events happen "somewhere," the map needs to be saturated with as many locations as possible so as to show meaningful differentiation between events. Of the locations in the database, only 11 percent appear on Faulkner's own maps.[3] Therefore, not entering anything outside of these knowable locations would still leave roughly 89 percent of all locations "unknown," a category that does not offer a lot of spatial insight. This is why the majority of locations are placed on the map by virtue of what the text says (29 percent) and contextual clues (45 percent). When the evidence is scant, other texts are relied upon (1 percent), and, failing that, locations are determined through speculation (14 percent). Whether this amount of speculation is low or high compared to other authors is hard to determine, even if it appears that Faulkner is fairly generous when providing distance and direction for locations. For instance, readers are informed of "Miss Joanna Burden's mailbox one mile west of the courthouse" (206) in *The Town*; and in *Go Down, Moses*, there is a logging camp "[t]hirteen miles below" De Spain's hunting camp (224). At other times, Faulkner is less clear with direction and distance. Hoke McCarron has a showdown with Eula's suitors at a "creek ford a half mile away" (*Hamlet* 146) from Varner's house in no particular direction, and there is a "weed-choked roadside ditch" just "down the drive" from the De Spain mansion in "Barn Burning" (24), but the length of the drive is never indicated. This ambiguity is to be expected, but what is unexpected is how consistent Faulkner can be with distances given the vast size of his corpus. True, Faulkner's maps are not to scale in any cartographer's sense, but he maintained many of the same distance ratios of his native Lafayette (Railton and Rieger).

In practical terms, all of these qualifications mean that the positions of locations and the distances between them are imprecise both within and among stories. It is even the case that across a number of stories, the same location is placed in a different position (Railton and Rieger). The inconsistencies between locations are not problematic when viewing texts individually, but they become a challenge when trying to create a consolidated map of all the locations. After all, prioritizing the position of one location over another suggests that the location is somehow more correct, as opposed to just one of several options. Furthermore, the shifting positions of different locations across the long span of Faulkner's career also speaks to his evolving vision, and by consolidating the locations onto one map, part of the vibrancy and indeterminacy of the corpus is lost. By and large, though, when all the locations across the entire corpus of fifty-four short stories and fourteen novels are projected onto the same map (fig. 1), the fluctuations in the locations of places are bounded by the imaginary limits of Yoknapatawpha's geography. The map demonstrates that places are consistently clustered within seven distinct areas in the county: the McCaslin plantation (northeast); Ikkemotubbe's land (north); Sutpen's Hundred and the Big Bottom (northwest); Sartoris and De Spain just north of town; Jefferson proper (center); the Compson place just southeast of town; and Frenchman's Bend in the southeast hill country.[4] There are virtually no events or locations in the southwest of the county. One final location of note is Memphis, where a significant share of events takes place.

Along with position, locations also have thematic attributes that can be used as proxies for features like social organization and narrative perspective. In this regard, the frequency of events at particular types of locations gives an indication as to what kinds of places receive more attention in the corpus. Out of the roughly 8,000 events, a significant number (602) take place at Courthouse Square, the beating heart of Jefferson. The next most-frequent location is the Sartoris plantation, which sees 354 events.[5] Numbers three and five on the list are two prominent locations from the Snopes trilogy, the law office of the Stevens family (191) and the Mallisons' House (149), with the Sutpen planation being the fourth most frequent. Since many of the events take place at the residences of major upper-class families, it is no surprise that mansions (1,083) are the most frequent type of site of an event. Meanwhile, events in domestic spaces (43 percent) are slightly less frequent than those in public spaces (46 percent). The remaining 11 percent take place in what can best be described as liminal spaces, which are neither strictly domestic nor public, such as prisons and brothels, or places outside of Yoknapatawpha whose type is not clear.[6]

Using location type as an indicator of narrative perspective suggests that many events occur in the homes of the wealthy and in public spaces, both of which privilege white men in the pre–Civil Rights South. There is room in Faulkner's fiction for African American, lower-class, and/or rural characters, but their homes are explored less. Cabins, mostly occupied by African Americans, see only one-third (369) of the events of mansions, as do farms (307) whose owners or sharecroppers are of a lower

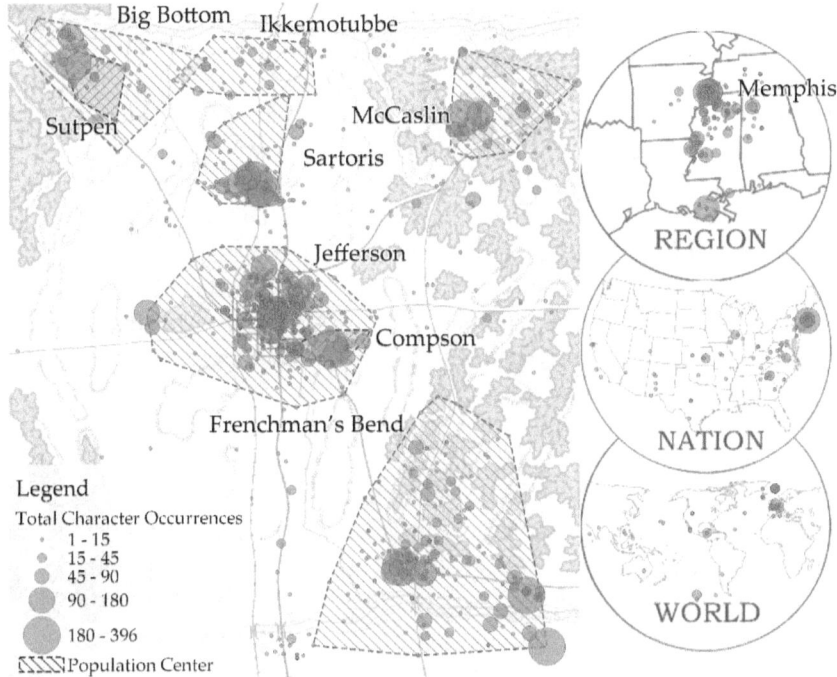

FIG. 1. Character frequency by locations. (Digital Yoknapatawpha at the University of Virginia)

social standing compared to the plantation families. Although suggestive of privileging the experiences of wealthy white men, the data does not reveal whether this location is portrayed positively or negatively. A case in point, Sutpen's place is a touchstone for many events throughout the Yoknapatawpha fictions, but his household is hardly portrayed as a model of virtue.

As fine-grained as the locational divisions are, one type of spatial organization is both missing from the database and unnamed in the fiction: racial segregation. Though race is a predominant theme in Faulkner, the color line is very rarely demarcated in the locations he describes. On only a few occasions are segregated spaces named, as when Horace Benbow peers into a "jim crow car" on the train in *Sanctuary* (168). This does not mean they do not exist. There are numerous examples of nonwhites who are seen as "intruding" into white spaces. After the lynching of Will

Mayes, one of Minnie Cooper's friends reassures her, "There's not a Negro on the square. Not one" ("Dry September" 181). The scene reveals how acts of brutal violence, like lynching, were a means of white social and spatial control. Segregation is all the more dehumanizing because there is no separation of space, as all space is functionally white. Part of segregation's effect on spatial organization is evidenced in the naming of nonwhite spaces, which are racialized explicitly, most notably "Nigger Hollow" in *The Sound and the Fury* (302). White space is so prevalent in the text that a full 699 (33 percent) locations have events where only white people are present. Only 21 (or 1 percent) are exclusive to African Americans and only 5 places (or 0.2 percent) are exclusive to Native Americans. Space for nonwhites in Yoknapatawpha is exceedingly rare. Another way to look at it, though, is that the majority of spaces (65 percent) are not exclusive to one race or another. One of the real limits of the data is that there is no basis for comparison with another author. It would be interesting, for example, to see if space is equally segregated in the work of other contemporary southern authors. Regardless, it is clear that locations in Faulkner are unevenly distributed across his map and receive different levels of attention.

Characters

Narrative theory offers a complex classification system for thinking through what constitutes a character in fiction (Jannidis 16–19). The encoding system used in DY does not take all of these permutations into account, but its more limited scope makes character entry easy, consistent, and scalable. If a character is present or mentioned at an event, he or she is entered into the character table. Since events slice the entire text into smaller textual units, there is no character who could exist outside of an event. Moreover, following other narrative scholars, DY treats all characters as ontologically independent entities, individuated by the explicit or implicit information the text provides (Lamarque 200–201; Margolin 405–9; Reicher 132; Ryan 34–35).[7] Stated more simply, if a character is described as an "unnamed farmer," it is assumed that he or she is a full-fledged person with a race, class, gender, and certain social standing, even if these are unknown. On the surface, this methodology appears straightforward, but there are still significant issues with regard to character countability, attributes, and, on a more fundamental level, ontology.

One of the biggest impediments to entering "all" of the characters who appear in the text is countability. For instance, in *Flags in the Dust*, the narrator describes how the good-natured country doctor Lucius Peabody never kept track of his patients' bills, and "from time to time a countryman enters his shabby office and discharges an obligation, commemorating sometimes the payor's entry into the world, incurred by his father or grandfather" (95). Strictly speaking, the countrymen, their fathers, and their grandfathers are all humans who exist in this fictional world. Even though they are individuated, each is part of a series of individuals, and there is, consequently, no way to establish their number. In similar fashion, designations like "couple," "crowd," "mob," and "Town of Jefferson" are all identifying groups of characters, each with a different order of magnitude, but establishing exact quantities for any of them is impossible. These are therefore identified as "groups," without any indication of their possible size. In this sense, DY does not count "all" the characters, because there is no way to individuate them. Grouped characters also raise a more philosophical question as to whether these are distinct entities or should be seen as part of the setting, especially if these characters do not play a role in a particular event (Lamarque 189).

Once a character or a group of characters has been identified, they have to be meaningfully and consistently described to individuate them from other characters. In the DY database, all characters have up to twenty-five different attributes associated with them, including but not limited to race, class, gender, and role in the narrative. While all of these attributes present interpretive challenges, the most contentious decisions have been those regarding the race and class of a character. As an editorial policy, the race and class of Faulkner's characters have been encoded from the perspective of his fictional world, and in a manner consistent with the social relationships of the early twentieth-century South. Consequently, many of the character descriptions do not comport with contemporary thoughts on race and ethnicity. For example, the race and class designations "Poor White," "Free Black," and "MixedWhiteBlack" are dated and perhaps offensive to twenty-first-century sensibilities, but they are commonplace in Yoknapatawpha. To be sure, Faulkner complicates and subverts many of the accepted beliefs about race, class, and gender, but this always happens within a context in which there are strict legal and social boundaries between different groups of people.

Determining class is rather less fraught. Faulkner's Yoknapatawpha is a highly hierarchical society, and the upper classes distinguish themselves from the other classes through various contextual clues such as family name, honorifics, and whether they have paid or enslaved laborers working for them. The differences between middle class, lower class, and poor white are less distinct, but usually inferred through a character's profession, which Faulkner mentions with some regularity. Still, the distinctions are not always cut and dried, because a character's class can change. Flem Snopes starts out his journey as a "Poor White" sharecropper, but ultimately becomes the president of the bank, a decidedly upper-class profession. Even though the DY encoding process captures the change in class across Faulkner's corpus, it cannot capture either the subtleties of Flem's slow climb on the economic ladder or whether the community will ever view him as anything other than "Poor White."

One valid objection to qualifying characters with certain race, class, gender, and other attributes is that it assumes that these are both necessary properties for a character to exist in a text, and, by extension, inherent qualities of a person. Some scholars, such as Roland Barthes, have argued that characters are purely textual entities and do not have an ontology outside of how they are being used as linguistic placeholders in a text; their race or class only becomes relevant when the text makes it relevant (67). Meanwhile, race, as a social construct, is not an inherent quality that a character or, to be clear, a person has, and as Toni Morrison so cleverly shows in "Recitatif," racial identity can be unwittingly projected onto characters by the reader through acculturated semiotic codes. Therefore, the DY editors run the risk of projecting their own preconceptions onto the text when they determine a character's race. While these are important and valid objections, Faulkner's Jim Crow social world would be inscrutable if characters were not seen as independent entities who embody a specific racial subject position. For example, a group of "unnamed jurors" in "Smoke" can only ever be white men, because at the time only white men served on juries (*KG* 19). What's more, Faulkner, with some consistency, marks his nonwhite characters with racialized designations like "negro driver" (*S* 306), "negro nursemaid" (*LIA* 59), "negro stevedores" (*AA* 167), in a similar fashion as he does his locations. In Faulkner, whiteness is the conspicuous absence of race (Watson viii–xi). White characters are very rarely identified by their race, and when their whiteness does become an issue, it is almost always in conjunction with their purported supremacy, as when Lucas Burch is questioned by the police and he denounces them, yelling, "Accuse the white man and let the nigger go free" (*LIA* 97).

Be that as it may, with any controlled vocabulary there will be exceptions. Sometimes a character's class is indeterminable because the text does not provide enough information. In a slightly different way, a character's race is "indeterminable" when the text makes the unknowability of a character's race a concern, as in the case of Joe Christmas. Other ambiguities that fall outside of the classification system are characters who are "not quite white," like the Jewish barnstormers in "Death Drag," or characters who engage in racial self-fashioning as, for example, Boon Hogganbeck does when he alternately affirms and denies (depending on his blood alcohol level) that he has Native American blood (*Reivers* 18). These cases are far and few between, however; and the race, class, gender, and other salient features of most characters is determined with a high degree of certainty.

These considerations notwithstanding, the statistical picture of Yoknapatawpha inhabitants mirrors the class, race, and gender divisions apparent in the locations. This is a corpus where the center of gravity is white, upper-class, and male. On the maps Faulkner drew, he indicated that his county was inhabited by "6298 Whites" and "9313 Negroes," a split of 40 percent to 60 percent respectively (Railton and Rieger). In contradiction to this claim, the data reveals that 77 percent of the characters in the fiction are white. What's more, when filtering out only major characters and counting how often they actually appear in events, whites are even more present, accounting for 85 percent of the characters in all of the events. The other types of characters in events are split among nine different groups, the largest share of which are African Americans (7 percent). Truly remarkable, though, is that nearly 96 percent of all events have at least one white character present. Narrative stretches with only non-white characters are exceedingly rare. A similar pattern emerges with gender and class. Men make up 81 percent of the characters present at events, and the upper-class men and women appear most often (51 percent). Characters who are not white, male, or upper-class are less represented in the corpus.

A more granular way to look at social organization is through a technique common in ecology called co-occurrence analysis. Co-occurrence and its close cousin, abundance analysis, measure the appearance of different species at different sites over a period of time. In a co-occurrence matrix, the incidence is measured as a simple binary present/absent, while in an abundance matrix the total number of species present at a site is measured. Based on this data, quantitative ecologists determine what the "rules of assembly" are for a particular ecosystem (Veech 252). That is, if species x occurs, is it more likely or less likely that species y occurs? While it would be a relatively simple procedure to tally the different co-occurrences in the corpus, this is mathematically unsatisfactory. As there are more upper-class white men in the corpus than any other character type, they are inherently more likely to co-occur with all other character types. To provide an accurate picture of which character interactions are patterned and which are random, any probabilistic model (used to arrive at the overall probability of co-occurrence) will need to account for the relative distributions of characters among the populations. Similarly, raw co-occurrence tallies do not establish negative interactions between characters; if one species occurs—say, a predator—what is the likelihood that another species—its prey—does *not* occur? Although the math for this is complex, Joseph Veech has created a highly predictive combinatorics model and, with the help of others, created a package for the statistical programming language R (Griffith).

Without going into too much technical detail, the DY corpus was primed to use the "co-occur" package, and characters were turned into "species" by concatenating—linking together in a series—all of their attributes. For instance, a white, lower-class female becomes White.LowerClass.Female as a character type or "species." The resulting concatenations lead to nearly 40 different possible combinations, which, in turn, can co-occur with each other in over 600 ways. Due to the large number of possible combinations, many of the character types never co-occur and even fewer co-occur positively. Table 1 shows the top 95 percent percentile of all positive co-occurrences that have less than a 5 percent chance of being random. These co-occurrence figures speak volumes about Faulkner's South and its distinct social constellations. There are three separate groups: upper-class whites, African Americans, and middle-class and lower-class whites. While the upper-class whites and African Americans interact by virtue of an economic relationship, middle-class, lower-class, and "poor whites" stand outside of this relationship and interact with neither. Meanwhile, gender relationships are intimately tied to class. Generally, cross-gender pairs are of the same race and class, likely indicating either marriage or kinship. The only context in which

TABLE 1. Co-occurrence of characters identified by race, class, and gender

Character type 1	Character type 2	Character 1 events	Character 2 events	Co-occurrence
White upper-class female	White upper-class male	1,214	3,667	914
Black free male	White upper-class male	802	3,667	505
White lower-class female	White lower-class male	736	2,146	500
White lower-class male	White poor-white male	2,146	869	384
Black enslaved male	White upper-class male	400	3,667	341
Black free female	White upper-class male	409	3,667	253
Black enslaved male	White upper-class female	400	1,214	206
White middle-class female	White middle-class male	593	1,300	205
Mixed black/white free male	White upper-class male	289	3,667	192
Black free female	Black free male	409	802	167

cross-gender relationships occur within different racial contexts is when African Americans are enslaved or employed by white families.

The above data represents co-occurrence patterns for the most abundant character types in the corpus, and does not take into consideration co-occurrence relative to their abundance. Normalizing the data brings to light social relationships between more marginalized characters (table 2).[8] All character types that have moved up in frequency due to normalization have been highlighted. Similarly, characters of the same type interact more frequently. As a rule, cross-gender co-occurrence happens within defined social spaces along the lines of class and race. This is obviously the case for enslaved men and women, who have few other options, but it is also true of poor white men and women. The notable exception is the relationship between Boon Hogganbeck, who is possibly of mixed Native American descent, and Miss Corrie, a white prostitute in Mrs. Reba's house of assignation.

TABLE 2. Normalized co-occurrence of characters identified by race, class, and gender

Character type 1	Character type 2	Character 1 events	Character 2 events	Normalized co-occurrences
White upper-class female	White upper-class male	1,214	3,667	584
White lower-class female	White lower-class male	736	2,146	540
Black enslaved female	Black enslaved male	110	400	490
Mixed Indian/white poor-white male	White poor-white female	136	172	412
Black free female	Black free male	409	802	411
Black enslaved male	White upper-class female	400	1,214	400
White poor-white female	White poor-white male	172	869	398
Black free male	White upper-class male	802	3,667	368
White middle-class female	White middle-class male	593	1,300	326
White lower-class male	White poor-white male	2,146	869	311
Mixed black/white free female	Mixed black/white free male	89	289	291
Black enslaved male	White upper-class male	400	3,667	288
Mixed black/white free male	Mixed Indian/white poor-white male	289	136	250

At the opposite end of the spectrum, the list of characters who co-occur negatively is, perhaps, more telling. This table is quite exhaustive, and it makes little sense to show a list where the co-occurrence is zero. Suffice it to say that one of the biggest divisions among characters is class. White upper-class characters, both male and female, co-occur with middle- and lower-class whites at a far less frequent rate given their relative proportions. Likewise, non-upper-class whites co-occur with African Americans at a lower rate than expected. This information is the inverse of the positive co-occurrences, and it underscores the strict social divisions in Yoknapatawpha.

The power of and also the problem with co-occurrence analysis is that it assumes that characters are independent actors moved by their own motivations. Of course, Faulkner's characters are where they are because he put them there. Writing each character was a deliberate act, so suggesting that a character co-occurrence is "random" is distorting. At the same time, it would be equally problematic to suggest, retrospectively, with the entire corpus in mind, that Faulkner intended for the total aggregation of character co-occurrences to have the same relative proportions. Clearly, this is the effect of character interactions following a pattern. Co-occurrence analysis pulls this pattern from the noise. These regular co-occurrence patterns are the social norms that form a backdrop to the individual transgressions that are the focus of much of the fiction. Upper-class white men are not meant to be with poor white women, yet Thomas Sutpen courts Millie Jones in "Wash." Lower-class white men and upper-class white men do not share the same social space, except when Wash and Sutpen drink together or Ratliff and Gavin find camaraderie through their fascination with the poor white Snopeses. Finally, sexual boundaries between races are not meant to be crossed, but there is no shortage of examples of such transgression. It would therefore be misleading to suggest that there is no diverse interaction in Yoknapatawpha; instead, this is the exception to the rule that drives so much of Faulkner's fiction: the constant high-wire act of tiptoeing on social fault lines, knowing that even a perceived misstep or change in the social winds can, and so often does, lead to disaster.

Mapping Demography

Throughout the course of this essay, a cautious attempt has been made to sketch a demography of Yoknapatawpha. With the quantity of data available, it is tempting to draw sweeping conclusions about Faulkner's writing. The data is certainly suggestive, but without any clear way to establish the margin of error across locations, characters, and events, it should be seen as exploratory and not evidentiary. Those qualifications aside, consolidating the data and projecting it back onto Faulkner's own map provides provocative insight into how Faulkner viewed the demography of his county.

Part of the real power of the DY data is that all locations have been given *x/y* coordinates based on their position on a digital rendering of Faulkner's map. This allows the data to be ported into GIS systems, such as Quantum GIS (QGIS), without requiring a georeferenced map or a projection system. QGIS treats the data like it would other GIS data, and a demographic map of Faulkner's county can be created based on any number of attributes. As the data is highly interpretive and fluid from text to text, many of the techniques available in QGIS are inappropriate to the data.[9] One available technique is to overlay descriptive statistics onto specifics areas of the map.[10] In figure 2, twelve different population centers have been identified by the number of times different types of characters appear there. The main area is Jefferson, and the second largest is Frenchman's Bend; both are a mix of private and public property. The other major population centers are plantations, including those of

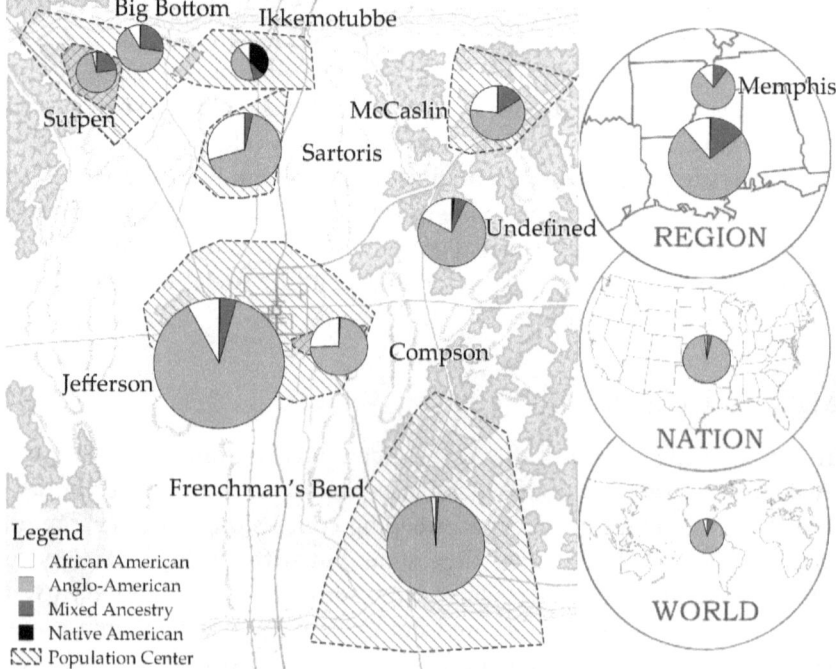

FIG. 2. Racial distribution by population center. (Digital Yoknapatawpha at the University of Virginia)

Sutpen, Sartoris, Compson, and McCaslin. The Big Bottom is the wilderness that includes the lands from Sutpen's Hundred that have fallen into disuse. Ikkemottube's domain is both a mix of public and private lands. The inset maps provide the demographic breakdown for Memphis, the region, nation, and the world. Finally, a thirteenth chart, "undefined," aggregates all of the statistics for the locations scattered across the country that fall outside of the major population centers. The population centers are outlined with a light gray overlay, accompanied by a pie chart scaled by the number of events that occur at that population center and broken down by character race. A table has also been provided to provide both the raw count and percentage of each specific area by race (table 3).[11]

The map makes clear that the different population centers in the county have their own unique racial politics. Even though the town has the highest density of character activity, the odds of characters from different races crossing paths is lower than most other areas. The majority of characters who interact with each other in town are white. In similar

TABLE 3. Racial makeup of characters by area (percentage)

Area	African American	Anglo-American	Mixed ancestry	Native American	Total
INSIDE YOKNAPATAWPHA					
Big Bottom	59 (8.6)	444 (64.3)	184 (26.7)	3 (0.4)	690
Compson	260 (25.4)	758 (74)	3 (0.3)	3 (0.3)	1,024
Frenchman's Bend	45 (1.5)	2,874 (97.7)	24 (0.8)	0 (0)	2,943
Ikkemotubbe	46 (10.7)	184 (43)	40 (9.3)	158 (36.9)	428
Jefferson	408 (7.8)	4,600 (88)	208 (4)	9 (0.2)	5,225
McCaslin	213 (23.4)	551 (60.5)	146 (16)	0 (0)	910
Sartoris	491 (29.6)	1,111 (66.9)	58 (3.5)	0 (0)	1,660
Sutpen	18 (3.5)	375 (73.5)	116 (22.7)	1 (0.2)	510
Undefined	252 (17.5)	1,084 (75.5)	80 (5.6)	20 (1.4)	1,436
OUTSIDE YOKNAPATAWPHA					
Memphis	69 (11.5)	466 (77.9)	63 (10.5)	0 (0)	598
Region	232 (11.2)	1,543 (74.4)	288 (13.9)	10 (0.5)	2,073
Nation	12 (1.7)	666 (95)	23 (3.3)	0 (0)	701
World	14 (3.9)	323 (90.2)	21 (5.9)	0 (0)	358
Total	2,119 (11.4)	14,979 (80.7)	1,254 (6.8)	204 (1.1)	18,556

fashion, the plantations close to town reproduce, to a large extent, the apartheid regime predominant in the pre–Civil Rights South. The Compson house has virtually no characters of mixed ancestry and sees a stark division between black and white. The Sartoris plantation does have one "mixed ancestry" character, Elnora Strother, but for the most part the possibility of white and black interracial relationships is muted. This is in contrast to the plantations farther from town, Sutpen and McCaslin, where there is a higher presence of "mixed ancestry" characters. In fact, when Sutpen's land later becomes the hunting grounds for the Big Bottom, the forest becomes the second most diverse place in the county after the Native American lands. Meanwhile, this land, governed by Ikkemotubbe, starts off as an exclusively Native American space, but over time the plurality of characters who appear here are white. Faulkner has reserved the southeastern part of the district for lower-class and poor whites. Indeed, the opening of *The Hamlet* describes this as an almost entirely homogenous region that in no uncertain terms is dangerous for nonwhites, as there is not "a negro landowner in the entire section" and "[s]trange negroes would absolutely refuse to pass through it after dark" (5). Within the wider world, Faulkner sees diversity as a possibility on a regional level, but at the national and the global scale his fiction is almost exclusively white.

The distribution of the data reveals a pattern that Faulkner, to a certain extent, consciously inscribed into his county. Evidence for this is found in the texts. In the same passage from *The Town* with which the editor of this volume begins, Gavin Stevens describes Yoknapatawpha as a series of concentric circles. He first notes the "rich alluvial river-bottom land of old Issetibbeha" that is the same as the "fat black rich plantation earth still synonymous of the proud fading white plantation names . . . Sutpen and Sartoris and Compson and Edmonds and McCaslin and Beauchamp and Grenier and Habersham and Holston and Stevens and De Spain." Then to the west, he observes, the "roadless, almost pathless perpendicular hill-country of McCallum and Gowrie and Frazier and Muir" and "last on to where Frenchman's Bend lay beyond the south-eastern horizon, cradle of Varners and ant-heap of the north-east crawl of Snopes" (331–32). DY, if anything, is proof that Faulkner's maps are more than just novelties; they are windows into his fiction. But beyond establishing what is already known, these demographic maps recover the spatial component of his writing—the most pronounced of which is racial segregation. Slavery and Jim Crow imposed legal and social boundaries in the communities of the South, and Yoknapatawpha was no exception. The preponderance of white characters and the lack of nonwhite spaces indicate a separate and unequal world. At the same time, the color line could be more or less divisive depending on class, gender, and, importantly, spatial context. Interestingly, events that take place farther from town have a higher likelihood of having interactions between different kinds of characters. The area where this is most pronounced is the Big Bottom where men find their common kinship through the age-old ritual of the hunt. On the exact opposite side of the map, the southeast, Frenchman's Bend, as birthplace of the "redneck," is a place with few possibilities for African Americans to be part of the social fabric.

Conclusion

The character distributions across time and space throw into question the traditional teleology of Faulkner's career as of one linear development. Instead, it may be more productive to think of Faulkner's interests with Yoknapatawpha as concurrent, multifarious, and conceived through different spatial contexts. These are different parts of the same story told in different places at the same time. This is not to suggest a totality but rather a ramshackle and fragmented unity of social connections that turn Yoknapatawpha from a shared space into a meaningful place. Thinking beyond the well-worn and scripted teleology of Faulkner's work opens up possibilities of understanding the relationships between texts across space absent of time, and de-hierarchizes assumed levels of canonicity within the corpus. As such, it complements work that has already been done by some of the DY editors using "traditional" scholarship, notably Theresa M. Towner. It also, in no small amount, underscores the potential impact of DY on Faulkner studies and DH scholarship more generally. By spatializing an entire corpus, patterns are revealed that in a strict chronological reading of an oeuvre are hidden. Ironically, DY itself organizes its site according to publication date, the sine qua non of author studies, but the ability to hop around in time at the push of a button rubs against this structure. DY has given users a publication date not so that they remember it, but that they might forget it.

Philosophical musing aside, DY is also a testament to practice-oriented DH. Though it might sound parochial that a major digital project involves learning by doing, the reality is that a mostly complete, mostly consistent database is better than a perfect theoretical one. There are certainly legitimate limitations to how the data can be used appropriately, but this should not detract from the fact that it can be used. As I hope this demography has shown, even in answering a relatively simple question—what type of people are where at what time in Yoknapatawpha—the database is, through some manipulation, able to produce a series of rich and multivalent perspectives that, at times, confirm already existing scholarly work and, at other times, disrupt it, but in all cases send the user back to the best source of all: Faulkner's own texts.

Notes

1. Currently, the exact numbers are 2,149 locations, 4,988 characters, and 8,433 events, all of which are subject to change.
2. Both can be viewed on the DY site with extensive commentary by Stephen Railton and Christopher Rieger.
3. Interestingly, these locations account for 31 percent of the events in the corpus, which demonstrates their centrality.
4. Faulkner refers to the Chickasaw lands to the north of Jefferson as alternately being ruled by Ikkemotubbe or Issetibbeha, and throughout the course of his career he appears to have conceived of two conflicting genealogies of the tribe. For more detail, see the genealogy on the Digital Yoknapatawpha site: http://faulkner.iath.virginia.edu/family/tree.php?name=Ikkemotubbe-Issetibbeha.
5. This number includes both the short stories that compose much of *The Unvanquished* in their earlier form and the final novel version of the text. One critique is that this overrepresents the Sartoris family in the corpus. The stories and the novel were different enough to merit individual encoding and are therefore treated as separate texts.
6. There is a plan in the works to label locations outside of Yoknapatawpha by type also.
7. This theory is not without its critics. While there is no time to revisit the debate fully here, the most salient criticism is that ontological independence necessitates that there will always be gaps in character description. After all, it would be impossible for an author to give a full account of every attribute that constitutes even one character, let alone all the

characters in a short story or novel. Some things about a character are meant to be inferred, while other things are simply unknowable. Yet, as there is no way to distinguish between what is open to interpretation and what is unknowable, it is possible to speculate whether Emma Bovary had a birthmark on her left shoulder. See Doležel.

8. Data normalization reduces the distance between the most frequent and least frequent character types. The data for the chart has been normalized using min-max feature rescaling where $X' = X - X_{min} / X_{max} - X_{min}$.

9. For example, in spatial analysis, population overviews are usually created through choropleths that denote the relative proportion of demographic groups within a bounded space; the bounding can either be done through an artificial human-created administrative area like a country, state, or voting district, topography, or, absent these, a regular grid superimposed on the point data. As there are no cartographically defined administrative areas in Yoknapatawpha, the former option is not viable. Meanwhile, since the population is very unevenly distributed, a predefined grid might seriously distort orders of magnitude between geometries. Finally, choropleths tend to view demographic data in relation to one static variable such as habitation or voting pattern. Since these are not places where people live, but rather where events take place, a choropleth would render these locations as deceptively static.

10. The images for this essay have been rendered in grayscale. To view them in color along with videos of the demographic shifts, see Burgers.

11. For the purposes of this map, race has been consolidated into four categories as opposed to the eight that are in the database. The key difference is that all "mixed" race and "indeterminable" characters have been collapsed into one category. Individually these numbers were so small that they did not register next to the more pronounced white and black presence in Yoknapatawpha.

Works Cited

Baroni, Raphaël, and Françoise Revaz. *Narrative Sequence in Contemporary Narratology.* Ohio State UP, 2016.

Barthes, Roland. *S/Z.* Translated by Richard Miller, Hill and Wang, 1974.

Bodenhamer, David J. "Making the Invisible Visible: Place, Spatial Theories, and Deep Maps." *Literary Mapping in the Digital Age,* edited by David Cooper et al., Routledge, 2016, pp. 207–20.

———. "Narrating Space and Place." *Deep Maps and Spatial Narratives,* edited by David J. Bodenhamer et al., Indiana UP, 2015, pp. 7–27.

Brindley, P., J. Goulding, and M. L. Wilson. "Generating Vague Neighbourhoods through Data Mining of Passive Web Data." *International Journal of Geographical Information Science,* vol. 32, no. 3, 2018, pp. 498–523.

Burgers, Johannes. "Race and Place: Mapping the Demography of Faulkner's Fictions." Digital Yoknapatawpha, University of Virginia, http://faulkner.iath.virginia.edu/racial_demography/index.html.

Chatman, Seymour Benjamin. *Story and Discourse: Narrative Structure in Fiction and Film.* Cornell UP, 1978.

Doležel, Lubomír. "Possible Worlds of Fiction and History." *New Literary History,* vol. 29, no. 4, 1998, pp. 785–809.

Evans, Elizabeth, and Matthew Wilkins. "Nation, Ethnicity, and the Geography of British Fiction, 1880–1940." *Journal of Cultural Analytics,* 2018, pp. 1–48.

Faulkner, William. *Absalom, Absalom!* 1936. Vintage International, 1990.

———. "Barn Burning." *Collected Stories.* 1950. Vintage, 1995, pp. 1–25.

———. "Dry September." *Collected Stories.* 1950. Vintage, 1995, pp. 169–83.

———. *Flags in the Dust.* 1973. Vintage International, 2012.

———. *Go Down, Moses.* 1942. Vintage International, 1990.

———. *The Hamlet.* 1940. Vintage International, 1991.

———. *Knight's Gambit.* 1949. Vintage International, 2011.

———. *Light in August.* 1932. Vintage International, 1987.

———. *The Reivers: A Reminiscence.* 1962. Vintage International, 1992.

———. *Sanctuary.* 1931. Vintage International, 1987.

———. *The Sound and the Fury.* 1929. Vintage International, 1990.

———. *The Town.* 1957. Vintage International, 2011.

Griffith, Daniel, Joseph Veech, and Charles Marsh. "Co-occur: Probabilistic Species Co-Occurrence Analysis in R." *Journal of Statistical Software,* vol. 69, 2016, pp. 1–17.

Guo, Q., Y. Liu, and J. Wieczorek. "Georeferencing Locality Descriptions and Computing Associated Uncertainty Using a Probabilistic Approach." *International Journal of Geographical Information Science,* vol. 22, no. 10, 2008, pp. 1067–90.

Jannidis, Fotis. "Character." *Handbook of Narratology,* edited by Peter Hühn, 2nd ed., De Gruyter, 2014, pp. 14–29.

Lamarque, Peter. *Work and Object: Explorations in the Metaphysics of Art.* Oxford UP, 2010.

Lane, Richard J. *The Big Humanities: Digital Humanities/Digital Laboratories.* Routledge, 2017.

Margolin, Uri. "From Predicates to People like Us: Kinds of Readerly Engagement with Literary Characters." *Characters in Fictional Worlds: Understanding Imaginary Beings in Literature, Film, and Other Media,* edited by Jens Eder et al., De Gruyter, 2010, pp. 400–415.

Morrison, Toni. "Recitatif." *Confirmation: An Anthology of African American Women*, edited by Amiri Baraka and Amini Baraka, Quill, 1983, pp. 243–61.

Murrieta-Flores, Patricia, Christopher Donaldson, and Ian Gregory. "GIS and Literary History: Advancing Digital Humanities Research through the Spatial Analysis of Historical Travel Writing and Topographical Literature." *Digital Humanities Quarterly*, vol. 11, no. 1, 2017.

Phelan, James. *Somebody Telling Somebody Else: A Rhetorical Poetics of Narrative*. Ohio State UP, 2017.

Piatti, Barbara. "Mapping Fiction: The Theories, Tools and Potentials of Literary Cartography." *Literary Mapping in the Digital Age*, edited by David Cooper et al., Routledge, 2016, pp. 88–101.

Railton, Stephen, and Christopher Rieger. "Faulkner Mapping|Mapping Faulkner." Added to the project: 2017. Digital Yoknapatawpha, University of Virginia, http://faulkner.iath.virginia.edu/FaulknerMapsHP.html.

Reicher, Maria E. "The Ontology of Fictional Characters." *Characters in Fictional Worlds: Understanding Imaginary Beings in Literature, Film, and Other Media*, edited by Jens Eder et al., De Gruyter, 2010, pp. 111–33.

Reuschel, Anne-Kathrin, and Lorenz Hurni. "Mapping Literature: Visualisation of Spatial Uncertainty in Fiction." *Cartographic Journal*, vol. 48, no. 4, 2011, pp. 293–308.

Ryan, Marie-Laure. "Story/Worlds/Media: Tuning the Instruments of a Media-Conscious Narratology." *Storyworlds across Media: Toward a Media-Conscious Narratology*, edited by Marie-Laure Ryan and Jan-Noël Thon, U of Nebraska P, 2014, pp. 25–49.

Towner, Theresa M. *Faulkner on the Color Line: The Later Novels*. UP of Mississippi, 2000.

Vasardani, Maria, Stephan Winter, and Kai-Florian Richter. "Locating Place Names from Place Descriptions." *International Journal of Geographical Information Science*, vol. 27, no. 12, 2013, pp. 2509–32.

Veech, Joseph A. "A Probabilistic Model for Analysing Species Co-occurrence." *Global Ecology and Biogeography*, vol. 22, no. 2, 2013, pp. 252–60.

Watson, Jay. "Introduction: Situating Whiteness in Faulkner Studies, Situating Faulkner in Whiteness Studies." *Faulkner and Whiteness*, edited by Jay Watson, UP of Mississippi, 2011, pp. vii–xxix.

Locations, Ownership, and Information Flow

Jennie Joiner

The courthouse in Jefferson, the county seat of Faulkner's fictional Yoknapatawpha County in Mississippi, is the center of all maps created for the fourteen novels and fifty-four short stories that comprise the Digital Yoknapatawpha Project. Depending on the text the map depicts, the courthouse is surrounded by various buildings with roads leading north and south and east and west. The four quadrants created by these roads are bordered to the north and south by rivers. These salient details of the maps are taken specifically from Faulkner's own maps that he drew and revised throughout his career (see Railton and Rieger). On his maps, Faulkner uses a circle and words to depict what happened at the courthouse: "Courthouse where Temple Drake Testified, & Confederate Monument which Benjy had to pass on his *left* side" (1936 map), or "Where Lee Goodwin was tried, jailed, and lynched" (1945 map). Digital Yoknapatawpha (DY) maps employ visual icons and cartography symbols rather than rely on words, and thus DY maps become a visual representation of locations. The courthouse icon is the symbolic center of DY from which all other locations, characters, and events radiate. Icons representing structures such as houses, public buildings, churches, cemeteries, farms, plantations, houses, and cabins populate the maps as well as stars and dots that depict locations of importance in the text. Rather than the words "Pine Hills" written across his 1936 map, DY uses contour lines to represent "hills" and green graphics to depict the "pine." Faulkner's 1936 map also contains the words "William Faulkner, Sole Owner & Proprietor" in the lower left quadrant, whereas each DY map contains the name of the Faulkner text and the DY editors who have contributed to the creation of that map in roles perhaps comparable to Faulkner's as "owner & proprietor."

Faulkner's distinct claim to ownership on his map raises interesting questions. As the map is a virtual duplication of the topography of the town of Oxford in Lafayette County, Mississippi, of what exactly is Faulkner claiming ownership? While it is reasonable to interpret this claim of ownership to his fictional Yoknapatawpha as a place, his ownership was also of the knowledge of "the larger world" that Stephen Railton and Christopher Rieger argue Faulkner had been building in his literary oeuvre through 1936: Faulkner became a cartographer by drawing a map for the publication of *Absalom, Absalom!*, "but on the map Faulkner drew, only 5 of the 27 different locations identify places that occur in the novel; the other 22 refer to places that figure in his five earlier Yoknapatawpha novels. The map appears in the first edition of *Absalom* as a two-color foldout at the very end of the book. When readers unfolded the map . . . , their attention was being directed well beyond this one novel, to the larger world that Faulkner had been building for almost a decade." This "larger world" that Faulkner depicts on his map does not consist only of places but more specifically what happens in these spaces. Despite his interest in drawing and imagery (the eye in *The Sound and the Fury* or the coffin shape in *As I Lay Dying*, for instance), Faulkner's map is surprisingly devoid of icons of any sort. Instead, he relies on words, short snippets of text that tell us what happens in the space rather than anything about the location itself, other than where it is located geographically. His map thus becomes an amalgamation of *his* understanding of Yoknapatawpha and the stories and novels he had written to that point in his career. Only Faulkner knows the information on the map. And for others to understand the map, they must acquire and read his other texts. In other words, Faulkner not only owns the landscape of Yoknapatawpha, but he also owns and controls the flow of information within it and about it. It becomes a somewhat coded understanding that is obscured within his complex narratives. In order to understand the landscape, one has to decipher the texts to comprehend the significance of the select information he reveals on his maps.

DY is an attempt to illuminate all locations in those texts and make information about them transparent and comprehensive. In the context of DY, what Faulkner did was record "Events" on his map, an endeavor that the collaborators of the project have expanded upon by locating at least 8,259 events on the map. Unlike Faulkner's attempt to draw attention to the "larger world" of Yoknapatawpha by creating an amalgamated map of specific events drawn from a multitude of texts, the DY Project creates a distinctive map for each text wherein readers click on location icons to learn more about the events that occur there. Even for stories like "Ad Astra" and "All the Dead Pilots," in which all the narrative action takes place outside Yoknapatawpha, the map remains the same, although for these stories inset maps of the Western Front are displayed. Thus, the map for each story stays static, with the courthouse as its center, and specific details on the map change to depict the information mined from the story. Some DY maps also contain more detailed inset maps of particular locations. *The Sound and the Fury*, for example, contains two inset maps. One of these maps is of the Compson Place, the other of Cambridge, Massachusetts, giving visual representation to these two significant locations. Similarly, *The Hamlet* contains an inset map of Frenchman's Bend, and *Sanctuary* contains two inset maps of Oxford, Mississippi, and Memphis, Tennessee. The descriptions of the locations are meant to do the opposite of what Faulkner does and not just describe what happens there (events), but extract descriptions of that location from the text when possible to highlight the imagery of that place for readers. For example, in the map of "A Rose for Emily," the description of the Grierson house is pulled directly from the story: "The Grierson house is 'a big, squarish frame house that had once been white, decorated with cupolas and spires and scrolled balconies in the heavily lightsome style of the seventies, set on what had once been our most select street. But garages and cotton gins had encroached and obliterated even the august names of that neighborhood; only Miss Emily's house was left, lifting its stubborn and coquettish decay above the cotton wagons and gasoline pumps—an eyesore among eyesores'" (119). In contrast, the clothing store located on the southwest corner of the square is a location created from the context of the story: "Although the story does not specifically mention a clothing store, it does tell us that Miss Emily buys 'a complete outfit of men's clothing, including a nightshirt' (127), implying the existence of such a location." The event then guides the creation of the location, the description—"clothing store"—and the description is what happens in that location rather than a description of the store.

DY maps expand Faulkner's practice of focusing on spatial positions on the map. Each specific location has *x/y* coordinates on the Yoknapatawpha map (or on the Region, Nation, and World maps located on the right of the screen). Locations in DY are defined as the following, as outlined in the DY Instructions for data entry:

(1) Places in or outside Yoknapatawpha where Events in your story occur are all Locations.
(2) In addition, all places *in Yoknapatawpha County* that are clearly identified in your story are Locations. (Ex: in "Spotted Horses" the narrator talks about trying to sell a sewing machine to Mrs. Bundren; narrative never takes readers there, but "Bundren Farm" is a Location that goes on the map.)
(3) In addition, places outside Yoknapatawpha that play a significant role in your story are Locations. (Ex: the spotted horses and Buck come from Texas, Flem and Eula spend a year in Texas, so even though narrative never takes reader to Texas, Texas goes on the map.)
(4) But places outside Yoknapatawpha that are simply mentioned in passing are not Locations. (Ex: Quentin remembers that his parents brought Jason a souvenir back from the Fair in St. Louis. St. Louis does not go on the map.)

Embedded in all the descriptions of locations is the term "place," a more enigmatic term that DY collaborators were required to interpret throughout the project in order to determine whether a place should become a "location" and thus be recorded within the database and on the map. In *Place: An Introduction,* Tim Cresswell points out the way in which interpreting place is currently at the forefront of interdisciplinary studies:

> At the other end of subjective-objective spectrum, place has also entered the lexicon of businesses and scholars who use geographic information systems (GIS). GIS are sophisticated computational software systems that can represent data spatially in the form of maps. Since their origin they have largely been centered on the manipulation and representation of quantifiable things in a spatial form. To many writers on the theme of place (as we shall see later), this has been the opposite of an interest in place. Recently, however, the fusion of mapping software with social media software has led to a new level of what we might think of as "augmented" place. (2–3)

Such understandings of "augmented place" are complicated: who defines the space, what understandings do they derive about that space, and for what purposes do they use that information? Cresswell points out that politicians, supermarkets, police forces, and security services are interested in these understandings for a variety of reasons—some for the local good, such as making data-driven decisions for public welfare, and some for more sinister reasons, such as getting into your wallet or affecting your voting habits. The DY editors are searching for new understandings of Faulkner's fiction by representing "quantifiable things in a spatial form." The data and the maps do not create "new" information. Seeing and looking at the map does not tell us anything that a very careful close reading of Faulkner's texts cannot do. However, looking at the maps can lead to new understandings by creating new ways of "seeing" the information on the map and in the novels and short stories. Moreover, mapping characters and events can allow other interpretations of locations, characters, and actions that affect understandings of the text itself.

Working with the DY map of the *The Unvanquished*, for example, I came to a metacognitive understanding of ownership and information flow both in the DY Project and within the novel. When looking at the map of *The Unvanquished*, as with all the maps, the first visual encounter one has is with the specific locations depicted on it. As a default, all natural and man-made locations are shown on the map without any characters. This visual creates a context for the novel. All locations shown have a character or event associated with them; there are no extraneous "larger world" understandings of Yoknapatawpha that can distract from the focus of this one. Clicking on Characters shows them at "home" (if known) or the location where they first appear in the text and thus where they appear on the map. All characters, therefore, have a specific site on the map, a spatial location to which they are anchored. White characters such as John Sartoris, Rosa Millard, and Bayard are at "home" on the Sartoris plantation, as are "enslaved" black characters such as Joby, Louvinia, and Ringo. Slaves who choose to leave their "home" are classified in the database as "free black," such as the large groups of slaves who walk the road to Jordan. The database does have a notation, however, that characters' class changes in the text for both of these categorizations when appropriate. Ringo, for example, is categorized as "enslaved black," but the character description contextualizes it this way: "Ringo, the grandson of Louvinia and Joby, was born a slave, though by the end of this novel, as a result of both the Emancipation Proclamation and the South's defeat in the Civil War, he is legally free—or, as he puts it in the story, 'I aint a nigger anymore. I done been abolished'" (199). Locating a character at "home," therefore, is complicated for black and white characters and necessitates interpretation. "Home" as described in the DY Instructions is "Where the character lives, if known. For most characters this won't be known, but when text does establish that, the 'Home' function will allow users to ask the map to display where the various characters in a text live." Once characters' homes are determined, they are permanently mapped to that location—they do not move. While this is clearly understandable for characters such as Joby and Louvinia, it is not as clear for characters such as Loosh and Philadelphy, who emancipate themselves and leave "home."

The static nature of the map, therefore, highlights thematic emphasis on ownership—of land, people, and information—in the novel. In *The Unvanquished*, Uncle Buck and Buddy have, according to John Sartoris, "ideas about land": "They believed that land did not belong to people but that people belonged to land" (48). This tension between ownership and mapping becomes apparent in the very first scene of the novel, which begins with Ringo and Bayard's map: "Behind the smokehouse that summer, Ringo and I had a living map." This map represents for the boys "the ponderable though passive recalcitrance of topography which outweighs artillery, against which the most brilliant of victories and the most tragic of defeats are but the loud noises of a moment" (3). The map represents Vicksburg, the place of resistance, of security, of sustenance for the South and the Confederacy. Moreover, it is a place, a location, through which information flows and about which information is vital. This map, though, is disrupted by Ringo's uncle, Loosh, who "with his hand . . . swept the chips flat." "There's your Vicksburg," he says as he destroys the map (5). This is the first moment in the text that Bayard's cognitive cartography is disrupted.

This term, "cognitive cartography," was coined by DY collaborator John Michael Corrigan as a way of contextualizing this project within the digital humanities:

> A cognitive cartography can be visualized as a temporal compression of movement, behavior and thinking in social space. In order to visualize this process, we need to consider how information is preserved both within and outside the body so that it is most likely to be replicated, copied or

adapted. Throughout Faulkner's fiction, the site for this preservation and replication of information can be located in numerous places at once, memory, textual surfaces and the architecture around us. Faulkner repeatedly depicts the process by which human movement and behavior cluster across time in particular social spaces, creating as a result institutional hierarchies in which information and resources are forced to flow through particular hubs of social space into the wider community. As much as these networks of power appear permanent, they are subject to new patterns of movement—and Faulkner thereby imagines how novelty, spontaneous individual interaction, can decenter these hierarchies, rearranging how such networks of power are constituted. In this respect, Faulkner suggests a modern form of individualism in which individual behavior, no matter how seemingly insignificant, can remake social space and with it the forms of cognition that are embedded in its structure.[1]

Loosh's "spontaneous individual interaction" of destroying the "living map" destroys all hierarchies for Bayard. Loosh does not behave as expected, and he underscores the weakness of Vicksburg as central to Confederate victory. The "living map" becomes dust, inseparable from the connotations of death and decay that we see so often in Faulkner's fiction. In his confusion, Bayard stoops and catches "both hands full of dust and rose: and Ringo still standing there, not moving, just looking at me even as I flung the dust. 'I'm General Pemberton!' I cried. 'Yaaay! Yaay!' stooping and catching up more dust and flinging that too. Still Ringo didn't move. 'All right!' I cried. 'I'll be Grant this time, then'" (6–7). Bayard flings dust at Ringo in an attempt to get him to submit to his will until he is defeated by Ringo's unwillingness to move and play the Union officer. The map that was once living has now become dust and Bayard's instinct is simply to use it as a weapon and throw it at Ringo.

This concept of dust is crucial to an understanding of ownership by (not of) the land. Once Loosh, the character who first embodies emancipation and leaves the Sartoris plantation, destroys the "living map," the land turns into dust. There are thirty-nine instances of the word "dust" in the novel; thirty-five of these occur exclusively between the moment Loosh destroys the living map and the point at which Granny, Ringo, and Bayard recover the silver and mules and find themselves "given," by the Union army, what Bayard says "looked like a thousand niggers, men women and children, with their wet clothes dried on them" (110). Between these framing events, former slaves who have emancipated themselves by leaving their "homes" to embody freedom are referred to repeatedly as a "dustcloud." For example, the family sees a "cloud of dust away to the west, moving slow, too slow for men riding" (82). Granny, looking at the "dustcloud" and also dislocated from her land, attempts to take a different direction by following the road into the east to track down the Yankees and reclaim her property. Nevertheless, the family, the emancipated slaves, and the Yankees all end up in the same melee at the river, which we can see as a piling up in a cluster on the map in this location in DY. The multitude of occurrences of the word "dust" allude to oppression, heat, decay, sterility, and death, but also, importantly, to movement. In this novel, freedom ceases to be simply an idea; it becomes an action. This movement is an embodiment of freedom for the former slaves, and the river offers a promise of life and relief from dust. Just like the "living map" that "drank water faster than [Bayard and Ringo] could fetch it from the well" (3), this "dustcloud" is seeking a return to life at "Jordan," a literal river in the South, but also a symbolic biblical river. The last instance of the term "dust" occurs when Granny addresses the former slaves from Alabama given her by the Union general:

> "I suppose you all want to cross some more rivers and run after the Yankee Army, dont you?" Granny said. They stood there, moving their feet in the dust. "What? Dont any of you want to?" They just stood there. "Then who are you going to mind from now on?"
> After a while, one of them said, "You, missy."
> "All right," Granny said. "Now listen to me. Go home. And if I ever hear of any of you straggling off like this again, I'll see to it." (114–15)

Bayard's use of the word "dust" ceases because the larger social structures of the plantation hierarchies are reinstated. The "novelty" to which Corrigan refers ends and the Sartoris family returns to the plantation along with the mules, the silver, and the former slaves who have been given to Granny by the Union army. Importantly, the fate of these former slaves who return with the family is never known, as Bayard never refers to them again. Thus, they disappear from the map, both temporally and visually. Information about these people is not relevant to the "social hierarchies" of Bayard's narration and thus not available within the "social spaces," as Corrigan points out, allowing Faulkner to maintain control of his spatial information and fictional geography.

The DY map intensifies such tensions surrounding ownership. Much like Uncle Buck and Uncle Buddy's "ideas about land," the DY map depicts people as being tied statically to a particular location on the DY map. Understandings of "home" are where people live, regardless of choice. For example, Loosh and Philadelphy choose to leave the plantation, to emancipate themselves, but the static nature of the map does not allow movement. People move within the text, but they do not move on the map. Movement is depicted on DY maps as red where action is occurring; it changes to purple once movement has passed, much like the "dustcloud" of emancipated slaves of which Bayard is aware but does not understand. Movement is occurring, but the movement is a faceless, nameless entity without distinction or specificity.

Just as editors of the Digital Yoknapatawpha Project are mapping characters' movements and locations in order to create a visual cartography, Ringo and Granny map movements of Yankee regiments and mules:

> It was the only window shade Louvinia had; Ringo had drawn it... with Granny showing him where to draw in the towns. But it was Granny who had done the writing, in her neat spidery hand like she wrote in the cookbook with, written on the map by each town: *Colonel or Major or Captain So-and-So, Such-and-Such Regiment or Troop* Then, under that: *12 or 9 or 21 mules* And around four of them, town and writing and all, in purple pokeberry juice instead of ink, a circle with a date in it, and in big neat letters *Complete*. (125)

They use the map to distinguish between branded mules to sort out ownership—where the mules were originally obtained, where they were sold, which Union regiment now owns them, and where that regiment is camped. As Cresswell points out, "Place is central to forms of struggle and resistance too. Recognizing the danger in Google mapping the world, others are producing an open source map (OpenStreetMap) project that does not allow corporations a monopoly on the production of place" (3). Comparing Ringo and Granny's map to Google may seem like a stretch, but in the world of Yoknapatawpha in the midst of the war, the information that Ringo secures and that is depicted on the painted window shade is incredibly valuable to them and also anticipates our current moment. The map that Ringo and Granny draw represents what I term the visualization of information flow.

As we know from recent Facebook and Cambridge Analytica concerns, this visualization is valuable. Where we are, how we move, and what we do when in social spaces is valuable, and mapping that data can be profitable, as Cresswell points out. Depending on who uses it, such a map can be useful in improving lives or it can be used to manipulate us in various ways and to create institutional hierarchies. While Google can compile data almost instantaneously and picture it on a screen, Ringo's travel and reconnaissance is dangerous and it takes days for him to gather the information to add to Granny's map. This map and the information it contains must also be protected, so Granny keeps it safely hidden under the loose floorboard in Louvinia's cabin. When Ringo returns from his travels, Granny and Ringo add information that Ringo has collected to the map and then they look at it. Bayard emphasizes this fact: "They looked at the map" (125). This looking at the map allows Ringo and Granny to determine risk assessments and opportunities for greater commerce. Similarly, DY captures as much information about characters as editors are able to discern: race, class, gender, ethnicity, and, importantly, where they first appear in the text. This information is then located on the map so we too can look at it, just as Granny and Ringo do, to better understand Faulkner's creative process. While our gaze is not meant to assess risk or commerce opportunities in Faulkner's oeuvre, we "look" to enhance understanding through objectivity and distance. It allows us a bird's-eye view of something that we cannot see unless we change our perspective. And in this case, we can see that what we are doing may utilize more advanced technologies than a window shade and pokeberry juice, but it constitutes the same kind of effort at visualization.

One of the challenges of mapping information is capturing its dynamic nature. A tendency has been to use Faulkner's 1936 map as a definitive understanding of Yoknapatawpha. Faulkner's uses of locations within the space of Yoknapatawpha, however, are not static. Some of the locations in his fiction do not correspond with the map. This becomes very clear in *As I Lay Dying*, for example. The 1936 map depicts in the lower left quadrant along the river a line with a circle along the river with this notation: "Bridge which washed away so Anse Bundren could not cross it with Addie's Body." It also contains a notation of

"Bundren's" farther south of Frenchman's Bend, and an arrow pointing south to "Mottstown," "where Jason Compson lost his niece's trail, and where Anse Bundren had to go in order to reach Jefferson." There are also notations for "Armstid's" and "Tull's" farther north in this quadrant. These notations seem to be helpful and definitive for mapping the story. Yet the narrative does not fit this map. For example, "Tull's" is located on the 1936 map significantly north of the river in the southeast corner and above Frenchman's Bend. But in *As I Lay Dying*, the bridge that the family has to cross to reach Jefferson is near Tull's farm. Because Tull's is on the same side of the river as Bundren's, Tull's farm must logically be on the south side of the river. There is simply no other way to make sense of the journey and, thus, DY relies on the narrative rather than Faulkner's map. In other stories, textual interpretations also locate Tull's farm differently than Faulkner mapped it. For example, in *Sanctuary*, Ruby Lamar gives the sheriff directions to get to the Old Frenchman place, mentioning Tull's farm in her directions: "[Y]ou pass Mr Tull's about a mile and turn off to the right" (105). The DY map for *Sanctuary* thus relies on Ruby's directions rather than Faulkner's map. Tull's farm is similarly located in both *The Hamlet* and *The Mansion* due to its proximity to Frenchman's Bend. The only DY map that locates Tull's farm close to where Faulkner himself placed it on his 1936 map is "Shingles for the Lord," which does not directly specify its location in the text; therefore, Faulkner's approximation on his map helps locate other buildings in proximity to Tull's.

The most difficult task in mapping *As I Lay Dying* is interpreting the role of the river in relation to the map. Again, the task of identifying a location means definitively situating something spatially. The interpretive journey to understand the river in the text is not unlike the Bundrens' attempt to locate the bridge and cross the river, since what looks definitive proves not to be. When the Bundrens finally reach the bridge, it is almost unrecognizable: "[I]t was mid-sunk and logs and such drifted up over it and it swagging and shivering like the whole thing would go any minute" (124). Moreover, Tull explains the confusion of the river itself: "It was nigh up on the levee on both sides, the earth hid except for the tongue of it we was on going out to the bridge and then down into the water, and except for knowing how the road and bridge used to look, a fellow couldn't tell where was the river and where was the land. It was just a tangle of yellow and the levee not less wider than a knife-back kind of, with us setting in the wagon and one the horse and the mule" (124). Tull, to whom "ownership" of the bridge is attributed, is the one who narrates the description of the bridge in both of these instances. Moreover, Tull "recognizes" the bridge, even in its damaged state: "But it was still whole; you could tell that by the way when this end swagged, it didn't look like the other end swagged at all: just like the other trees and the bank yonder where swinging back and forth slow like on a big clock" (138). But as Tull also demonstrates in his narration, "seeing" something is not the same as using it:

> It was like when we was across, up out of the water again and the and the hard earth under us, that I was surprised. It was like we hadn't expected the bridge to end on the other bank, on something take like the hard earth again that we had tromped on before this time and knowed well.... And when I looked back and saw the other bank and saw my mule standing there were I used to be and knew that I'd have to get back there someway, I knew it couldn't be, because I just couldn't think of anything that could make me cross that bridge ever even once. (139)

Tull's understanding of the bridge clarifies it as a location; he owns it and understands it much better than the Bundrens do, and his descriptions help readers understand it.

The flood, however, obscures the landscape for Darl and Cash, making it difficult for them to "read" the latter. Darl and Cash talk through the logic of finding and using the ford by means of which people got across the river before 1888, before the bridge was built:

> "I reckon we're still in the road, all right."
> "Tull taken and cut them two whiteoaks. I heard tell how at high water in the old days they used to line up the ford by them trees."
> "I reckon he did that two years ago when he was logging down here. I reckon he never thought that anybody would ever use this ford again." (142)

Much like DY collaborators who are looking for solid ground and clues in the text to map, Darl and Cash are reading the landscape for clues to find the ford. But the landmarks that discern the ford have been removed. Like readers, however, who plunge forward into the depths of Faulkner's confusing prose hoping to find solid ground, so do Darl and Cash wade forward into the river: *"I felt the current take us and I knew we were on the ford by that reason, since it was only by means of that slipping contact that we could tell that we were in motion at all. What had once been a flat surface was now a succession of troughs and hillocks lifting and falling about it, shoving at us, teasing at us with light lazy touches in the vain instances of solidity underfoot"* (147–48). In the midst of the river, Darl grounds his narrative in understandings of topography. In the incredible tension of the scene, he refers twice to the space "between two hills" where the log shoots up "from the bottom of the river" (148) and where the mules stand "when they had lost contact with the earth" (149). The metaphor of the hills helps Darl describe what he sees literally and metaphorically.

I focus on this narrative confusion in the text in which Tull, Darl, and Cash are searching for meaning as they read the landscape because it is similar to the reading and interpretive experience of looking at Faulkner's 1936 map and reading the text. We have markers that have been laid out for us but which Faulkner has chosen to relocate for his narrative purposes and thereby caused great confusion for DY. In particular, after the Bundrens have crossed the river, they learn from Armstid that "the levee through Haley bottom had done gone for two miles and that the only way to get to Jefferson would be go around by Mottson" (185). On both of Faulkner's maps, Mottstown (with different spelling than is used in the novel) is located south of Jefferson and, since it is not on the map, presumably south of the river that the family has just crossed. Logically, then, the narrative journey makes no sense in relation to the maps. DY, therefore, had to make decisions to change the map, as Stephen Railton outlines in the note on the text:

> The "explanation" our map provides by bending the river southward is essentially a pure speculation, and probably says more about the needs of our project than the work of Faulkner's imagination. Throughout his career he was always willing to sacrifice consistency to the demands of the particular story he was trying to tell, and he probably never felt our anxiety to make sense of the Bundrens' route. In any case, in 1930 he was still at the beginning of the process of creating "Yoknapatawpha"—*As I Lay Dying* is in fact the first time Faulkner bestows that name on his fictional world (it was Yocona before)—and so his landscape was probably still imaginatively very fluid in his mind.

The DY map, therefore, looks very different from other maps with its sharp bend to the south rather than running along the bottom of the map. Mottson is a location where the river would normally be on other Yoknapatawpha maps. This map becomes an interpretation of the information flow within *As I Lay Dying*, which editors have tried to make clear.

As owners and proprietors of DY, editors have made interpretive decisions and choices that affect the "reading experience" of viewing maps. For instance, on the map for *Go Down, Moses*, one can view all locations in the novel (the default option), or a specific "story" within the novel can be chosen, at which point the map changes to reflect only locations in that section. In the section for "Was," only four locations appear: Ike McCaslin's house in Jefferson, the McCaslin-Edmonds plantation, the road leading from the McCaslin-Edmonds plantation, and Hubert Beauchamp's plantation (located on the Region map, as it is outside Yoknapatawpha). Within the narrative, however, more granular spaces appear. For instance, on the McCaslin-Edmonds plantation within "Was" are "the cabins in the quarters," in one of which Uncle Buck and Uncle Buddy live; the "big house" built by L. Q. C. McCaslin in which the slaves now reside (6); and the gate (7). Similarly, on the Beauchamp plantation, even more distinct locations exist that depict the race to find Tomey's Turl. DY collaborators chose not to depict these locations on the map. These choices reflect the interpretive tension between distinguishing narrative function from social function in a text such as *Go Down, Moses*. The simplicity of the map for "Was" illustrates the social emphasis on ownership. Tomey's Turl and Tennie either belong to (or are owned by) the McCaslin-Edmonds plantation or the Beauchamp plantation. (Tennie, for example, is located at "home" on the Beauchamp plantation, not the McCaslin plantation where most of her life is spent, again demonstrating the static nature of maps rather than the dynamics of change.)

In contrast to the map for "Was," the map for "The Bear" in *Go Down, Moses* is much more detailed. Major de Spain's hunting and fishing camp, previously part of Sutpen's Hundred, and before that Issetibbeha's Chickasaw Grant, contains twelve separate interstices: ridge, trail, tree stand, logging company railroad, gum tree, glade/landmark tree, bayou, down log, blowdown, crossing in Big Bottom, coon bridge, and riverbank. One way to interpret these more specific locations is that in the environment of the Big Bottom, emphasis is placed on natural spaces rather than on ownership. The visible contrast between the McCaslin-Edmonds plantation—the upper right quadrant of the map—with only two structures, the McCaslin-Edmonds plantation and the Commissary, looks bare in contrast to the upper left quadrant that contains such interstices. While Ike McCaslin repudiates ownership of the McCaslin-Edmonds plantation, which is rightfully his inheritance, its boundaries and social function remain absolute. The Big Bottom reflects a location free of the taint of ownership, an understanding that is challenged throughout the novel. In contrast to Ike's repudiation of his inheritance, Lucas Beauchamp claims his inheritance on his twenty-first birthday and stays on the plantation: "Within the year he married, not a country woman, a farm woman, but a town woman, and McCaslin Edmonds built a house for them and allotted Lucas a specific acreage to be farmed as he saw fit as long as he lived or remained on the place" (106). His "ownership" of his own home on the McCaslin plantation thus becomes a symbol of his masculinity and his freedom, and thus, in "The Fire and the Hearth," "Lucas Beauchamp's Place" is clearly depicted on the map on the McCaslin-Edmonds plantation.

Perhaps the most perplexing of all places to locate is Oxford, Mississippi, as it is widely understood that Jefferson and Yoknapatawpha County are fictional representations of Oxford and Lafayette County. In "Faulkner Mapping|Mapping Faulkner," Railton and Rieger compare Faulkner's 1936 map of Yoknapatawpha with one of Lafayette County, noting the similarities: "It's easy to see how closely Yoknapatawpha resembles Lafayette. The two county seats—Oxford and Jefferson—sit near the center, beside the railroads that bisect each county vertically and in the middle of the major roads that lead from town in every direction except southwest." When characters from Faulkner's fictional Jefferson travel to Oxford, it is particularly disconcerting. Most characters, however, go to Oxford to visit or attend the University of Mississippi, which is absent from Faulkner's fictional Jefferson. The physical distance between Jefferson and Oxford is significant. In *The Unvanquished*, for example, Ringo rides "forty miles" from the Sartoris plantation to Oxford to fetch Bayard where he is studying law at the university after Bayard's father is murdered (213). Similarly, in *The Hamlet*, Will Varner tells Labove, who is playing football at the university, that "it aint but forty miles to Oxford" from Frenchman's Bend (118). In *The Town*, Flem Snopes gives Linda permission to attend the "State University" fifty miles away in return for Eula's agreement to sign the document giving him half of any inheritance she receives (303). DY has chosen consistently to locate Oxford a bit north of its actual location on the map, in the Region but, of course, outside the boundaries of Yoknapatawpha. The forty or fifty miles' distance between Faulkner's Oxford and Jefferson symbolically underscores the space between Faulkner's understanding of real and fictional places. Oxford is the locus for higher learning and thought; Jefferson becomes what Oxford might be without the state university as its center. Unlike Faulkner, who didn't have to leave his hometown to attend the University of Mississippi, his characters do: Temple Drake, Labove, Bayard Sartoris, Gavin Stevens, Charles Mallison, and Linda Snopes all leave their homes in Jefferson to attend university. Perhaps Faulkner leaves the university in Oxford because there is a flow of information in a university system that is outside of his control, even in a fictional space. If he cannot control it, he cannot own it.

Jefferson gleans so much of its tangibility from its replication of Oxford, complete with its town square surrounding the iconic courthouse with the Confederate monument. The courthouse is the geographic center of Faulkner's novels as well as the civic and legal center of the community; it is where deeds of ownership are kept. Ownership as a thematic concept runs throughout Faulkner's Yoknapatawpha fiction. Ownership for some characters reflects independence; for others, a choice to assume responsibility. Faulkner, in laying his claim of ownership to Yoknapatawpha, clearly communicates both. Not only does he own Jefferson, but he also has exclusive rights to control and use it to fit his narrative purpose. Everything that happens within Yoknapatawpha is under his purview and he has control of all the information generated within this space, including the manipulation of the space itself. Nothing reflects this more than his use of Oxford as a location within his fiction. The juxtaposition of Oxford and Jefferson in the same text seems to be a rhetorical move that Faulkner uses to highlight the fictionality of Jefferson, a place that he spent his career creating, and in doing so, he also highlights his ownership of that world. By reminding his readers that Oxford exists in the "larger world," he prohibits readers from merging these two spaces. Jefferson and Yoknapatawpha become a distinct world in which he can bend the rules to shape his narrative purposes. He can create and move locations to meet his needs. Yoknapatawpha is Faulkner's place, not simply a location: it becomes his way of seeing, knowing, and understanding the world, a vision often obscured by his difficult and complex prose. Digital

Yoknapatawpha attempts to make that world more comprehensible, but in doing so it lays its own claims of interpretive ownership to Faulkner's world.

Note

1. John Michael Corrigan provides an analysis of Faulkner's cognitive cartographies in "Murder in the House of Memory: Faulkner and the Plantation Prototype of Flags in the Dust," *modernism/modernity*, vol. 4, cycle 2 (2019), https://doi.org/10.26597/mod.0119. This particular quotation is from his as yet unpublished monograph *Cartographies of Consciousness*.

Works Cited

Corrigan, John Michael. *Cartographies of Consciousness: Self and Social Body in Faulkner's Yoknapatawpha*. Unpublished manuscript.

Cresswell, Tim. *Place: An Introduction*. 2nd ed., Blackwell, 2015.

Faulkner, William. *As I Lay Dying*. 1930. Vintage International, 1990.

———. *Go Down, Moses*. 1942. Vintage International, 1991.

———. *The Hamlet*. 1940. Vintage International, 1991.

———. *Sanctuary*. 1931. Vintage International, 1993.

———. *The Town*. 1957. Vintage International, 2011.

———. *The Unvanquished*. 1938. Vintage International, 1991.

Railton, Stephen, and Christopher Rieger, "Faulkner Mapping|Mapping Faulkner," Added to the project: 2017. Digital Yoknapatawpha, University of Virginia, http://faulkner.iath.virginia.edu/media/resources/DISPLAYS/FaulknerMapsHP.html.

"Around a Hundred and at Least Triplets"
EXPLORING CHARACTERS IN DIGITAL YOKNAPATAWPHA

CHRISTOPHER RIEGER

> Old Het, having just walked in from the poorhouse, ran down the hill toward the kitchen, shouting in a strong, bright, happy voice. She was about seventy probably, though by her own counting, calculated from the ages of various housewives in the town from brides to grandmothers whom she claimed to have nursed from infancy, she would have to be around a hundred and at least triplets.
>
> —Faulkner, "Mule in the Yard" (with thanks to Jim Carothers)

EACH OF the approximately 5,000 characters in the Digital Yoknapatawpha (DY) database has a wealth of different data points entered for him or her, all of which can be searched by users. The DY editors enter obvious markers like gender and race, as well as all texts in which the characters appear. For class, there are twelve categories from which to choose, as well as a checkbox for "Class Changes in Text." Other fields entered for each character are Name; Rank (Major, Minor, Secondary, or Peripheral); Family; Date of Birth; Vitality (Alive, Dead, Dies, Born, etc.); Occupation (eleven choices of job classes, plus the ability to enter a specific job); Origin; Ethnicity; Disability (twelve choices); Ontological Status (Historical/Real, Literary/Mythic/Biblical, and Created by a Character in the Text); Narrator; and Cause of Death. Each of these categories is searchable in combination with any of the others, creating a dizzying, even overwhelming, array of options for combing through the data. Obviously, covering all or even most of these options is beyond the scope of this essay (or even this book). The hope is that individual researchers will come up with uses for all of this data that go beyond anything the editors had in mind when creating the site. This essay will introduce some of the ways characters can be searched and provide examples of various results that can be found with the hope that these suggestions and examples can help readers use the database in their own ways.

Faulkner's characters provide a cornucopia of opportunities for exploration and discovery in DY. Because many characters appear in multiple works, the DY database can provide insights into a single character as he or she changes and develops across Faulkner's fictional universe. What may be less obvious to even serious Faulkner scholars is the sheer number of characters with which Faulkner populates his postage stamp of native soil. Print guides, such as Edmond Volpe's *A Reader's Guide to William Faulkner* (1964) and Hamblin and Peek's *A William Faulkner Encyclopedia* (1999), are indispensable; yet they cannot, by their nature, provide the same types of searchability, scale, and results that a large database such as DY can.

Cleanth Brooks's *William Faulkner: The Yoknapatawpha Country* and *Who's Who in Faulkner* by Margaret Patricia Ford and Suzanne Kincaid, both published in 1963, have some similarities with the DY database. *Who's Who* is largely made up of an alphabetical index of characters with a one-sentence description for most and up to a paragraph for major figures. Those who appear in multiple works get something like the cumulative biography in DY, and the book also includes genealogies of the Compson, McCaslin, Sartoris, Snopes, and Sutpen families. Brooks's book is more a collection of short essays, mostly organized around the novels, along with a section of shorter "Notes" on a variety of topics. Brooks adds the Stevens family to his genealogies, and he also includes a character index listing works in which characters appear without any biography. Harry Runyan's *A Faulkner Glossary* (1964) is similar to *Who's Who*, though it adds entries on locations and published works to its alphabetized list. Longer entries on the "principal families of Yoknapatawpha" replace the family trees.

Volpe's guide is very helpful in terms of summarizing major themes and providing analyses of major characters in each novel, and it is later reissued as *A Reader's Guide to William Faulkner: The Novels,* along with a companion volume on the short stories. Volpe includes genealogies for the major families as well as chronological reorderings of the events in some works. Robert W. Kirk's *Faulkner's People* (1963) is also organized book by book, but it goes further as a reference guide. In addition to short biographies of each named character, there is a list of each page on which he or she is named. Kirk also includes a Master Index of Characters that lists each work in which a character appears. Thomas Connolly's *Faulkner's World* (1988) provides something closer to the events table in DY, listing characters by work in order of appearance with a brief synopsis of his or her action in that scene. Connolly also seems the first to attempt to include all unnamed characters, except for "those who have no connection with the plot at all, but serve merely as part of the background scene" (xiii), in his chronologically organized guide. *Critical Companion to William Faulkner* (Fargnoli et al. 2008) combines elements of all these previous guides. Alphabetized entries on each work include summaries of plot and critical reception, as well as excerpts from reviews for the novels, with short stories getting a shorter synopsis and critical commentary before an alphabetized character list that provides biographies ranging from one sentence to multiple paragraphs, along with helpful cross-references to characters' appearances in other works.

DY contains all of the information in these print guides and much more, leveraging the advantage of being online to include every named and unnamed character, no matter how minor or seemingly insignificant. But DY should not be thought of as merely a web version of these print guides; the voluminous amount of data and the variety of tools for exploring it makes the DY database capable of much more. There are 4,983 characters entered in the database at the time of this writing, including 2,728 unnamed characters.[1] These unnamed characters include individuals with labels like "Negro Youth in Jefferson," "Arkansas Girl Who Lives Near Hineses," and "Man Killed by Calvin Burden" (all from *Light in August*), as well as groups of people entered as single characters with labels including "Unnamed Possum Hunters," "Caddy's Sexual Partners," and "Imagined Squad of Soldiers" (all from *The Sound and the Fury*). As is clear from some of the labels, 4,983 characters in the DY database does not equate to 4,983 people in Yoknapatawpha County. Some of these characters exist in the Yoknapatawpha fictions but reside outside the county (like "Harvard Crew Team" or "Babe Ruth"), so removing these would lower the number. In fact, over 500 characters are dead but are still included. (In some cases, they are more important dead than they were alive.) Additionally, there are about 900 characters who are only mentioned but never present in the action of a text. While this occurs for any number of reasons, those characters might skew any attempt at a population count using DY. On the other hand, most groups have an unknown number of people in them and are simply entered as one character, so those characters are undercounting the number of people who appear in the body of Yoknapatawpha fiction. Additionally, we should keep in mind that named characters who reoccur in multiple texts (Quentin Compson, for instance) get a new entry each time they appear.

On the map he drew for *Absalom, Absalom!,* Faulkner famously listed the population of the county as "Whites, 6298; Negroes, 9313" for a total of 15,611, which is less than the actual Lafayette County's 19,978 (1930 census) or 21,257 (1940 census). Just as Faulkner's fictional county is an approximation of Lafayette County, the DY database is a representation of Faulkner's fictional realm, a rough guide as opposed to a census. Rather than provide a complete tally of Yoknapatawpha's citizens, DY instead collects all the people Faulkner found it worth mentioning—even if only in passing—in his novels and short stories set in Yoknapatawpha County, and this also includes many characters from its past. While this may not give us a complete picture of the county, it surely can tell us important things about it.

The sheer volume of information available in DY, as well as the various ways it can be retrieved and organized, can be intimidating or bewildering to new users. Some guides for how to start using DY are provided in this essay and book, but we can only point people in a general direction. Most of DY's digital terrain is yet unexplored. For example, unnamed characters are understandably left out of the print guides nearly entirely. Since many African American characters are never named,[2] they are vastly underrepresented in the print guides. Leaving unnamed characters out is perhaps understandable, but it also severely distorts our understanding of the racial makeup of Yoknapatawpha County by effectively erasing a large part of the African American population. However, DY is not bound by the costs of printing or concerns about unwieldy size, so these characters can be discovered more easily, which may lead in turn to seeing them differently. For example, the "Unnamed Blind Negro Musician" who sits in front of Rogers' restaurant in *Flags in the Dust* does not appear in any print guides, but by clicking on him in DY, we can see that he is mentioned nine separate times, while Stuart MacCallum appears in only eight events and Caroline Sartoris in thirteen. This character becomes, in essence, more visible since he appears in search results alongside named and more prominent characters. Is he perhaps more significant than he seems? Is he a Tiresias figure in disguise? Whatever the conclusions may be, scholars using DY are more likely to discover him, to notice his presence, and perhaps to link him to other characters, themes, and interpretations.

Character Biographies

Each character is given a brief biography in the database, and this biography is unique to each text if a character appears in more than one. These brief, usually one-paragraph, biographical summaries provide a quick overview of the characters' importance in their respective texts. Cumulative Character biographies draw on all appearances of a character to create an overview of his or her role in the Yoknapatawpha fiction as a whole, and I discuss these in more detail in a section below. The brief biographies linked to a single text may be accessed numerous ways, but a good starting point is to choose a text from the list at the bottom of the home screen which will bring up a map showing the locations associated with that narrative. The "Display Controls" box on the left side of the map allows you to tweak what the map shows, including the option to add characters. Choosing to show all characters will fill the map with a unique icon for each character, and for novels that can mean a very crowded map. There are different icons for men and women, and white, black, or mixed white/black icons denote white, black, and mixed racial categories, while red icons are used for Native American characters.

In order to reduce crowding and allow for more exploration of individual characters, it helps to limit those shown to either "Major" or "Major and Secondary" (zooming in on the map can also provide separation of sometimes overlapping character icons). Even more useful can be checking the box for "Alphabetic List," which will create a new pop-up window on the right listing every character present or mentioned in the text. Now you can check the box of one or more characters from the list, and clicking the "Show" button will remove all characters except those you have checked. Clicking on one of the character icons brings up an extremely useful set of tools in a new pop-up window with three tabs: Biography, Character Information, and Events. The Biography tab provides a quick overview of the character's role in that text, and the Character Information tab lists the fifteen categories mentioned at the beginning of this essay. The Events tab gives users clickable links to every Event in which the character appears in that text, making it incredibly easy to examine every action, word, and mention of any and all characters.

Groups of Characters

While the features mentioned in the previous section are helpful to learn more about individuals, there can also be value in searching for large groups of characters within a single work. A search for all of the black characters in *The Unvanquished*, for example, yields just ten named black characters and another nineteen unnamed characters (or character groups), which is perhaps surprisingly few in a Civil War–era novel in which emancipation plays a major role. The lack of naming suggests that African Americans are important primarily in their identities as slaves, not as individuals. Ringo has a prominent role early in the novel, but by the end he is largely irrelevant, taking on a subservient role. The freed slaves trying to cross the river in "Raid" are described as a "tide" (104), a "mob," and a "wave" (106); they are faceless, nameless, and unimportant as individual subjects: "We couldn't see them, and they could not see us" (83). One character whose description jumps out from the anonymous characters in the novel is "Unnamed Lynched Negro." This is the man apparently killed by Grumby and left hanging from a tree as a warning to Bayard and Ringo. While this character is perhaps easy to overlook, once you notice him in DY, you may also notice how Faulkner has constructed him as a disposable character, unimportant outside of his dead body's significance to the novel's main white characters. The name chosen for him by the DY editors calls attention to his disposability in the world of Yoknapatawpha, and his character biography reminds us that Faulkner describes him initially as a "thing hanging over the middle of the road from a limb" (177). In DY, our attention is drawn to something that Faulkner wanted to be unobtrusive mise-en-scène, and we may note the ways in which the culture of Faulkner's time and place similarly wants to erase the humanity of black people through objectification and through culturally sanctioned violence.

So if *The Unvanquished* has surprisingly few black characters, which Faulkner novel has the most? *Go Down, Moses* might be a reasonable guess, and indeed it does top this list with 71 different black characters, while *Flags in the Dust* has 63 (of course, many of these are groups of people in each novel). Interestingly, *The Mansion* has 54 black characters,

Light in August has 48, and *The Reivers* has 44, while novels that we might think of as dealing primarily with race have fewer: 40 in *Absalom* and just 27 in *Intruder in the Dust*. It turns out that the Snopes trilogy also comes out near the top when it comes to female characters (though the women are not so culturally diverse). *The Mansion* has 76 female characters (66 of whom are white), *The Town* has 66 (57 white), and *The Hamlet* has 57 (52 white), making them three of the top four novels in terms of sheer numbers of female characters. If we look at the largest number of black and female characters, *Go Down, Moses* has the most with 16 (along with 14 white females), which might be expected by many Faulkner scholars, while perhaps less-expectedly, *The Reivers* includes 15 (with another 28 white females). Ranking third by this metric is *Light in August* with 11 black females (and an additional 39 white women), and *Flags in the Dust* has 10 black women and 51 white women, which ranks it third in terms of total female characters. *Sanctuary* might be a novel expected to rank high in terms of female characters, and while it does have 46 total, that is significantly fewer than each of the books in the Snopes trilogy. Any of these searches could be refined in multiple ways, such as filtering out characters who are only mentioned but never present in the text. The results of any such searches can be used to generate a new map of the text populated with only the search criteria, facilitating further exploration.

It is important to note that a simple tally of numbers of characters tells only one part of the story. It does not tell us, for instance, how significant a role those characters may play, something which might well be of more interest. Of course, a concept like significance is not one easily handled by a database. The DY editors do begin to address this question with the category of Rank, with the choices being Major, Secondary, Minor, and Peripheral. This is one of many places where the subjective judgments of editors necessarily intrude on a seemingly objective database. In reality, there are many subjective choices and interpretive judgments that must be made in order to present the data in usable forms. One advantage of being able to sort by Rank, for instance, is the less-cluttered visual representation on maps and graphs when looking at smaller sets of characters. Secondary characters are those who have dialogue or do things reported in the narrative (and as DY events) but are not important enough in the editors' view to be considered Major. Minor characters would be those who appear directly, speak rarely (if ever), and act only in ways not significant to the story. Peripheral characters are referred to but do not appear directly in the narrative. These are not rigid categories, and some decision-making is necessary for editors. Is Tobe in "A Rose for Emily" Major, Secondary, or Minor, for example? The case could be made that he is a Major character, but his infrequent appearances could also suggest he is a Minor character. Ultimately, despite his lack of action and dialogue, the editors deemed him significant enough to rank as Secondary, though some users might disagree. Of course, characters can also be different Ranks in different texts. For example, "Colonel Sartoris" is a Major character in *The Unvanquished*, a Minor one in *The Sound and the Fury*, and a Peripheral one in "Barn Burning."

With those definitions and caveats in mind, we can consider some examples from among the character ranks. When we look for black women who are Major characters, there are just seven in the entire corpus, no more than one in any given text, compared to fifty white women considered Major. *Flags in the Dust* and *Sanctuary* each have three Major white female characters; *The Sound and the Fury* also has three, and, with Dilsey also considered Major, it ranks as the only novel with four major female characters. By comparison, *The Sound and the Fury* also has four male characters considered Major, while the texts with the highest number of Major male characters are *Flags in the Dust*, "Smoke," and *The Hamlet* with seven each. Which characters get to narrate in a first-person voice might also be deemed significant, and by that metric it is interesting to note that the only female characters who speak directly are Cora, Addie, and Dewey Dell in *As I Lay Dying* (1930). No black characters are given first-person narrator status. All of this should make clear that search results in DY are starting points for study and scholarship, not definitive conclusions. The database can alert us to topics worth exploring further, but raw numbers tell only partial stories.

Moving the line of inquiry to Native American characters, we can see that there are just twenty-six female Indian characters. This lack of representation is probably not shocking, but looking deeper shows an even greater degree of marginalization than that of the African American women. Only one of these characters is given a name. Mohataha, who is Issetibbeha's sister and Ikkemotubbe's mother, appears three times on the list because she is in "A Name for the City," *Requiem for a Nun*, and *The Mansion* (where her name is spelled Mahataha). She also has two more entries as "Doom's Mother" in "Red Leaves" and "A Justice," and another as "Ikkemotubbe's Mother" in "The Old People," meaning this one character accounts for 23 percent of all Indian females in the database. Why does an apparently obscure character appear so often? Why does only this one Native American woman have a name? Different scholars may have different answers, but it seems significant that her biography on the site tells us that she is the "Chickasaw matriarch" who signs land deeds for many of the early settlers of Yoknapatawpha, including Quentin Compson II in 1821, providing legal backing for the dissolution of her son's kingdom. She is important for giving birth to a male and because, like Eve before her, she is credited for giving away the garden of earthly paradise and instigating the Fall.

Further confirmation of this patriarchal world comes from the fact that none of the other Indian women characters are named, and, in fact, eighteen of the twenty-six are identified by terms that denote their relationships to men, such as "Issetibbeha's Second Wife," "David Colbert's wife," and "Herman Basket's Aunt's Second Cousin." In other words, these women are often only identifiable by their relationships to men; they are unimportant in their own right, and this connects them to black and white women in patriarchal Yoknapatawpha County. The possessive appellations for the women are redolent of the people-as-property connotations of slave names like Tennie's Jim and Tomey's Turl; they reflect these women's positions and value in their societies and their roles in the stories. Boon Hogganbeck's grandmother accounts for another four of the twenty-six entries (another 15 percent), although she is designated as Peripheral in all of them (the least significant of the four ranks). Why might she appear so (relatively) often? Each of her appearances serves to underscore the same point: that her sexual relationship with a white man is the source of Boon's plebeian pedigree.[3] We can then expand the parameters to put these numbers in a wider context and see that overall there are 261 unnamed female characters and almost 69 percent of them (179) are white. There are 1,456 unnamed male characters, and 78 percent of those (1,139) are white. DY cannot tell you what to make of facts like these, but it can illuminate such occurrences and make them visible in ways that the texts themselves or traditional print guides cannot.

Although black, white, and Indian racial groups are, of course, the most prominent in Yoknapatawpha County, the DY database does tabulate some other racial categories as well. Faulkner's fictional universe is certainly not known for including Asian or Asian American characters; indeed, a search for all Asian characters returns just eleven total results (by comparison, Ulysses S. Grant appears ten times). What jumps out more than their paucity is that none of them gets a name, with the possible exception of Das in "Ad Astra." As the DY editors note in their description of him, though, Das is a common term for servant, "so it may be used by the subadar in the story not as a name but as a respectful title of address." Not only are all (or virtually all) of the Asian characters unnamed, but most of them are only referred to in passing; they are not actual characters present in action of the text. That is, characters use references to "Polynesian Chiefs" or "The Bornese" to connote something exotic, completely foreign, and essentially unknowable. This suggests just how insular Mississippi and the South were during Faulkner's writing life, particularly its early years. Ethnicity beyond African American, Native American, and European American was culturally almost nonexistent, something only experienced vicariously. In fact, the 1940 Census lists the Asian and Pacific Islander population in Mississippi as 0.0 percent, while in 1950 it is 0.1 percent.

Race, class, and gender may be the most obvious groups to start with, but the database contains many other ways to group characters that may be quite illuminating. For example, a search using the Vitality field reveals that 220 characters die in the narrative events of a text (*Absalom* has the most). However, only twenty characters are born across all the Yoknapatawpha short stories and novels. A check of the site's Genealogies page (discussed below) confirms that the prominent founding families of Yoknapatawpha are dying out over the course of the saga. Even those famously proliferating Snopeses are whittled down in the last generation to Byron's "four half-Snopes half-Apache Indian children" (*The Town* 389–90; *The Mansion* 327) who are sent back to Texas.

Occupations

The Characters Search function also allows for combining Occupation with other search parameters. For example, searching for all white characters whose Occupation is Domestic Service yields just three results, all of them men. So few whites in this line of work may not be surprising, but the absence of women might be. Additionally, the same search for blacks in Domestic Service results in 101 characters, 38 of whom are female. A similar search for black characters identified as Criminal for their occupation produces just five characters, while there are 104 whites who are labeled Criminal.[4] Does this mean that Faulkner is working against stereotypes of dangerous, immoral, criminal blacks? Perhaps, although some researchers might conclude that blacks are simply underrepresented in all walks of life in Faulkner's fiction, that his world is disproportionately white. Or as a correlative, is Faulkner engaging in stereotypes of poor whites? Of the 27 white female criminals, 26 are from either the Lower Class group (25) or Poor White (1), and 68 of the 77 white male criminals are from the Lower Class (58) or Poor White (10) categories. Perhaps this tells us less about Faulkner's attitude toward the lower class or poor whites and more about the socioeconomic realities of the north Mississippi hill country. It is simply not an area rife with white-collar crime. Nonetheless, the relative paucity of black criminals suggests that Faulkner is intentionally working against the racist stereotypes of his era. Users can employ this feature of the site to create their own lists of, say, all the doctors or all the sheriffs or all the prostitutes who appear in the Yoknapatawpha saga.

Recurring Characters

Of course, many characters appear in multiple Faulkner texts, and the DY database allows for comparisons and analysis of different iterations of the same character. Lucas Beauchamp, for instance, appears in six different texts. Interestingly, his race is identified as "Black" in four of them but "Mixed Black White" in the other two. This apparent inconsistency is due to the DY editors relying on the internal evidence from each text rather than assuming authorial intention in one story based on details in another. A close look at the data reveals more than a Faulknerian quirk; rather, he developed Lucas into a more complex character as he returned to him throughout his career. The four texts in which he is categorized as "Black" are the four earliest in which he appears: "A Point of Law," "Pantaloon in Black," "Gold Is Not Always," and "Go Down, Moses." As Faulkner reworked those stories for the novel *Go Down, Moses,* he developed the more complicated backstory of Lucas and his mixed-race ancestry, eventually making him, by the time of *Intruder in the Dust,* perhaps the strongest, most complex, and most interesting African American male character in the entire Yoknapatawpha saga. Yet even as the DY data reveals, it can also conceal. Editors are forced to choose an Occupation for Lucas, and his is listed as "farming" in all six texts. While this is certainly accurate, we might consider the limiting effects of this choice when arguably his bootlegging is perhaps just as important in some of the texts. An occupation of bootlegger would, for instance, capture his rebelliousness and rejection of racist codes in *Go Down, Moses,* a text in which readers see Lucas working with a metal detector and an illegal still but not doing much farming. This choice also affects the numbers in the search example above for black criminals. Lucas would not be captured in that search, though arguably his behavior in some texts might qualify him for inclusion.

Cumulative Characters Index

The Cumulative Characters Index allows users to explore recurring characters like Lucas Beauchamp in yet another way. There are 3,725 cumulative characters entries—which is all of the unique characters Faulkner created, filtering out multiple entries for Lucas, Quentin Compson, John Sartoris, and the like. For characters who only appear in one text, these cumulative biographies are virtually identical to the ones that appear when you click on that character from the map of his or her text. The cumulative index is especially useful for characters who recur in multiple texts, as their biographies have been rewritten to account for their various iterations. For example, there is a single entry for V. K. Suratt/Ratliff despite his name change, while the entry for Ringo shows how he shifts from a Major character in six texts to a Minor character in one to Secondary in two more. Henry Armstid's cumulative biography notes how much his character traits shift from "generous, reliable, and sane" in *As I Lay Dying* to abusive and foolish in *The Hamlet,* pointing out what seems to be a contradiction in the way Faulkner presents the same character in different texts. Res Grier is another character who is presented very differently in "Two Soldiers," "Shingles for the Lord," and "Shall Not Perish." The Cumulative Characters Index is also able to note how Faulkner renames this character Eck Grier when he reuses him in the 1950s.

Mapping Characters

The mapping features of DY allow visualization of characters' movements in unique and revealing ways. Searching for all Events in which Benjy Compson is present in *The Sound and the Fury,* for instance, creates a map upon which you can watch his movement across the entire novel. Clicking the play button on either the Page Order or Chronological Order bars under the map lets you see Benjy's movements as represented by purple flashes on the map. Immediately noticeable is how Benjy virtually never leaves the Compson Place. He is constantly in motion but circumscribed within a tiny box on the map, contained within the fences of the Compson estate, peering out through the fence at the larger world from the novel's opening line. Playing the Events using Page Order, you can also watch the dizzying time shifts on the Chronological Order bar in a way that, again, allows readers, and perhaps students in particular, to see clearly just how much Benjy jumps around in time. (A similar effect can be achieved by clicking play on the Chronological Order bar and watching the Page Order jump seemingly randomly along its continuum.)

Performing the same search for Quentin Compson (Caddy's brother, not daughter) provides an interesting comparison. While the same wildly jumbled chronology is evident (as we might expect), the difference between Quentin's geographical movement and Benjy's is jarring. For the first ten or fifteen events (a few seconds, depending on the speed at which you set the bars), Quentin's movements look like Benjy's, confined to the Compson house and yard, but then the map begins flashing on the Cambridge inset as well as all over Jefferson. While Quentin may sometimes seem as mentally trapped as Benjy, the map visualizations might suggest a freedom that Quentin fails to appreciate. This is analogous to what we see thematically in the novel: Quentin is as obsessed with Caddy as Benjy is, and both brothers relate to her as a surrogate mother, but Quentin's preoccupation with her sexuality is a major difference between his and Benjy's relationships with her. Quentin chases (or does he run from?) the specter of his more worldly sister, while Benjy plaintively waits for her to come home.

Location-Character Graphs

Following a single character across multiple texts can also be illuminating. Flem Snopes makes appearances in nine different texts, and by looking at a map for each, you can track his movements through each text and through the fictional universe as a whole. In his earliest appearances in "Spotted Horses," "Centaur in Brass," and "Lizards in Jamshyd's Courtyard," we see him mostly confined to Frenchman's Bend with a few forays into Jefferson. The Location-Character graphs that are available as a link in the Display Controls sidebar allow for an alternative visualization than the map. The Force Directed Location-Character graph with Flem Snopes entered in the Name field produces a graphic with Flem represented as a blue square at the center, surrounded by green circles for each location with which he is associated: the bigger the circle, the more often he is in that place. This graph could show Flem across all nine texts or be limited to one text. The resulting graph for only *The Hamlet* shows the specific Locations that Flem visits, and most of them are in Frenchman's Bend or other places out in the county. Clicking "play" on the Chronological Order slider bar on the map shows how Flem's early activity is in Frenchman's Bend in the novel; then he moves into Jefferson proper fairly quickly. By the midpoint of the narrative, Flem is popping up frequently on both the regional and national inset maps, as well as continuing to make appearances in Jefferson, Frenchman's Bend, and the northern part of the county. Toward the end of the novel's action, he is mostly back in Frenchman's Bend, completing his pattern of spreading out into the wider world and then going back to where he started: first Yoknapatawpha County, then the world.

By the time of *The Town*, Flem's appearances are almost entirely within Jefferson, illustrating how he has moved from sharecropper to interloper to fixture of the community. In *The Mansion*, Flem's appearances are spread across Jefferson and from the northern to the southern ends of Yoknapatawpha County, as well as in Memphis and Pascagoula. (My, my, a body does get around.) Varner's Store and the Jefferson Power Plant stand out as the largest circles on the Force Directed Graph, indicating that he appears at these locations more frequently than the far-flung locales where he may only show up once, a nice reminder that Faulkner's narratives spend more time and energy concerned with Flem's roots and rise than with anything else. Also available for the same data is the Character-Location Bipartite Graph, which presents the information in a different format. Here the list of locations appears in a column on the right with the selected character(s) on the left with connecting lines of different thickness indicating strength of association. Both versions of the Character-Location Graph can be configured in a plethora of ways, so that you could determine, for example, which locations in *Absalom* are visited most frequently by female characters or how often are African American characters appearing in the Jefferson town square. Rather than groups of characters, you can also see which specific characters are connected to a specific location or even types of locations. Who visits cemeteries most frequently, for instance, is now a simple question to answer definitively.

Character-Character Graphs

There is a similar option for Character-Character Force Directed Graphs, and these reveal connections between various characters. For example, simply entering *The Sound and the Fury* as the text while leaving all other fields blank produces a somewhat chaotic jumble of blue boxes (the characters) and red lines indicating connections between characters. Most often, these connections show characters who interact, although they can also mean one character mentioning another. Together, these create meaningful links, and the thicker the red lines are, the more closely the characters are linked. Limiting the search to only male characters in *The Sound and the Fury* creates a less chaotic, though still crowded, picture of connections. Unsurprisingly, Benjy, Quentin, and Jason appear as hubs with many lines branching out, though Shreve also has a surprising number of connections. More interesting is running the same search with just female characters selected. The visual difference is striking, with a vastly reduced number of characters present and far fewer connections among them. Quite a few women are floating in space on the graph, not connected to other women at all, while many others have solitary lines linking them to just one other woman. The only thick and therefore strong connections are between family members or between domestic servants and employers, namely Dilsey and the Compson women. The same search for black characters generates a graph almost identical looking to the one for women. Both groups are restricted to domestic connections with little joining them to the wider world of political and economic power. No matter what Jason may think, it is, indeed, a white man's world.

Character-Event Graphs

Since you can also search DY for entire families, you can watch as all of the Snopeses spread across the country, a process that Maxwell Cassity compared to a contagion's spread when he showed this visually at the 2019 Faulkner and Yoknapatawpha Conference. The Event Search feature allows for searching for associations between characters—that is, when characters are present or mentioned together. One interesting application of this ability is to see where Faulkner's most notorious declining (Old South) family, the Compsons, might meet his most notorious rising (New South) family, the Snopeses. Only one Compson ever interacts with any Snopes, and this distance seems appropriate given their respective family trajectories. Perhaps equally appropriate is the fact that it is Jason Compson (the younger) who is the only member of the once-proud and once-prominent Compsons to deal with any of the Snopeses (in passing at the telegraph office in *The Sound and the Fury* and more directly with Flem in *The Mansion*). These two scheming, materialistic, and selfish men perhaps encapsulate Faulkner's negative vision of the New South better than anything else. DY helps point out that they cross paths, and it confirms that no other Compsons and Snopeses ever do—all in a search that takes a few seconds.

Genealogies

A wonderful tool for exploring aggregate data is the page on Yoknapatawpha's First Families, comprising the eleven most significant families in the Yoknapatawpha fiction displayed as family trees. Clicking on a family name displays the aggregate family tree across all texts. For Sartoris, we see, for example, all thirty members of the extended family, who appear in a total of twenty-six texts. A group biography for each family is also included, briefly introducing their importance in the world of Yoknapatawpha. Clicking on an individual family member brings up a cumulative biography, summing up the person's role across the fiction rather than the individual biographies available for each story and novel. Additional tabs show a list of all texts in which the character appears, further differentiated visually by those in which he or she is present versus only mentioned. Two more tabs provide links to Events and Locations for that character arranged chronologically by text. What this means is that with a couple of clicks, you can have a complete list of every single time and place a major character appears or is mentioned across all of Faulkner's work. This is quite remarkable, and the research potential of such tools is virtually unlimited.

Furthermore, across the top of the page with the family tree is a clickable display of every text in which the family appears. Clicking on one will highlight those characters on the family tree who are in that work while greying out those who are not. Doing this also shifts the family biography to a short essay focused just on that one text, while the individual character tabs for biography, Events, and Locations are also now limited to just that work. (A demonstration video on the site shows all these features in action with the Sartoris family.) Moving text by text, you can see how Faulkner reimagines families from one text to another. In fact, the family of Ikkemotubbe is so complicated and shifts so much in Faulkner's various retellings that two different family trees are provided, capturing how Faulkner could not or would not settle on a consistent history. DY allows these inconsistencies and evolutions to be captured, whereas in the print guides of the past, definitive and sometimes contradictory choices were made; for example, Volpe includes Elnora in the Sartoris family tree, but Brooks does not. The DY genealogy allows you to see both versions almost instantaneously. This lack of limitation, in fact, is perhaps the chief advantage that a database like DY has over printed volumes. The types of searches and uses envisioned by the project's designers and editors are only starting points. While I have barely scratched the surface of what's possible to learn about Faulkner's characters by using DY, I hope to have offered enough suggestions, tips, and examples to help scholars explore the database and discover what else can be done with this digital humanities tool.

Notes

1. For reference, Connolly says he identified about 1,700 named characters.
2. About 400 character names contain some form of the term "Unnamed Negro" or "enslaved." Though many other unnamed characters can be classified as black, many of these characters are groups of people, and many more could possibly be black, though the race is indeterminate for characters like "Unnamed Bystanders" and "Unnamed Feedstore Customers."
3. This blame-the-women mentality finds an echo in *Go Down, Moses* when Lucas Beauchamp denigrates the "woman-made" line of McCaslins (54).
4. An additional five Criminals are identified as either MixedBlack/White, Multiracial Group, or Indeterminable (the last group including Joe Christmas).

Works Cited

Brooks, Cleanth. *William Faulkner: The Yoknapatawpha Country.* Louisiana State UP, 1963.
Carothers, James B. *William Faulkner's Short Stories.* UMI, 1985.
Cassity, Maxwell. "The Yoknapatawpha Outbreak: An Epidemiological Reading of the Snopes Family." Faulkner and Yoknapatawpha Conference, 23 July 2019, University of Mississippi, Oxford, MS. Forthcoming publication.
Connolly, Thomas E. *Faulkner's World: A Directory and Synopses of Actions in His Published Works.* UP of America, 1988.
Fargnoli, A. Nicholas, Michael Golay, and Robert W. Hamblin. *Critical Companion to William Faulkner: A Literary Reference to His Life and Work.* Facts on File, 2008.
Faulkner, William. *Go Down, Moses.* 1942. Vintage International, 2011.
———. *The Mansion.* 1959. Vintage International, 2011.
———. "Mule in the Yard." *Collected Stories.* 1950. Vintage, 1995, pp. 249–64.
———. *The Town.* 1957. Vintage International, 2011.
———. *The Unvanquished.* 1938. Vintage International, 2001.
Ford, Margaret Patricia, and Suzanne Kincaid. *Who's Who in Faulkner.* Louisiana State UP, 1963.
Hamblin, Robert W., and Charles A. Peek, editors. *A William Faulkner Encyclopedia.* Greenwood Press, 1999.
Joiner, Jennie J., John Padgett, and Dorette Sobolewski. "Faulkner's *The Unvanquished.*" Added to the project: 2016. Additional editing 2019: Theresa M. Towner. Digital Yoknapatawpha, University of Virginia, http://faulkner.iath.virginia.edu/?text=UV.
Kirk, Robert W. *Faulkner's People: A Complete Guide and Index to Characters in the Fiction of William Faulkner.* U of California P, 1963.
Runyan, Harry. *A Faulkner Glossary.* Citadel Press, 1964.
U.S. Census Bureau. "1930 Census of Population." Census.gov, www.census.gov.
———. "1940 Census of Population." Census.gov, www.census.gov.
Volpe, Edmond. *A Reader's Guide to William Faulkner.* Farrar, Straus, and Giroux, 1964; reissue subtitled *The Novels,* Syracuse UP, 2003.
———. *A Reader's Guide to William Faulkner: The Short Stories.* Syracuse UP, 2004.

Events in Digital Yoknapatawpha
MAKING FAULKNER'S WORLD MOVE

Lorie Watkins

> The aim of every artist is to arrest motion, which is life, by artificial means and hold it fixed so that a hundred years later, when a stranger looks at it, it moves again since it is life.
>
> —Faulkner, "Interview with Jean Stein Vanden Heuvel" (253)

ALL READERS of William Faulkner have experienced at least one moment (and probably many more) when they suddenly realize that they have absolutely no idea what just happened in a text. This first happened to me when I read *As I Lay Dying* as a junior in high school. I became quite lost in Faulkner's multi-authored, multi-layered text, and I thought that Lafe McCallum was just being helpful by picking cotton into Dewey Dell Bundren's sack. I was pretty stunned to learn that by doing so, he was advancing his own very specific agenda. In retrospect, I probably wasn't ready to read the book, but let's face it—Faulkner is hard at whatever age you begin to read his work. That is one of the reasons that the Events category is such a key component of Digital Yoknapatawpha (DY). At base, by entering textual events into the database, scholars contributing to the project seek to outline what actually happens in a text. Those of us teaching Faulkner and working on the database realize that readers and students are going to seek help somewhere, and we want them to turn to DY for that guidance. That said, we are very committed to making the site a supplement to the text, not a replacement for it. To that end, this essay offers a definition of events in the text, describes how we construct them, and suggests ways that using the events features of the site can change a reader's textual experience.

An event in DY consists of a continuous scene—what happens within a single setting, during an unbroken length of time, with one main focus, and an unchanging narrative style. This means that occurrences like shifts of time (even mental ones), arrivals or departures, and memories can make a new event. However, as is so often the case with Faulkner, it's not necessarily that simple. As project creator and director Stephen Railton notes in his instructions on our data entry site, "When we did the data for *Flags*, for example, we decided the entire week that Bayard spends at the MacCallums' is 1 Event, but others could decide 'a new day' in such a case makes a new Event." Another such example comes from senior collaborating editor Erin Penner: "When I was doing 'Pantaloon in Black' with Dotty Dye, we were struck by the difficulty of addressing Rider's lynching. It happens parenthetically. So, is the lynching an 'event'? Does it rise to the level of an event in the narrative, even if it's nearly obscured by the narrator?" I have had many such questions myself as I've worked on various texts, but none were odder than the ones that stemmed from "Beyond." The story chronicles Judge Howard Allison's moment of death and continued existence after it in a place known simply as "Beyond." Theresa M. Towner and I faced some pretty unusual dilemmas as we edited this story for the site. First of all, where do you locate the events that occur in "Beyond" on the map? We located it to the left of South America in the "World" map inset simply as a matter of visual practicality. I created the events for the story, and Towner and I had some interesting discussions about the nature of narrative consciousness after death and how that affects the division of events. Does his realization that his servants can't see or hear him constitute an event? What about the moment of his death? Is that an event, even though his consciousness doesn't seem altered? As problematic as such questions were, they paled in comparison to the dilemma I faced when entering events for chapter 20 of *The Town*. Gavin Stevens narrates that chapter and spends most of it speculating about the nature of Eula Snopes and Manfred de Spain's affair. My first instinct was to present his entire reverie as a single event, but my colleagues Towner and Railton pointed out that while not exactly incorrect, such a categorization would be so broad as to render it useless for users searching the database. While there is room for interpretation, thanks to multiple readers and Railton's consistent editing of all events, they are remarkably uniform.

    Consistency also comes from the format we use for data entry. As those of us working on the project enter events, we have several items to consider. We enter the events last, after other editors have entered the locations and character fields. This is a matter of necessity, as we need to populate and locate the events as we create them. First, we select the text and the page number where the event begins. There are often several events within a single page, and in that case we enter the order of events within the page—which one happens first, second, and so on. This ranking is invaluable later on when we arrange the events in chronological order. We then enter the first eight to ten words of the event and note the page on which the entire event concludes. Next, we take note of the location of the event, and list all characters present or mentioned in the scene.

We have several options for the next section, narrative status, or who/what is responsible for the source of the event. If an event is "narrated," then a first- or third-person narrator shares it with the reader. It is "told" if one character tells the event to another character. It's not surprising that the text containing the most "told" events is *Absalom, Absalom!*, beginning with Rosa Coldfield's story of Thomas Sutpen, then shifting to Mr. Compson, and later to Quentin and Shreve. "Remembered" events occur when readers see a character remembering an event, even if the event may have only happened that way in that character's perception; to that end, *The Sound and the Fury* contains the most "remembered" events. Events that characters create in their own minds or imagine from are "hypothesized," and *The Mansion* contains the most of those. Finally, an event can be "narrated+consciousness," to record, as Railton puts it on the data entry site instructions, "those times when Faulkner combines third-person *and* stream-of-consciousness narrative techniques in a single paragraph. I think most such Events occur in *Light in August,* as in the novel's very first paragraph: 'Sitting beside the road ... Lena thinks, "I have come from Alabama ..." Thinking *although I have not been ...*'" In addition to *Light in August, The Mansion* and *Go Down, Moses* also feature quite a few of the "narrated+consciousness" events.

Next, we assign a date to the event as best we can. As I entered events for several short stories and for *The Town,* I found this process of assigning a date was by far the most complicated aspect of creating an events entry. Sometimes I got lucky, as with the title detective story of Faulkner's collection, *Knight's Gambit.* As Michael Wainwright notes in the key to the text of "Knight's Gambit," "The story's main action transpires on the three days before December 7th, 1941, the date of the Japanese attack on Pearl Harbor that lives in infamy." Each day was clearly marked in the text, so assigning a date to this text was extremely easy. With other texts,

I more commonly found myself making a judgment call. For example, the events of "The Tall Men" technically could have happened in 1941; but given the publication date of May 1941 and the attendant historical circumstances—the enactment of the first peacetime draft in September 1940—a date of 1940 seemed more reasonable. Such choices often come down to an educated guess, and I do mean educated. Dating events required me to read Faulkner as I never had before. Taylor Hagood perhaps puts it best when he writes of reading "Barn Burning" for DY, "The first step was to reread the story in a completely new way, and oh what kind of a reading this required. I found myself undertaking a type of close reading so intricate that it would surely have made Cleanth Brooks proud" (477).

After dating the events, editors assign each one to a prominent historical era: Pre-Removal (–1830), Antebellum (1831–1860), Civil War (1861–1865), Reconstruction (1866–1889), Turn of the Century (1890–1913), World War I (1914–1919), The Twenties (1920–1929), The Depression (1930–1940), and Midcentury (1941–). These eras and dates are crucial, because after we enter all of the event categories, we use the dates to arrange events in chronological order. Often, the most confusing thing about a Faulkner text is how the narration of it moves around in time, so being able to view a text like "A Rose for Emily" or *The Sound and the Fury* chronologically is invaluable for users.

Next, the editor enters a brief overview of the event. This summary is tricky because we want to describe what happens in a textual event, but we cannot give too much information or editorialize lest we risk replacing the text rather than supplementing it. For instance, the editors who tackled *The Sound and the Fury* summarize the first event of the novel, which spans pages 3 to 4, as follows: "Benjy watches the golfers while Luster is trying to find the quarter he lost." There's no explanation of Benjy's mental state, no discussion of his extreme reaction to hearing the golfer call for his caddie, no note of Benjy's birthday, or any examination of the nature of his relationship with Luster. The editors resist the urge to give too much information while guiding readers through the maze of Faulkner's fiction. I used their reticence as a model when, in "Knight's Gambit," I summarized the first event on page 145 as follows: "Charles marvels at his Uncle Gavin's reaction to the visit from the Harriss children." The key is to focus on what happens and avoid the temptation to reveal too many details, as I did here with the nature of Stevens's reaction.

Keywords are the other, infinitely more descriptive feature of the events entry form. As we entered the events, we chose two or three words that seemed crucial to describing what was going on during the scene. From this experience and the initial suggested keywords, we developed a more codified list during our editorial meeting in 2018. We agreed to adopt broad first-level categories of actions, aesthetics, cultural issues, environment, relationships, and themes/motifs. Under these categories are second- and third-level terms that will be searchable in the final product. As Railton notes of creating keywords on the data entry site, "Attaching useful and consistent Keywords to each Event is going to require a lot of work. But in the project's long run, it may turn out to be the most valuable contribution DY makes to Faulkner studies. If we can create a rich and supple enough database, scholars and students will be able to query the entire Yoknapatawpha at one time." Railton then provides the following example: "A scholar writing on an issue like 'racial violence' or 'environmental degradation' in Faulkner could use keywords like 'violence' and 'race,' 'land use' and 'farming,' to locate all the scenes in the stories and novels that might be relevant to such analyses." Although the codified keywords aren't searchable yet, the original keywords are. Many of us working on keywording looked to those as a guide as we developed new second- and third-level terms, so such a search could be useful. Although fully searchable keywords are, for now, a thing of the future, we're working to make them a reality in the current phase of the project. Two separate readers have already given several texts a first and second pass and added keywords to the data entry site at each level.

Even without fully searchable keywords, the events category can already give users much information about a text. When users access the home page of the site, they see a bookshelf at the bottom of the screen that serves as the entry point for each text. The default arrangement is in chronological order of publication, but users can change the order to alphabetical if they want to do so. They can also limit the bookshelf to novels, uncollected or collected short stories, and the *Knight's Gambit* stories. When users open the icon for a text, they see a map that cartographers created specifically for that text based on the two maps that Faulkner himself drew for *Absalom, Absalom!* and *The Portable Faulkner.* Users can see more information about the maps by clicking the "Commentary" tab at the top left side of the site and choosing the tab titled "Faulkner Mapping|Mapping Faulkner." How the maps change from text to text is one of the many larger narratives that DY tells about how the place was always changing and growing in Faulkner's mind. There are also maps for the region, nation, and world inset on the right to show places mentioned in the text outside of Yoknapatawpha, illustrating how Faulkner's county fits into the larger scheme of things. The maps are interactive, and when users click on a location, tabs appear to describe the location, the events that happen there, and the characters connected to it. Users can manipulate which locations, characters, and events display on different levels of the maps.

In addition to simply viewing events, users can also search them using the search button at the top of the site's main screen. Clicking this button allows users to search by events, characters, and locations. The events search allows for searching by the following parameters: text, characters (present, mentioned, or either), characters with another character, a date or range of dates, the era, location, first words of the event, summary, narrative status, date or range of dates of publication, and keyword. Users could then search for a list of events in a story and use those as a sort of reading guide as they go through the text.

Users might also search for all of the events in a text that include a particular character. Searching for Caddy Compson in *The Sound and the Fury* reveals that she is present in far more events than she is mentioned in, yet she is commonly known as the absent center of that text. Also useful is a search of characters that appear with another character. To give an example, I realized when I searched "Centaur in Brass" for events in which Eula Varner Snopes appears with her husband, Flem, that the couple never appears together outside of their home. She is mentioned once with Flem in the grocery store, but their actual relationship plays out behind closed doors, so readers really know nothing about it except the conjecture of other characters. Likewise, in *The Town,* the couple is mentioned almost twice as often as they're actually present together in public or in private, so they are definitely the subject of *much* conjecture. This type of search also made me rethink another common pairing, Lucas Beauchamp and Chick Mallison in *Intruder in the Dust.* In this novel that is ostensibly about their maturing relationship and its attendant growing mutual respect, they appear in fewer than thirty events together. Lucas appears in almost fifty events, and Chick appears in over three times that number. This distance would suggest that any change in their relationship is the result of internal individual growth more than mutual association.

Jenna Grace Sciuto presented a paper about using DY in the classroom at the 2019 Faulkner and Yoknapatawpha Conference, and in it she supports this revisionary thinking: "In a number of my students' papers, *Digital Yoknapatawpha* led them to view events and interactions between characters in a different, and often more complex, light." DY seeks to foster exactly this sort of changed perspective.

Another feature that supports such change is the ability to search by a year or a range of years. If a user searches for what Faulkner published the year before he won the Nobel Prize for literature in 1950, he or she might be surprised to learn that the only text published that year was *Knight's Gambit,* hardly one of his most well-known works. In addition to years, we can also search the site by eras. For example, the result of a search for texts that are set during the Great Depression yielded far more texts than I expected. I knew that the Depression was a major influence on Faulkner's life and work, but I had no idea that thirty-six of his texts involve that era.

Users can then create their own map of the search using the MapIt feature. One issue that several of us working with the project have noted at our various meetings is that the maps, when judged by modern online standards, look a bit dated. My students assure me that according to their expectations, informed largely by modern video games, the maps look "retro" or "basic" (their words). This means that, as a teacher of Faulkner, I have to convince my students of the value of the maps, and of the information they can yield. One way that I've done this in my classes is to take a short story, divide it into events, and have the students use a worksheet to go through the process that DY scholars have undertaken to input the data for various events. After they spend a week working out the dates, characters, locations, and descriptions of each event, I introduce them to the site, and show them how much work we've already done to make the text more accessible to them through the maps. Going through the data gathering process themselves makes them much more appreciative of the information that the maps can provide, even if they only follow the events chronologically or in narrative order to get a sense of what's actually happening in the text.

Regardless of their appearance, the maps yield something quite amazing in that they make Faulkner's fiction "move again," as my epigraph describes, when users play the events of each narrative. They can play them in their entirety, or by section, using the first two controls under the map. The speed feature on the right of each option controls the speed of displayed events. The "page order" option displays events as Faulkner orders them in the text. The "chronological order" option rearranges the events in the order that they occur in real time. There is a black bar on this line that marks the opening point of each text. When users display events using any of these options, the event first appears as a red icon, then fades to purple as a new event occurs and turns red. Users can reset the maps multiple times for multiple views of the events of a story.

To take a practical example, in the map for "A Rose for Emily," users can display all of the characters to get a sense of who, exactly, makes up the town for which the narrator claims to speak. However, when filtered for major characters, there are only four: Mr. Grierson, Emily, Homer Barron, and the unnamed narrator. If users narrow the search to just Emily by selecting only her from the alphabetic list of characters and putting the events of the story into play, the map yields a visual representation of just how contained her life is. Her story plays out primarily within the confines of her own home, and exclusively within the town of Jefferson. Perhaps this is why the narrator says that when she was alive she was "a tradition, a duty, and a care; a sort of hereditary obligation on the town" (119). Thomas Dilworth suggests that the duty that the town feels toward Emily extends to covering up the role she inevitably plays in Homer Barron's death: "The way the story is told is determined by the narrator. In the process of telling it, he implies his own and his society's cultural values, which influence attitudes and behavior toward Emily in a way that implicates him and the townspeople in her fate" (251). The most confusing aspect of this story is the telling of it, as DY confirms. Resetting the story's map and viewing it chronologically simplifies the plot and illustrates this claim. This chronological chart shows that everything, the entire story, has already happened—only the final climactic scene occurs in the present tense of the story. The jumps in time that readers experience happen because of the way the story is told, and the narrator could very well be telling the story of the town's complicity in Barron's murder.

Chronological searching can also display an accurate model of multiple events occurring at the same time. DY illustrates that while Dilsey seeks and finds solace at her church in *The Sound and the Fury*, Jason is simultaneously searching for his money in Mottstown. As a reader, I previously experienced these events separately and did not realize how contiguous they are. Faulkner can't narrate them at the same time, but DY can, and it tells a similar story with many other texts.

In addition to manipulating the presentation of events, users can also limit them to a specific period of time. For example, Railton pointed out to me in a personal interview that if users search *The Sound and the Fury* for the events of the year that Damuddy dies in 1898, the map reveals that the events are carefully ordered chronologically—all of the chaos occurs as a result of Benjy's narration. Moreover, he adds that playing the events of Benjy's section of the novel also reveals that he is incredibly constrained physically as well as mentally. While that section of the novel "jumps around," if you will, the map shows that all of the jumps occur in Benjy's mind.

In addition to these maps, users can also search events using the "character by locations in events graphs" under the tab marked "visualizations." The searchable categories are as follows: text, name, family, race, gender, class, date of birth, vitality, occupation, specific job, origin, ethnicity, cause of death, biography, and date of publication for a single year or a range of years. The combinations are endless, and endlessly surprising in part because this feature allows users to search all of the texts simultaneously or separately. Take Flem Snopes, for instance. When I think of Flem, the locations that immediately come to mind are his various homes in Jefferson and the bank, but such a search shows that he actually appears a whopping eighty-nine times in Varner's store. The bank and Varner's house run a distant second and third with fifty-seven and fifty-six appearances, respectively. This type of search interestingly reveals that the most common places where black people appear are first on the Sartoris plantation and then on the courthouse square; conversely, white people appear most often at the courthouse square and second most commonly on the Sartoris plantation. Also, the most common location for murder is Sutpen's plantation—the least is New York City. Not surprisingly, the most characters assigned the vitality status of "dead-ghost" appear on Sutpen's plantation. Users can also generate different visual representations of this information by creating "location-character graphs" and choosing a "force-directed" or "bipartite option."

Another option designed to help users bring the events of Faulkner's texts to life is found under the "About" tab at the top of the site. When users click the tab, several options pop up. The first is labeled "Credits," and it acknowledges those scholars and groups working on and funding the site. The "Dedication" tab memorializes Robbie Bingler, the lead programmer who pioneered the technical implementation of the project, and who passed away in 2019.

The "Index of Manuscripts" tab will take users to sample illustrative manuscript pages. The originals primarily come from the William Faulkner Foundation Collection at the University of Virginia's Albert and Shirley Small Special Collections Library. Others are located in the Louis Daniel Brodsky Collection of William Faulkner Materials, Special Collections and Archives, Southeast Missouri State University. Scholars try to include manuscript pages that illustrate the evolution of Faulkner's thinking about a text. As Railton and I write in the description of the pages that we chose to display for "Knight's Gambit,"

> The pages here are from the 23-page typescript of "Knight's Gambit" that Faulkner sent his agent in January, 1942—seven years, at least three rewritings, and over a dozen rejections from magazines before he completed the 150-page typescript of the novella that was published in 1949 as final story in the collection *Knight's Gambit*. Even this typescript is not the earliest version of the story, as we can tell from the cancelled version of the first page that is on the back of the sheet that the ever-frugal author reused when he typed the next version of page one.... That ur-story has been lost.

The "Index of Illustrations" tab allows users to access the magazine illustrations that accompanied Faulkner's Yoknapatawpha fictions as they appeared in magazines like the *Saturday Evening Post, Scribner's,* and *Collier's*. These materials are drawn from the William Faulkner Foundation Collection at the University of Virginia's Albert and Shirley Small Special Collections Library. Although Faulkner generally had little say in the matter of these illustrations, they're still of interest in that they offer users an initial look at how various artists first interpreted Faulkner's fiction. To wit, Weldon Bailey's first illustration for "A Rose for Emily" from the *Forum Magazine* depicts Miss Emily's home as looking like a stereotypical haunted house. George Howe's only illustration for the *Collier's Magazine* version of "Go Down, Moses" is an expressive full-color depiction of Mollie Beauchamp. Perhaps even more dramatic are Harold Von Schmidt's illustrations of "Two Soldiers" for the *Saturday*

Evening Post. Railton writes of the picture of the young boy following his brother Pete to volunteer to serve in World War II: "The larger, two-color illustration . . . is a little faded, but you can still see how Von Schmidt represents the story's young protagonist marching toward Memphis against the background of Americans who have fought in the country's earlier wars." Also included in the illustrations for "Two Soldiers" is a copy of the full-page United States Army recruiting ad captioned "First-Class Fighting Man" that faced Faulkner's story in the magazine.

The last two items under the "About" tab are the "Bibliography" and "Re-Presenting DY" tabs. The first offers a list of source materials that scholars consulted in writing entries for the site. The second is an ever-growing list of representations of DY in print, online, at conferences, and in the media.

Also of relevance to this consideration of "Events" are the materials under the "Commentaries" tab at the top of the site. Currently there are three sections. The first one, "Faulkner & Maps," is an exploration of both the maps that Faulkner drew and the website's appropriation and modification of them in various texts. The locations change with Faulkner's imagination. For instance, as the website notes,

> Where possible, we rely on Faulkner's maps, but there are quite a few places where that is not possible. The Armstid place, for example. Faulkner includes it on the 1936 map . . . , locating it southeast of Jefferson and northeast of Frenchman's Bend, along a road that comes into Yoknapatawpha from still further east. This is where Armstids' Farm appears in *Light in August* (1932): the road is the one on which Lena Grove is walking after leaving Alabama, Armstids' is the place where she spends her first night in the county, and our map of that novel locates the road and the place where Faulkner does. . . . But the Armstids' farm is also a location in *As I Lay Dying* (1930), where it is *south* of Frenchman's Bend—on the river that the Bundrens have to cross on their journey to Jefferson.

The "Faulkner's Cemeteries" tab in this section chronicles the final resting places of various characters, or, as the website says, "This display allows you to see where and how he buries the bodies." The third tab labeled "First Families" gives users access to family trees of key Faulknerian families who appear in at least four texts over three generations. As the website states, "The goal of our genealogies here is to represent the people and patterns in Faulkner's major families more dynamically and interactively, thanks to the capabilities of electronic technology." Once users search for a family, they can narrow the family tree to a specific text via the bookshelf that appears above it. All of these tools help users to envision Faulkner's changing world, especially the recently added section on pedagogy and another section featuring photographs to illustrate key points of the fiction.

This chapter simply offers an overview of some of the most interesting things that I've learned so far about ways to use events in DY, and readers should not underestimate the value of the simple search. The feature that my students have found most useful is the ability to click from event to event narratively to get a handle on a text during a first reading. As my former student Ian Pittman said after learning how to use that feature at Faulkner and Yoknapatawpha in 2018, "It's really like a living map of what's happening." I like his analogy quite a lot, and I mention it here because it is a map, both literally and figuratively. As I mapped the events of Faulkner's fictional world, they became real to me in a way that they weren't before. I began working on this project because I was interested in the digital humanities, I knew a lot about Faulkner, and I thought that I could usefully contribute to something new in Faulkner studies. I've learned much more about Faulkner than I've contributed, though. Before I started working on the project, I always read Faulkner's writing as somehow independent from the era of its production. DY made that fictive world more tangible for me. At the 2017 Faulkner and Yoknapatawpha Conference, I spoke of working on "The Tall Men," an obscure story that Faulkner wrote just before the United States became involved in World War II in early 1941. Faulkner wrote the story with a clear financial imperative to pay off owed back taxes. He anticipated its reception correctly and the story sold in less than a week to the *Saturday Evening Post*. In plotting these events for DY, I realized that the story's commercial success was largely due to Faulkner's timing. It appeared after two key events: In 1933, the United States enacted the Agricultural Adjustment Act to regulate farm surpluses, and on September 16, 1940, the first peacetime draft went into effect. "The Tall Men" joins these two events in the McCallum family's refusal to be governed by either law—the family won't take a subsidy for a crop that they didn't plant, and the twins have failed to register for the draft, even though they fully plan to enlist when and if the United States enters the war. To paraphrase my epigraph, that's when "The Tall Men" began to move again for me. To my mind, the McCallums went from being stubborn, backwoods throwbacks to an earlier generation and became contemporary Mississippians distrusting a federal government that has lied to them before, even as they continue to swear allegiance to it.

Or at least that's my understanding of it for now. I will add in closing that the really remarkable thing about DY is that, much like Faulkner's fiction, readers in the future will do things with it that he/we never imagined. Namely, I've mentioned the data entry site for the project several times in this chapter. Careful readers will notice that there isn't a corresponding entry for it in my Works Cited page. For various reasons, most of them economic ones related to data storage, that site is private and password-protected. However, in the future, the project editors plan to make it public. Johannes Burgers, the project's associate editor, has already started working with the raw data. He writes in "Digital Yoknapatawpha Visualizations," "What is more exciting about . . . a complex database is that the data can be user-driven and interactive. This is why I am currently working on a dashboard that allows a range of data views determined by the user. . . . This version allows for multiple data views on the fly and enables users to 'drill down' into the data. As a version of this is being developed in HTML for the main project website the functionality has been largely stripped down at this point to forefront the interface." Who knows what some other bright data analyst who reads Faulkner for fun might find when he or she can click directly into the data we've entered and interpreted for the general user site? Surely something that I can't even imagine, and something that Faulkner never dreamed of. Towner perhaps describes DY best in her contribution to the *Mississippi Quarterly*'s roundtable on DY when she dubs it "a twenty-first-century monument to the work of America's greatest writer" (466). Remarkably, it may grow for centuries to come.

Works Cited

Burgers, Johannes H. "Digital Yoknapatawpha Visualizations." Digital Pedagogy Lab, https://joostburgers.wordpress.com/digital-humanities-projects/digital-yoknapatawpha-visualizations.

Burgers, Johannes H., and Elizabeth Cornell. "Faulkner's 'A Rose for Emily.'" Added to the project: 2012. Additional editing 2018: John Corrigan and Jennie J. Joiner. Digital Yoknapatawpha, University of Virginia, http://faulkner.iath.virginia.edu/?text=RE.

Burgers, Johannes H., John Corrigan, and Ben Robbins. "Faulkner's *The Mansion*." Added to the project: 2018. Digital Yoknapatawpha, University of Virginia, http://faulkner.iath.virginia.edu/?text=M.

Dilworth, Thomas. "A Romance to Kill for: Homicidal Complicity in Faulkner's 'A Rose for Emily.'" *Studies in Short Fiction*, vol. 36, no. 3, Summer 1999, pp. 251–62.

Faulkner, William. "Interview with Jean Stein Vanden Heuvel." *Lion in the Garden: Interviews with William Faulkner, 1926–1962*, edited by James B. Meriwether and Michael Millgate, Random House, 1968, pp. 237–56.

Hagood, Taylor. "Humanism, Faulkner, and the Digital." "*Digital Yoknapatawpha*: A Written Roundtable." *Mississippi Quarterly*, vol. 68, nos. 3–4, 2015, pp. 476–80.

Joiner, Jennie J., Mike Wainwright, and Lorie Watkins. "Faulkner's 'Knight's Gambit.'" Added to the project: 2019. Digital Yoknapatawpha, University of Virginia, http://faulkner.iath.virginia.edu/?text=KGB.

Napolin, Julie, Johannes H. Burgers, Taylor Hagood, Robert Coleman, Sarah Perkins, and Ren Denton. "Faulkner's *The Sound and the Fury*." Added to the project: 2014. Digital Yoknapatawpha, University of Virginia, http://faulkner.iath.virginia.edu/?text=SF.

Padgett, John, and Stephen Railton. "Faulkner's *Flags in the Dust*." Added to the project: 2012. Digital Yoknapatawpha, University of Virginia, http://faulkner.iath.virginia.edu/?text=FD.

Penner, Erin. "Re: Events Chapter." Received by Lorie Watkins, 19 July 2019.

Railton, Stephen. "Illustrating 'Go Down, Moses.'" Added to the project: 2018. Digital Yoknapatawpha, University of Virginia, https://faulkner.drupal.shanti.virginia.edu/content/godownmosesillustrations.

———. "Illustrating 'A Rose for Emily.'" Added to the project: 2018. Digital Yoknapatawpha, University of Virginia, https://faulkner.drupal.shanti.virginia.edu/content/emilyillustrations.

———. "Illustrating '2 Soldiers.'" Added to the project: 2018. Digital Yoknapatawpha, University of Virginia, http://faulkner.drupal.shanti.virginia.edu/node/16323?canvas.

———. Personal interview, 19 July 2019.

Railton, Stephen, and Christopher Rieger, "Faulkner Mapping|Mapping Faulkner." Added to the project: 2017. Digital Yoknapatawpha, University of Virginia, http://faulkner.iath.virginia.edu/media/resources/DISPLAYS/FaulknerMapsHP.html.

Railton, Stephen, and Lorie Watkins. "Faulkner's 'The Tall Men.'" Added to the project: 2016. Additional editing 2019: Johannes Burgers and Erin Penner. Digital Yoknapatawpha, University of Virginia, http://faulkner.iath.virginia.edu/?text=TM.

Railton, Stephen, Theresa M. Towner, and Johannes H. Burgers. "Faulkner's *Absalom, Absalom!*" Added to the project: 2017. Additional editing 2019: John Corrigan. Digital Yoknapatawpha, University of Virginia, http://faulkner.iath.virginia.edu/?text=AA.

Pittman, Ian Alfred. Personal interview, 9 Sept. 2019.

Sciuto, Jenna. "Faulkner's Families: *Digital Yoknapatawpha* in the Classroom." Faulkner and Yoknapatawpha Conference: Faulkner's Families, Oxford, MS, July 2019.

Towner, Theresa M. "*Digital Yoknapatawpha:* Where We Are." "*Digital Yoknapatawpha:* A Written Roundtable." *Mississippi Quarterly*, vol. 68, nos. 3–4, 2015, pp. 464–66.

Towner, Theresa M., James B. Carothers, Elizabeth Cornell, Chad Jewett, Cheryl Lester, and John Padgett. "Faulkner's *Light in August*." Added to the project: 2013. Digital Yoknapatawpha, University of Virginia, http://faulkner.iath.virginia.edu/?text=LA.

Towner, Theresa M., James B. Carothers, Jennie J. Joiner, and Lorie Watkins. "Faulkner's *The Town*." Added to the project: 2018. Digital Yoknapatawpha, University of Virginia, http://faulkner.iath.virginia.edu/?text=T.

Towner, Theresa M., and Lorie Watkins. "Faulkner's 'Beyond.'" Added to the project: 2018. Digital Yoknapatawpha, University of Virginia, http://faulkner.iath.virginia.edu/?text=BE.

Towner, Theresa M., Robert Coleman, Erin Kay Penner, and Ben Robbins. "Faulkner's *Go Down, Moses*." Added to the project: 2016. Digital Yoknapatawpha, University of Virginia, http://faulkner.iath.virginia.edu/?text=GDM.

Watkins, Lorie. "Digital Yoknapatawpha in 2017 and Beyond." Faulkner and Yoknapatawpha Conference, Oxford, MS, 25 July 2017.

Watkins, Lorie, and Stephen Railton. "Manuscripts &c: 'Knight's Gambit.'" Added to the project: 2019. Digital Yoknapatawpha, University of Virginia, http://faulkner.drupal.shanti.virginia.edu/node/20263?canvas.

Visualizing Narrative Modes

THE NARRATOLOGICAL MAPPING OF TRAUMA IN FAULKNER'S *SANCTUARY*

BEN ROBBINS

THIS CHAPTER will demonstrate the effectiveness of Digital Yoknapatawpha (DY) as a tool for pursuing narratological readings of Faulkner's literature, in particular as a means to illuminate the spatial and temporal organization of the author's narratives. DY's MapIt feature allows users to plot the different events in a given text according to their narrative status under five categories: narrated, told, remembered, hypothesized, and narrated-plus-consciousness. When displayed on the map of Faulkner's fictional county, they visualize how the different narrative modes the author employs are spatially distributed. Additionally, when one sets the timelines for a particular text in motion, one can observe the extent to which different kinds of narrative mode move across space and time.

Using Faulkner's 1931 novel *Sanctuary* as a case study, a novel that contains each of the five "narrative statuses" under which we categorize events, I will show how the MapIt function reveals the relationship between authorial choice of narrative mode and the representation of a traumatized consciousness. In particular, it becomes clear that the manner in which the traumatic events Temple Drake endures at the Old Frenchman place and Miss Reba's place are remembered, hypothetically processed, or psychologically rendered in the text is, to different degrees, geographically and temporally restricted. The mapping of each narrative mode within the novel reveals the following: First, Temple's rape at the Old Frenchman place and the abuse she experiences in Memphis become a marked absence in narrative memory; second, free interior monologue, when used as a break from omniscient narration, is exclusively used to access Temple's thoughts in the text, but its limited employment demonstrates the severe restrictions placed on the reader's access to Temple's psychological state as a victim; and, third, Temple is the character most frequently attached to hypothesized narrative events, which are principally deployed to imagine alternatives to her subjugation at the Old Frenchman place, suggesting that her trauma is narratively processed through her adoption of a different perspective on the violence she has undergone. These findings have significant implications for trauma theory, since the core tropes that populate literary works about trauma are evident when one conducts both close and distant readings of *Sanctuary*. Finally, I will suggest that digital humanities (DH) projects such as DY, which embed speculative and interpretative functions within them, can chart the movements of modernist narratives in revealing new ways.

How Digital Yoknapatawpha Categorizes Narrative Modes

For the purposes of data entry, DY considers each event in a Faulkner work to have a single setting, one main focus, and one narrative style, and to take place over an unbroken length of time. As collaborative editors on the project, we attribute each event to one of five categories of narrative status, after considering who or what can be identified as the event's source. First of all, "narrated" events are produced by a third- or first-person narrator, and this is the category to which events are attributed with most frequency. Second, "told" events are flagged when a character (or characters) in a Faulkner fiction tells an event to another (or others). Third, "remembered" events are used to indicate instances when readers are presented with an event as a character remembers it, whether or not the veracity or accuracy of the recollection can in fact be trusted. Fourth, "hypothesized" events pinpoint instances where characters construct a possible version of what has happened, the kind of speculative narrative reconstruction in which, for example, Quentin and Shreve engage in piecing together the life of Thomas Sutpen in *Absalom, Absalom!* (1936).

Finally, "narrated-plus-consciousness" events are used to indicate occasions when Faulkner employs both third-person and stream-of-consciousness narrative techniques in a single paragraph. This is a hybrid narrative category, since it flags moments in which omniscient or external narrative becomes mediated by the consciousness of an individual. However, it is also a somewhat capacious category, since it captures a range of narrative techniques that differ in levels of formality. For example, in the opening lines of *Light in August* (1932), the narrative engages in one such narrative shift: "Sitting beside the road, watching the wagon mount the hill toward her, Lena thinks, 'I have come from Alabama: a fur piece.' . . . Thinking *although I have not been quite a month on the road I am already in Mississippi, further from home than I have ever been before*" (401). Here the narrative moves from third-person omniscient narration to quoted interior monologue and then to free interior monologue, which is unquoted and rendered in italics. This example, however, stops short of moving to full-blown stream-of-consciousness narration, which is less formally structured. As Monika Fludernik explains, interior monologue is used "to reflect the feel of the character's incoherent musings . . . in incomplete sentences, random words and phrases or in repetitious language. . . . If the mental world is rendered as a flow of thoughts and associations, with one incomplete sentence tumbling out after the other, then the interior monologue turns into so-called *stream of consciousness*" (81). An example of a shift between stream-of-consciousness and omniscient narration in a single paragraph occurs in *Flags in the Dust* (1929), when Horace Benbow observes two female characters playing tennis: "Girlwhite and all thy little Oh. Not pink, no. For a moment I thought she'd no. Disgraceful, her mamma would call it. Or any other older woman. Belle's are pink O muchly 'Oaten reed above the lyre,' *Horace chanted, catching the ball at his shoe-tops with a full swing, watching it duck viciously beyond the net*" (187; emphasis added). Here the narrative shifts from rendering the disconnected and syntactically incomplete internal thoughts of Horace, in response to the tennis attire of the women, to omniscient narration describing the wider scene. Both of the passages from *Light and August* and *Flags in the Dust* would be categorized as narrated-plus-consciousness events, despite their technical differences. Importantly, DY does not use this narrative status to flag events that *only* employ stream-of-consciousness narrative, such as those that appear in the first three sections of *The Sound and the Fury* (1929) or many of the chapters of *As I Lay Dying* (1930), which are instead identified as (first-person) narrated events. The only exception here would be instances when the character remembers another event within an unbroken stream-of-consciousness narrated passage, in which case it would be placed separately under the category of a remembered event. These five definitional categories do not follow a traditional narratological typography, but they nevertheless capture a spectrum of narrative instances whose spatial and temporal logics ultimately diverge.

The particular function of DY that enables users to map narrative modes from Faulkner's fictions is the MapIt button, which can be found on the Event Search page once results have been generated. The Event Search page allows a user to select a particular Faulkner text or search all events in the database for aspects such as featured characters (either present or mentioned), date of event, location of event, or key words associated with events. Once the events have been called up for a particular search, they can be plotted for an individual text on the DY map using the MapIt button. For my analysis of *Sanctuary,* I select each narrative status from the drop-down list for the novel on the Event Search page to call up all the novel's events for each of the five categories, and then I plot each narrative status separately on the DY map using the MapIt function. This then generates a map that shows how the events that fall under each narrative mode are distributed across space in Faulkner's imagination.

What Digital Yoknapatawpha Can Tell Us about Narrative Modes in *Sanctuary*

Sanctuary offers a productive case study for contrasting differences in the spatial distribution of these modes, as it contains each of the narrative statuses for which DY collects data. By plotting these on the DY map and conducting a comparative analysis, it becomes apparent that Faulkner places different spatial and temporal boundaries around each narrative type.[1] In making these comparisons, I am particularly interested in the ways trauma structures narrative patterns in the novel. *Sanctuary* focuses on Temple Drake, a teenage student and sexualized New Woman, who loses the protection of her date Gowan Stevens after he crashes their car while driving to a bootlegger's homestead—the Old Frenchman place—looking for liquor. Temple becomes the victim of assault and rape by a series of bootleggers and gangsters, led by Popeye, at both the Old Frenchman place and a brothel in Memphis owned by Miss Reba, where she is taken against her will. As I will demonstrate, the narrativization of these events is dictated by the representation of trauma.

The two narrative modes that have the widest spatial distribution in *Sanctuary* are narrated and told. Narrated events take place not only in Yoknapatawpha, Oxford, and Memphis in the novel, but the inset maps show both regional and global narrated events (the latter is the novel's final scene, in Paris's Luxembourg Gardens). Told events also take place in Yoknapatawpha, Oxford, and Memphis in the novel, but they can be additionally found on the regional, national, and global inset maps (in San Francisco, Kansas's Leavenworth, and New York on the national stage and in the Philippines on the global stage). Such wide spatial distribution in both cases can in part be attributed to the frequency with which told and narrated events occur in the novel; using the Narrative Analysis visualization feature in DY, one can see that 77 percent of the novel's events are narrated and 15 percent told. There is, however, a significant difference in temporal distribution between these two narrative modes; narrated events range from 1862 to autumn 1929, whereas told events only range from 1902 (Popeye's birthday on Christmas Day) to June 1929. As such, omniscient narration is substantially more temporally mobile (by forty years) in *Sanctuary* than told narration. It should also be noted that both modes of narration move little beyond the point in time at which the text begins; the first event in the text (where Popeye watches Horace Benbow drink from the spring) is dated 7 May 1929, but narrated events only take the reader as far into the future as autumn 1929 in the Luxembourg Gardens. Similarly, told events only propel us to mid-June 1929 in Miss Reba's Memphis brothel, where Temple is bribed to remain during Popeye's absence. Consequently, the text's temporal mobility serves to dramatize the past, as well as the past's shaping influence on the present, moving little into the future.[2]

When one plots the five remembered events in *Sanctuary* using the MapIt feature, it becomes apparent that differences in narrative memory's mobility can, in part, be attributed to the gender of the character who is the source of the remembering. Events are remembered by three characters in the novel: two by Temple Drake; two by Horace Benbow (the middle-aged lawyer who investigates the crimes at the Old Frenchman place); and one by Ruby Lamar (the devoted common-law wife of the bootlegger Lee Goodwin and mother of their infant son). Of these, Horace's memories are by far the most temporally mobile. His first remembered event (in page order) takes him from 13 May 1929 back to 7 May 1929, where the novel begins, as he recalls first seeing Ruby's child at the Old Frenchman place "lying in a wooden box behind the stove" (121), an environment he found to be oppressively suffused with "Popeye's black presence" (121). While of course this flashback evidences very little temporal mobility, the recollection functions as the stimulus for a deeper excavation of Horace's memory. Two events later in the text (again in page order), Horace goes on to remember playing with his sister Narcissa as a child on the street in front of the family home in Jefferson in 1897 in a reverie of sentimental, premodern nostalgia; before the street was paved, the rain would form a canal before the Benbow house, through which he and his sister would paddle and make mudholes "with the intense oblivion of alchemists" (122), and he thinks back on "the prints of his and his sister's naked feet in the artificial stone" (123). Deep memory, for Horace, serves as an escape from the criminal excesses of the narrative present and its attendant abuses of the innocence of childhood.

In contrast, remembered events do not have such a liberating function for the female characters of the text. Ruby recalls visiting her lover Lee Goodwin in Leavenworth Prison in the immediate post–World War I period, working night shifts as a waitress so she could visit him on Sundays, elaborating that "I lied to him and made money to get him out of prison, and when I told him how I made it, he beat me" (61). Ruby's memory presents the criminal back story to the murder plot unfolding in the present, a murder for which Lee has been falsely charged. Temple's remembered events evidence even less temporal depth. At Miss Reba's brothel, she remembers dressing for dances at the university in Oxford, Mississippi, during the semester that ran up to her fateful date with Gowan on 11 May 1929; in this scene, Temple witnesses her fellow female students victimizing one woman due to her presumed sexual experience, "their eyes like knives until you could almost watch her flesh where the eyes were touching it" (152). Her mind also casts back slightly to a moment earlier in the same day of her date with Gowan when he buys a bottle of hair-oil to drink in Dumfries, Mississippi. The memory is triggered after his drunken driving causes them to crash their car near the bootleggers' mansion. Temple's memory, in both of these examples, traces the causation of events that led to her sexual subjugation at the hands of Popeye. First, she recalls a university culture in which the virgin/whore dichotomy is strictly policed; as Diane Roberts argues, Faulkner in fact disables the virgin/whore opposition through Temple, as she is a virgin forced into sexual knowledge (129). And second, Temple thinks back to how Gowan's reckless actions put her in a highly vulnerable situation. Female-remembered narration, then, roves around the map, but not deep in time, seeking out events in the not-too-distant past that have produced their current desperate situation, wherever that may take them in the region or nation outside of Yoknapatawpha (whether elsewhere in Mississippi or Kansas). Male-remembered narration, on the contrary, is temporally mobile but relatively spatially static; Horace's memory takes him home, to the Benbow House in Jefferson at the center of the map, more than thirty years earlier, finding refuge in a past at odds with a present he perceives to be devoid of innocence. A clear difference is struck here between masculine nostalgic remembered narration (spatially static, temporally mobile) and feminine narrative memory that unearths a painful past which informs the present (spatially mobile, relatively temporally static).[3]

Temple's memory does not grant the reader access to events at the Old Frenchman place and Miss Reba's brothel, meaning that the sites of her abuse are a marked absence in narrative memory. This may indicate that the rape has become a psychological void, since only the events that lead up to it can be recalled by the victim. The text, however, does give us limited access to Temple's thoughts at the Old Frenchman place and Miss Reba's through three narrated-plus-consciousness events that contain snatches of her free interior monologue. The rape itself still remains a mental blank space, but the three events establish a pattern: when omniscient narration dips into Temple's thoughts, she questions or invokes the authority of men with whom she is associated to protect herself from Popeye and his gang. Her interior monologue is first activated at the spring and road location by looking on in horror at Gowan's wild driving, observing him "braced and clinging as the car leaped and bounced in the worn ruts" (37). Temple's thoughts surface in the omniscient narration again when she notices Gowan walking down to the barn at the Old Frenchman place to continue drinking after the crash: "[H]e's getting drunk again. That makes three times today" (51). In both instances, Faulkner highlights Gowan's inability to provide safety and protection in this new environment. In the third and final narrated-plus-consciousness event, Temple imagines at Miss Reba's that it is the Sunday morning before the rape rather than the evening after it: "Maybe it was half-past-ten this morning, that half-past-ten-oclock. Then I'm not here, she thought. This is not me. Then I'm at school. I have a date tonight" (152). Her free interior monologue meditates here on her disembodiment and displacement through a brief shift back in time, and she again imagines the presence of alternative male figures that could have averted her current situation. To sum up, when Faulkner provides us access to Temple's thoughts as free interior monologue, snippets that are couched in omniscient narration, they may invoke the protection of absent men or try to rewind time, but they shy away from the psychological processing of the abuse and rape itself. It is remarkable, too, when the three narrated-plus-consciousness events are plotted on the map, how little temporal and spatial mobility they evidence: all take place in the vicinity of the two locations where Temple is held against her will (the Old Frenchman place and Miss Reba's) and within twenty-four hours of each other from 11 to 12 May 1929. Thus the narrative mode of free interior monologue itself illustrates Temple's physical and mental imprisonment on the DY map, ironically not presenting its narrative freedom at all.

These patterns do in fact appear to be typical of Faulkner's spatial and temporal representation of trauma in modernist narrative. A key character in *Flags in the Dust*, (Young) Bayard Sartoris, returns to Jefferson in 1919 after serving in the Royal Air Force during World War I in Europe, where his brother was shot down and for whose death he feels responsible. If a user plots, as I did for Temple, all the narrated-plus-consciousness events in *Flags* that give us access to Bayard's thoughts as free interior monologue (by selecting him as a "present" character in the Event Search options), a similar pattern can be observed: each of the eight narrated-plus-consciousness events occur in Yoknapatawpha either at the county jail (where Bayard spends a night for carousing), the Sartoris plantation, or the MacCallum place in the central and northeastern parts of the map between 1 May 1919 and 20 December 1919. In contrast, the narrated-plus-consciousness events for the *whole* novel range from April 1862 to June 1920 and move outside of Yoknapatawpha to other parts of Mississippi and Virginia. A close reading of these events reveals that this can in part be attributed to Bayard's sense that his traumatized mind is shackled to a suffering and weary body. In the county jail, his thoughts lament his indivisibility from a "body which he must drag forever about a bleak and barren world" (155), and later in the text (in page order), Bayard's interior monologue describes a waking nightmare in which the memory of aerial combat returns as a form of physical imprisonment: "[H]e was a trapped beast in the high blue, mad for life, trapped in the very cunning fabric that had betrayed him" (211). Bayard's thoughts cannot detach themselves from the reality of a sick body that somatically manifests his trauma; his mind is confined to the temporal and spatial environment in which his body is situated, even in moments of deep introspection. Again, as is the case for Temple, the traumatized consciousness cannot escape its immediate temporal and spatial context when mediated through narrative.

Similar to narrated-plus-consciousness events in the novel, hypothesized events are almost exclusively associated with Temple; they form the dominant narrative mode through which she processes the trauma she has experienced. Of the fourteen hypothesized events that occur in the text, twelve are associated with Temple and two with Horace. Horace's hypothesized events are characterized by whimsy and pleasurable fantasy; he speculates that Pap, the old blind and deaf man at the Old Frenchman place, might have been left there one hundred years ago by the "old Frenchman" (110) himself, who originally built the place, and he imagines watching his stepdaughter being intimate with a young suitor by the "grape arbor in Kinston" in a passage saturated with a transgressive desire expressed in the most lyrical terms (166).

Temple's hypothetical events have quite a different function in the narrative; most significantly, six of them also imagine that she is present in the hypothetical scene, and it is within these that trauma causes her to repeatedly create fantastical alternatives to the abuse at the Old Frenchman place. First (in page order), when Popeye attacks her in the crib, she sees herself screaming, "'Something is happening to me!'" to Pap, "the old man with the yellow clots for eyes" (102), in a moment of potential psychosis. In her account to Horace of the rape, she imagines a number of hypothetical scenarios: that her legs were those of a boy (216); that she was wearing a medieval chastity belt (217); that she was lying dead in a coffin (219); that she was a teacher in command at school (219); and then, finally, that she was "an old man, with a long white beard," causing her to sprout a penis while Popeye is groping her (220). Temple's six hypothesized events where she is also present, and which collectively provide an account of the rape, are completely temporally and spatially static: they all take place within twenty-four hours at the Old Frenchman place. Although Temple can imagine vivid narrative alternatives to what occurred there, there is no equivalent escape in time or place, indeed no sanctuary. In these instances, the text is focalized through Temple's consciousness. David Herman defines hypothetical focalization as "the use of hypotheses, framed by the narrator or a character, about what might be, or might have been or perceived—if only there were someone who could have adopted the requisite perspective on the situations and events at issue" (231). By assuming a hypothetical perspective, Temple discursively grants herself the authority and power she lacked at the Old Frenchman place when she finally comes to elaborate upon the traumatic events. Narrative moments such as these illustrate the gap between discourse and content in the description of events, since Temple's account highlights the "peculiar epistemic modality" of hypothetical focalization in which "the *expressed world* counterfactualizes or virtualizes the *reference world* of the text" (Herman 231). For Temple, discourse (the expressed world) becomes a means of agency over the material reality of subjugation (the reference world).

Trauma's Tropes and Structures: Distant, Surface, and Close Readings of Narrative

From studying the DY maps plotted according to narrative status, it becomes apparent that the abuse Temple suffers remains absent from several narrative modes, either in spatial or formal terms: the sites of the rape and sexual abuse at the Old Frenchman place and Miss Reba's are a void in Temple's remembered events; we have limited access to her interior monologue in the very few narrated-plus-consciousness events, which invoke absent protector figures and avoid processing sexual violence; and her hypothesized events establish a figurative relationship to her suffering. Consistent with these patterns, narratological approaches to *Sanctuary* have tended to highlight the text's formal evasiveness to varying degrees, drawing attention to Faulkner's reluctance to plumb the psychological depths of his characters' consciousnesses through internal monologue or speech. Irving Howe argues that the novel's focus on the surface details of violent events conceals "a void [that] may result from Faulkner's fastidious distance from his material, a profound unwillingness to breathe the foul air of Temple and Popeye" (144). In Howe's understanding, Faulkner, in a putatively anti-modernist move, eschews the radical representation of subjectivity in favor of a "behaviorist" (144) technique; he elaborates that the novel "concentrates on sheer events, seldom examining the sources of conduct; and in several crucial sections, particularly the rape scene, displays an opacity which comes from a crowding of action, a blurred jam of scurrying and commotion" (145). Taking a DH perspective on the "sheer events" of *Sanctuary,* one can assert that while the novel's events, taken as a whole, light up all parts of the Yoknapatawpha map, the regional, national, and global inset maps, and a large section of the timeline (1862 to 1929), very few of them offer a psychological interpretation of the spatial and temporal movement of the action.

While Howe pays attention to the lack of psychological interpretation of action in the novel, John T. Matthews also identifies a void at the novel's center but principally attributes this to a lack of probing speech. Matthews argues that the device of ellipsis shapes both the psychological and narrative structure of the text; after pointing out that the central "incident" of the novel (Temple's rape) is essentially left out, he describes how Faulkner's use of "vague diction, vacancies in syntax, breakages in thought and utterance, and violations of place, time, and character conspire to blur the presentation of the novel's crucial event" (246).[4] Florence W. Dore similarly argues that the narrative is organized around its lack of articulation of sexual violence, "a tendency not to say" (79), silence that she finds indicative of self-censorship on Faulkner's part. These readings are indeed reflected in Temple's hypothetical narrative mediation of the account of her rape, which returns the reader to the site and location of the novel's central incident, but they are verbally indirect as they conceal while telling. As techniques, however, I would argue that these narrational decisions should not be attributed either to Faulkner's moral shrinking from his characters or to self-censorship. Faulkner instead offers the reader a narrative rendering of trauma. Theresa M. Towner similarly stresses the importance of recognizing that Temple's account of the rape registers her suffering, particularly in its narratorial stance of numb detachment, an account that also expresses racial prejudice by encoding Popeye as a black, male aggressor that she is able to Other (18–19). Additionally, *Sanctuary*'s narrative modes evidence the impact of trauma when they are mapped, since their spatial and temporal organization illustrate that Temple is a victim of sexual violence whose memory is occluded, whose mind cannot process the disturbing event itself, and who speaks in hypotheticals as a coping mechanism.

These narrative patterns, which discursively present Temple's mental engagement with her rape, reveal how much the incident sits outside of her comprehension since it cannot be assimilated into her psyche. The first wave of scholarship on trauma and narrative theory drew attention to precisely this incomprehensibility of the traumatic incident in literature. These scholars innovatively brought together psychological theories of trauma and poststructural approaches to narrative to perform analyses of literary texts that articulate pain. Joshua Pederson summarizes the commonality of these two fields: "For poststructuralists, there is a break between word and world; for trauma theorists, there is a break between word and wound" (100). In other words, just as poststructuralists challenge the putative close relationship between signifier and referent, so too trauma theorists question how much the traumatic event can be processed in language, since it is essentially unknowable. Within this field, Cathy Caruth's groundbreaking book *Unclaimed Experience* (1996) employed psychoanalytic theory to demonstrate how catastrophic events repeat in the lives of victims in ways that are fully out of their control; these repetitions "seem not to be initiated by the individual's own acts but rather appear as the possession of some people by a sort of fate" (2). When trauma is explored in literature, Caruth argues, writers focus on the limits of the victim's knowledge: "It is . . . at the specific point at which knowing and not knowing intersect that the language of literature and the psychoanalytic theory of traumatic experience precisely meet" (3). In formal terms, the traumatic event appears actually to resist narrativization.

Despite its impalpability in narrative, trauma does manifest in narrative structure through its close association with a number of recurring tropes, which Pederson identifies as absence, indirection, and repetition (101). First, since the traumatic event is of such force that it cannot be registered in memory, narratives such as *Sanctuary* employ "lacunae [that] serve as markers of traumatic experience" (101), and one must therefore pay attention to the gaps, silences, instances of aporia, and ruptures in the text. Second, narrative may engage with trauma by establishing an indirect relationship to the pain its memory evokes, and it is principally "metaphor [that] mediates the relationship between reality and catastrophe" (103). Third, as Caruth first explicated, traumatic experiences repeat and return to the victim in literature, demanding not only that they be relived but that they be retold (104). Early trauma theorists were consistently attracted to modernist texts as illustrations of these features, since their formal complexity evidences the aporia, silences, and fragmentation that attend the experience of trauma (106).

These three core tropes can be found in the events that explore Temple's mental state in response to the trauma of sexual violence, whether present in memory, interior monologue, or hypothetical description. In terms of absence, when Temple's mind recalls the day of the rape, her interior monologue is populated by gaps and omissions. When she imagines at Miss Reba's that it is the morning before the rape, she leaves some key information out: "I have a date tonight with. . . . . . . thinking of the student with whom she had the date. But she couldn't remember who it would be" (152). The ellipsis here is telling: the failure to recover the name of her date. The traumatic incident does not manifest directly in Temple's consciousness, but the omissions within her mental evocation of a previous self are in fact created by trauma, since her life before the rape is at this moment psychologically inaccessible. Trauma, then, makes its presence felt even when absent from the narration. To give an example of indirection from a remembered event, Temple recalls the college dances that preceded her victimization. The passage below describes Temple's recollection of the women in the dormitory readying themselves for one such occasion: "The hour for dressing for a dance, if you were popular enough not to have to be on time. The air would be steamy with recent baths, and perhaps powder in the light like chaff in barn-lofts, and they looking at one another, comparing, talking whether you could do more damage if you could just walk out on the floor like you were now" (151). Although this memory comes to Temple after the rape, it is still figuratively mediated by its violence. Temple is violated by Popeye in the "crib" (the grain or corn storage room) in the barn just behind the Old Frenchman place, and Temple's memory of the competitive sexual attractiveness of her fellow female students is grimly described through a simile that returns her to the site of her abuse. Here trauma indirectly intrudes on her consciousness as figuration. Finally, when Temple describes the rape to Horace in the series of hypothetical events, trauma is repeated in the retelling; in imagining herself as a boy, a medieval queen, a corpse, a teacher, and an old man during the abuse, she changes her relationship to the incident, but the trauma itself recurs through her forced inhabiting of a series of roles. Temple moves through these personae under duress, since none of them are effective in overcoming her subjugation. Trauma therefore produces its repeated retelling in narrative.[5]

Through such a close reading of *Sanctuary*'s events, one can demonstrate how tropes of the traumatized narrative structure Temple's memory, consciousness, and discourse through omission, indirection, and repetition. Additionally, the DY maps show how these patterns are manifested in the text's overall spatial and temporal organization. Plotting the remembered events on the map demonstrates the trope of absence, since the Old Frenchman place is omitted from the map of Temple's narrative memory. In relation to indirection, if one plots all the told events in which Temple is either present or mentioned, it is remarkable that none of them take place in Jefferson, the putative center of Faulkner's fictional county.[6] In contrast, if one plots the events for the whole of *Sanctuary*, Jefferson is crowded with locations; when Temple or other characters tell her story, the map has an absent center, since the narration of trauma appears to decenter Faulkner's imagination. Finally, the map for the six hypothetical events at which Temple is present as a character demonstrates repetition, since these discrete retellings return her to the Old Frenchman place on the day of her rape. Trauma, then, not only establishes the patterns of recurring tropes throughout the text but also informs the way in which its various narrative modes travel across time and space.

In these analyses of tropes from trauma narratives as they appear in *Sanctuary*, I have moved among distant, surface, and close readings of the novel. I would like to outline how these different practices can productively inform each other through the use of a DH tool such as DY. Franco Moretti coined the term "distant reading" to encapsulate critical approaches in which an analysis of a large amount of aggregated data permits new understandings of literary texts; it describes the use of "statistical, quantitative methods to 'read' large volumes of text at a distance, using 'graphs, maps, and trees' as forms of abstract representation that enable the study of patterns over time" (Kirschenbaum 2). Moretti asserts that close reading is limited by the size of the samples it uses and "necessarily depends on an extremely small canon" (48). In contrast, distant reading, by using amassed data, "allows you to focus on units that are much smaller or much larger than the text: devices, themes, tropes—or genres and systems" (48–49). Without the distant reading method, when a literary scholar recognizes a pattern in a text, its repetition across a corpus, oeuvre, or genre can only be studied up to the limits of the scholar's reading. As Stephen Ramsay highlights, in contrast, "a machine . . . can unerringly discover every instance of such features across a massive corpus of literary texts and then present those features in a visual format entirely foreign to the original organization in which these features appear" (17). This mechanistic method creates opportunities for new and original readings of texts beyond the scope of human close reading, but Moretti's thoroughgoing rejection of qualitative analytic methods seems too absolute. In the analyses of passages from *Sanctuary* presented in this chapter, once I have observed patterns within the aggregated data for Faulkner's corpus, I return to the text itself and perform further close reading, rather than keep it at a distance. By oscillating between close and distant readings, I believe I have been able to illuminate how the data on narrative modes and their temporal and spatial distribution is reflected in the stylistic and aesthetic decisions Faulkner makes to narrate trauma. In other words, the omission, indirection, and repetition that typify the narration of trauma can by identified by reading the text both closely and distantly.

Surface reading treads the middle ground between distant and close reading and is invested in the belief that the *reorganization* of texts through DH tools can make overarching patterns in literary texts apparent. Unlike the purism that can sometimes characterize distant reading, the emphasis of surface reading is to return to the text once these patterns have been foregrounded through the systems of categorization that new technologies enable. As Stephen Best and Sharon Marcus outline, surface reading emerged, in part, as a reaction against symptomatic readings, where the various elements present in the text are taken to be "symbolic of something latent or concealed" (3), such as Freudian or Marxist readings would argue. They advocate, instead, for attention to be paid to "what is evident, perceptible, apprehensible in texts" (Best and Marcus 9). Their argument resonates with Susan Sontag's essay "Against Interpretation" (1964), in which she similarly challenges symptomatic, or interpretative, readings of the content of works of art, lamenting that "the modern style of interpretation excavates, and as it excavates, destroys; it digs 'behind' the text, to find a sub-text which is the true one" (6). Here, surface is ignored in favor of excavating hidden or concealed meanings through the use of theoretical interpretations. Sontag perceives such critical practices to be particularly rife in the field of literary studies, in which the constituent elements of a poem or novel are translated into something altogether different, and she in fact names Faulkner as one of the authors whose work has attracted a high degree of (over-)interpretative activity (8). She calls instead for a return to the sensory surface of the work of art through the use of critical faculties that seek to illuminate *"how it is what it is, even that it is what it is, rather than to show what it means"* (Sontag 14).

In a sense, Best and Marcus offer a practical guide to avoiding critical over-interpretation. Among the types of reading they introduce, the treatment of the textual surface "as the location of patterns that exist within and across texts" (11) is the most suited to the incorporation of DH methods. The intention here is to move away from the localized identification of patterns, by close reading an isolated textual unit, in order to comprehend wider networks of recurrence and reconfiguration. This is not carried out, however, in the service of an ideological (or symptomatic) reading, since the critical eye is still trained on the surface of the text and the narrative structures and abstract patterns that manifest on this level. Best and Marcus compare the surface reader to an anatomist and taxonomist, who either divides texts up into their component parts or arranges texts into larger categorical groups, respectively; consequently, surface readers "rearrange texts into new forms but nonetheless attend to what is present rather than privilege what is absent" (11). Computers are naturally central to this work because, although they have a limited interpretative function in and of themselves, they are highly successful anatomizers and taxonomists (17). Instead of valorizing distant over close reading, surface readers use digital methods to *expand* literary critical activity. My approach to *Sanctuary* fuses distant, close, and surface readings, since my analyses rely on both the aggregation and the visualization of data on narrative modes (distant) but also the categorization and reorganization of these modes on the DY map (surface) as a means to return to the text (close). The close readings I have carried out differ in part from those pursued by a surface reader, as they are symptomatic to some extent, since I consider the omissions and silences of the text (what is suppressed or concealed) to be as revealing of the narration of trauma as the stylistic and aesthetic features evident on the surface. The study of complex literary texts is perhaps best served when these reading practices are used in tandem to observe the ways in which narrative structures can be seen to move across time and space both at a remove and up close.

Mapping Subjective Ambiguity: Digital Humanities and the Modernist Narrative

The modernist text has been an enduring object of analysis in trauma theory, since its disruptions of form seek to mimic the spatial and temporal discontinuities of consciousness. The DY project can visualize the omissions, absences, spatial displacements, and event repetitions that trauma produces in a modernist narrative such as *Sanctuary* or *Flags in the Dust*. It is, however, precisely the subjective ambiguity of the modernist text that has led many humanist scholars to be skeptical about visualizations of works of art, as such complexity would seem to resist any definitive translation into stable data categories. Such skepticism can be partly attributed to a disjuncture between text and image in approaches to modernist aesthetics. As Johanna Drucker argues, "Critics trained in or focused on the modern tradition... have difficulty letting go of the longstanding distinction between textual and visual forms of representation—as well as of the hierarchy that places text above image" (435). The use of visualizations, such as graphs and maps, to perform distant readings of modernist literary texts can be considered at odds with these works' indeterminacy, openness, and subjective ambiguity. Addressing such concerns, Drucker has championed DH practices that embed speculative, subjective, and intuitive functions within them, "premised on the conviction that logical, systematic knowledge representation, adequate though it may be for many fields of inquiry, including many aspects of the humanities, is not sufficient for the interpretation of imaginative artifacts" (432). This is especially important for modernist narratives, which resist logical temporal and spatial organization. A number of recent modernist mapping projects have pursued this speculative approach; the Z-Axis Research Initiative, for example, has constructed 3D maps of familiar locations that are warped by the individual author's imagination. Their work is based on the understanding that the coordinates of a map for a city such as Paris cannot be directly applied to a modernist work that uses Paris as its principal setting, such as Djuna Barnes's *Nightwood*, since Barnes distorts the city for her own creative purposes. The project's 3D images visually interpret the ways in which "canonical modernist novels warp or transform historical cities to produce fictitious, highly biased, and subjective versions of them" (Christie). Their approach crucially reflects the incomplete and subjectively filtered evocation of space in modernist narration, which "constructs multiple situated and partial expressions" (Christie) and therefore results in multiple maps of a given location, city, or county.

In the case of Faulkner, we are not dealing with a modernist writer who evokes a space that has real coordinates as reference points, such as Barnes's Paris, James Joyce's Dublin, or Christopher Isherwood's Berlin. Faulkner's Jefferson in Yoknapatawpha County is a fictional town, which only roughly corresponds to Oxford in Lafayette County, Mississippi. Faulkner produced two of his own maps of his literary county, on which the DY maps are based. However, DY consciously resists creating a definitive map of Yoknapatawpha, since each of the maps is customized according to the text that it serves to visualize. A speculative or interpretive function is embedded into DY's digital visualizations, since the maps for each Faulkner work shift and reconfigure according to the author's imagination at a given point in time. This extends to the project's tool for mapping narrative modes; the five narrative statuses are themselves of course interpretive categories, but the ability to select and plot a narrative status, such as remembered or hypothesized, according to a character's presence visually demonstrates how much events in the modernist text are filtered through the specific spatial knowledge and imagination of individual characters. If one plots told narration for the whole of *Sanctuary*, every part of the map generates events, but when filtered by character, levels of fixation (marked by high levels of activity) or disregard (those parts of the map that remain blank) in relation to different spaces become visually apparent. DY, therefore, speculatively visualizes modernist narratives, offering new insights into the spatial and temporal boundaries of narrative modes. These maps vividly illustrate the malleability of spatial and temporal narrative structures in Faulkner's work and how contingent these structures are on the consciousnesses of the characters the narration inhabits. Consequently, DH projects such as DY offer innovative new tools to chart the activities of the mind as they shape narrative structure.

Notes

1. The analyses that follow are based on the state of the data for *Sanctuary* in DY in spring 2020, which may be subject to small changes.
2. This is also apparent from the Narrative Analysis visualization feature, which shows that *Sanctuary* mostly progresses between events in a linear manner (48 percent of events) or through flashback (31 percent of events), with flashforward only accounting for 20 percent of progression between events.
3. The first wave of theorists to bring the fields of gender studies and narratology into dialogue with one another in the late 1980s speculated that data aggregation could benefit their analyses. In *Gendered Interventions* (1989), Robyn R. Warhol charts gender's effect on discourse in the Victorian novel, focusing on whether a narrator's interventions have a distancing (coded masculine) or engaging (coded feminine) effect on the reader (22). Warhol decides against a computational approach by means of which one could "scan hundreds of novels looking for the word *you* outside of

quotation marks (and therefore occurring in interventions, rather than dialogue)" since "it could not begin to account for how direct address functions in individual texts" (23–24). Through DY, I am able to pursue a gendered approach to narratology that first establishes the overall recurrence of a discursive feature and then allows me to return to the text to examine the particular gender dynamics at work in a selected passage.
4. The Narrative Analysis visualization feature bears out the claim that this is the novel's crucial event; the most frequent start date for events in *Sanctuary* is 11 May 1929 (56 events in total), the day of the car crash and the beginning of Temple's abuse at the Old Frenchman place.
5. These assumed roles do also reflect the indirection of traumatized narrative. In the process of retelling what happened to her, Temple is only able to talk figuratively; for example, the raincoat that she puts on at the Old Frenchman place is transformed into an imagined tool of self-defense, "a kind of iron belt in a museum a king or something used to lock the queen up in" (Faulkner, *Sanctuary* 217).
6. These events are also temporally static on the timeline, suggesting that to speak of Temple in the novel is to be rooted in the present.

Works Cited

Best, Stephen, and Sharon Marcus. "Surface Reading: An Introduction." *Representations*, vol. 108, no. 2, 2009, pp. 1–21.

Caruth, Cathy. *Unclaimed Experience: Trauma, Narrative, and History*. Johns Hopkins UP, 1996.

Christie, Alex, et al. "Modeling How Modernists Wrote the City." *Maker Lab in the Humanities*, 1 Aug. 2014, maker.uvic.ca/dh14.

Dore, Florence W. "Free Speech and Exposure: Obscenity, the Phallus, and William Faulkner's 'Sanctuary.'" *Narrative*, vol. 9, no. 1, 2001, pp. 78–99.

Drucker, Johanna, and Bethany Nowviskie. "Speculative Computing: Aesthetic Provocations in Humanities Computing." *A Companion to Digital Humanities*, edited by Susan Schreibman, Ray Siemens, and John Unsworth, Blackwell Publishing, 2004, pp. 431–47.

Faulkner, William. *Flags in the Dust*. 1973. Vintage International, 2012.

———. *Light in August*. 1932. Library of America, 1985.

———. *Sanctuary*. 1931. Vintage International, 1993.

Fludernik, Monika. *An Introduction to Narratology*. Routledge, 2009.

Herman, David. "Hypothetical Focalization." *Narrative*, vol. 2, no. 3, 1994, pp. 230–53.

Howe, Irving. *William Faulkner: A Critical Study*. Random House, 1952.

Kirschenbaum, Matthew G. "The Remaking of Reading: Data Mining and the Digital Humanities." 2007, www.csee.umbc.edu/~hillol/NGDM07/abstracts/talks/MKirschenbaum.pdf.

Matthews, John T. "The Elliptical Nature of 'Sanctuary.'" *NOVEL: A Forum on Fiction,* vol. 17, no. 3, 1984, pp. 246–65.

Moretti, Franco. *Distant Reading.* Verso, 2013.

Pederson, Joshua. "Trauma and Narrative." *Trauma and Literature,* edited by J. Roger Kurtz, Cambridge UP, 2018, pp. 97–109.

Ramsay, Stephen. *Reading Machines: Towards an Algorithmic Criticism.* U of Illinois P, 2011.

Roberts, Diane. *Faulkner and Southern Womanhood.* U of Georgia P, 1994.

Sontag, Susan. *Against Interpretation.* Penguin, 2009.

Towner, Theresa M. *Faulkner on the Color Line: The Later Novels.* UP of Mississippi, 2000.

Warhol, Robyn R. *Gendered Interventions: Narrative Discourse in the Victorian Novel.* Rutgers UP, 1989.

Reading the *Portable Faulkner* through Digital Yoknapatawpha

RECOVERING THE "PROBLEMS" AND "DIFFICULTIES" OF "APPENDIX COMPSON 1699-1945"

Erin Penner

"It's not a new work by Faulkner. It's a new work by Cowley all right through" (Cowley 66): a decade after inscribing "William Faulkner, Sole Owner & Proprietor" on a map of Yoknapatawpha County, Faulkner had new reason to doubt the strength of his property claim.[1] The *Portable Faulkner* (1946) that bore his name clearly attested to the editorial vision of Malcolm Cowley. Cowley's letters to Viking Press indicate that even his language occasionally, if accidentally, trumped that of Faulkner: "There is one change I made in pencil on the ms. of his Appendix . . . that it turns out he didn't approve of" (Cowley 64). That is why, as the manuscript made its way through production, "Quentin still escapes from Jason's locked room by climbing down a pear tree" (64), rather than the "drain pipe" Faulkner mentioned in correspondence with Cowley two months earlier (32). Cowley overlooked the reference to the drain pipe in Faulkner's September letter (32), did not incorporate Faulkner's handwritten correction to Cowley's revision in November (57), and then failed to ensure Faulkner's choice was reflected in the final proofs. Once restored, Faulkner's drain pipe became the subject of considerable critical discussion, and is one of the most notable discrepancies between *The Sound and the Fury* and the Compson "Appendix." Cowley appears to have simply forgotten to follow through with Viking, but his repeated failure to recall Faulkner's preference—much less the author's exact wording[2]—exposes the cost of his desire to unify and therefore simplify Faulkner's Yoknapatawpha County for the *Portable Faulkner*.

In a letter to Faulkner dated 9 August 1945, Cowley five times expressed his desire to present Faulkner's work "as a whole" (Cowley 21–24). Cowley's preference for Faulkner's short fiction reflected his view that a stable, static vision underlay Faulkner's published work, and that the stories simply needed to be arranged and framed by a good editor for the pattern to be evident to all.[3] As Cheryl Lester notes, Cowley's emphasis on completeness emerged from the broader turn to New Criticism in literary studies, which set the terms for Faulkner criticism from its early decades onward (373–74). Lester argues, "The effect of the *Portable* was thus to legitimize the celebration of Faulkner in the United States as the celebration of a literary realization and consciousness of wholeness and aesthetic totality" (374). Even as Cowley's interests were shaped by New Criticism, so, too, his claim that Faulkner created a unified picture across different texts enhanced Faulkner's reputation for well-ordered vision.

Cowley's vision, however, is not that of the editorial team at Digital Yoknapatawpha (DY). As Stephen Railton avows, "A major goal of our project is to enable users to visualize that lifelong ferment: the acts of re-creation that were shaped by Faulkner's continuously evolving social, historical, artistic, and moral preoccupations, as these in turn were shaped by changes in American culture across the arc of his career" ("Digital Yoknapatawpha" 459). But rather than reject outright the project Cowley undertook with the *Portable Faulkner,* DY allows Faulkner readers to consider the trade-offs of competing desiderata. DY helps readers recognize where and how Faulkner's churning imagination expands and alters the worlds he creates, but it can also help users to identify points of contact between Oxford and Faulkner's imagined town of Jefferson, for example, or between the characters of *The Sound and the Fury* and *Absalom, Absalom!* To investigate the latter, however, is not to assume that such entities can be conflated.

In mapping only the texts Faulkner set in Yoknapatawpha, DY seems to echo Cowley's parameters for the *Portable Faulkner.* But if the DY editors replicate Cowley's textual selections, to a large extent, their choices stem from different motivations. They assume the burden of grappling with Faulkner's complex relationship to place. If place or regionalism does not constitute everything that is remarkable about his fiction, neither is it, as Faulkner suggested in 1944, "not very important" (Cowley 14). Through its emphasis on place, both fictional and real, DY enables readers to examine what may be their own tendency to draw a "unified" vision from Faulkner's texts. DY's data set has been constructed one text at a time, and thus prioritizes detail at the level of the individual story or novel. Comparisons of similar elements across Faulkner texts must be drawn out of data that preserves the distinctions between different published narratives. DY is perhaps most useful as a check on readers' impulses to create their own consistent view of Yoknapatawpha at great cost to the particularities of individual Faulkner works. Consistency is, of course, what Cowley asked of Faulkner, but DY equips users to call consistency into question. Rather than follow Cowley's lead in assembling a "whole" from Faulkner's work that could be extended to the South more generally,[4] DY invites Faulkner readers to identify precise relationships among his fictions. The digital project offers a third way: not Cowley's insistence that discrepancies be resolved, nor Faulkner's refusal to return to earlier work to integrate the worlds he has created. Instead, the data of DY is grounded in particular texts, but it also facilitates comparisons across Faulkner's body of work.

Faulkner's Compson "Appendix" and its different treatments by Cowley, Faulkner, and the DY team reveal how Cowley's and even Faulkner's desire for "wholeness" obscured the fiction writer's unruly inventiveness. It is a testament to Cowley's fixed vision that he saw even the "Appendix" as a key to Faulknerian wholeness: "After one reads the Compson genealogy, the whole book does fall into pattern" (39). By contrast, Joseph R. Urgo is one of many critics who see Faulkner's "Appendix" as an act of resistance to Cowley's "authoritative, orthodox program of discovery and canonization" (41–42). Cheryl Lester goes further: "The appendix constitutes itself as a literary text precisely insofar as it is essentially a refutation of the proper and correct" (372). But it was Faulkner, rather than Cowley, who suggested using Jason Compson's narrative to represent *The Sound and the Fury* in the *Portable Faulkner*, since it would give the collection a unified vision of the "new South": "What about taking the whole 3rd section of SOUND AND FURY? That Jason is the new South too. I mean, he is the one Compson and Sartoris who met Snopes on his own ground and in a fashion held his own. Jason would have chopped up a Georgian Manse and sold it off in shotgun bungalows as quick as any man" (Cowley 25). In Faulkner's description, Jason Compson IV emerges as the victor in a modern race to capitalize on southern nostalgia. Jason insists on his freedom from the entanglements of southern history, a declaration that has narrative ramifications: a story that does not acknowledge other influences lends itself to excerpting. Cowley's and Faulkner's desire to present a "whole" picture of Yoknapatawpha in short extracts makes them more likely to select stories that feature characters who shake off history than those who court a complex relationship with it.

Faulkner considered the Dilsey section of *The Sound and the Fury* for the *Portable Faulkner* but hesitated because it "depends too much on what has gone before" (Cowley 28). Both author and editor were reluctant to include texts that insist on interconnectedness. By contrast, DY offers a forum for sophisticated renderings of complex texts, which can then be used to educate a general readership that is accustomed to tidy plot summaries, print or online. Faulkner's and Cowley's premise, that material should be eliminated if it "depends" on other texts, suggests that the "wholeness" they sought could easily become a tenuous edifice: one that leans hard on shared geography and recurring characters to form the walls of a closed world, as opposed to a posited reality that suggests further stories than what the reader has encountered or Faulkner has written. In a decision that proved pivotal for the arc of the *Portable Faulkner*, both Faulkner and Cowley swerved from a vision of the "new South" that concluded with the union of the Snopeses and Jason Compson. Instead, both author and editor were compelled by the eloquence of the black characters in the final section of *The Sound and the Fury*; their decision to include Dilsey's "dependent" narrative over Jason's fierce independence led to the creation of the Compson "Appendix," a text that further extends the Yoknapatawpha world.

James B. Meriwether argues that the "Appendix" is the fulfillment of Faulkner's desire to write a "Golden Book of my apocryphal county" (Meriwether 95; Faulkner quotation from Cowley 25). Even if Meriwether's claim too tidily knits Faulkner's ambitions to his writing, Faulkner's phrasing speaks to his desire to draw together his material. As Thadious Davis argues, the "Appendix" "strains toward the production of a completeness, a self-containment, that is not technically the Compson family genealogy" (245). In presenting the "Appendix" to Cowley, Faulkner wrote, "I should have done this when I wrote the book [*The Sound and the Fury*]. Then the whole thing would have fallen into pattern like a jigsaw puzzle when the magician's wand touched it" (Cowley 36). That Faulkner would say that he "should have" constructed the "Appendix" at the time of writing *The Sound and the Fury* comes as a surprise, given that both the organization and the scope of the "Appendix" suggest he responded to the narrative arc Cowley outlined for the *Portable Faulkner*. Cowley wanted the reader to have "a picture of Yocknapatawpha [sic] county . . . from Indian times down to World War II" (22). Cowley charted a course that began with "Red Leaves" and "A Justice" and moved toward "Spotted Horses." Faulkner responded with an "Appendix" that begins with Native American stories[5] of early Yoknapatawpha and, when it eventually moves to the Compson characters of *The Sound and the Fury*, highlights the modern voice of Jason Compson IV.

Even though Faulkner and Cowley settled on the "Dilsey" section of *The Sound and the Fury* for the *Portable Faulkner*, Jason's influence lingers in the evaluative tone of the "Appendix," in which he is declared the "first sane Compson since before Culloden and (a childless bachelor) hence the last" ("Appendix" 338). It is unlikely that an impartial observer would deem Jason the one "sane" Compson. The anti-Semitism in the "Appendix" also renews the bigotry that Jason voices in the third section of *The Sound and the Fury*: "I have nothing against jews as an individual . . . It's just the race. You'll admit that they produce nothing. They follow the pioneers into a new country and sell them clothes" (191). A passing reference to "Jew owners of Chicago and New York sweatshops" in the "Appendix" seems strikingly at odds with post-WWII public sentiment, and thus one of the most significant indications that the "Appendix" is shaped by a particular character's perspective (343).

Most notably, the "Appendix" resolves Jason's family members' fates with a twist that satisfies his desire for revenge. When a glossy photo of what is presumed to be his sister Caddy is thrust before him, he refuses to claim her (334). Since her life has already shaped so much of his own, he will give her no more attention. Caddy's daughter, Quentin, runs off with Jason's savings in *The Sound and the Fury*, but at the end of the "Appendix" the carnival pitchman with whom she escapes is noted to be "already under sentence for bigamy," a fact that undercuts her romantic trajectory (342).

Perhaps the cruelest revision, however, appears in the "Appendix" characterization of Jason's brother Benjy. As Stephen Railton remarked to me, Benjy is never referred to by that nickname in the "Appendix." Given the prominence of his nickname in *The Sound and the Fury*, it may well sadden readers that he is no longer aligned with his sister Caddy through the aural and visual similarity of their names. In the novel,

Benjy's mother stripped him of a family name to avoid linking his disability to her lineage, but Caddy insisted on the nickname by which readers would know Benjy, despite her mother's protests. The "Benjamin" of the "Appendix" is not treated with the intimacy of the "Benjy" of *The Sound and the Fury*. Instead, the "Appendix" defines Benjy as a sacrificial lamb, claiming he "was rechristened Benjamin by his brother Quentin (Benjamin, our lastborn, sold into Egypt)" (340). The elaborate telling and retelling of Benjy's naming should remind readers that a different story can emerge from slight shifts in narrative perspective.

The "Appendix" also takes aim at Benjy Compson's role as an innocent. It would seem to resolve the question of whether he sexually assaulted a passing girl, or whether he simply scared her by approaching her on her way home from school. The text of *The Sound and the Fury* aligns the incident with his childhood habit of meeting his sister Caddy on her way home from school, thus supporting readings of the event as simply another moment in which Benjy is misread by others. The "Appendix," however, includes a reference to "a fumbling abortive attempt by [Jason's] idiot brother on a passing female child" (339), simultaneously identifying Benjy through his relationship with Jason and assigning Benjy malicious intent. To read in this way, however, is to ignore the signs of free indirect discourse at work, as the text gradually becomes focalized through Jason Compson IV. Just above the reference to the "abortive attempt," the narrative glosses over the fact that Jason's savings were not primarily composed of "niggard and agonised dimes and quarters and halfdollars" from his paychecks (339), but rather of crisp bills from the bank at which Jason committed fraud by cashing his sister's checks. The influence of free indirect discourse can be seen in what the text elides as well as what it provides.

Faulkner wrote to Cowley that "the purpose of this genealogy is to give a sort of bloodless bibliophile's point of view. I was a sort of Garter King-at-Arms, heatless, not very moved, cleaning up 'Compson' before going on to the next 'C-o' or 'C-r.' ... He knew only what the town could have told him" (Cowley 44). Cheryl Lester reads this explanation as an indication of Faulkner's increased testiness as Cowley continued to press for textual consistency: "Faulkner's description of the Garter K/A suggests an unflattering double for Cowley" (385). To her point, Faulkner's description of the Garter King-at-Arms was immediately preceded by a curt acknowledgment that the French in his text was ungrammatical and, yes, he was aware of the correct French term. If Faulkner invented the Garter K/A as a sly dig, Cowley appears not to have gotten the joke. He not only continued pressing Faulkner for information, but also appended to the above Faulkner letter in *The Faulkner-Cowley File* a description of the duties of the Garter King-at-Arms from the *Britannica*, thus doubling down on his attempts to tie Faulkner's world to the rules of the real one. Cowley noted, however, that such an "avatar" conveniently freed Faulkner from adhering to the details of *The Sound and the Fury* (45).

Whether the source of the tonal inflection in the "Appendix" is free indirect discourse of Jason Compson or a Garter King-at-Arms who heard Jason's complaints, its influence on the authority of the "Appendix" has been overlooked. Instead, the "Appendix" is too often read as Faulkner's final word on the world of the Compsons, as is evident from the frequency with which the work appears in critical discussions without quotation marks. The lack of punctuation suggests that Faulkner produced an appendix, a work outside his fictional realm that is accountable for the veracity and consistency of the claims made within it. Instead, however, Faulkner's "Appendix Compson 1699–1945" continues, extends, and reimagines his fictional realm, and should be punctuated accordingly.

When Stephen Railton and I edited the DY data for the "Appendix," he noted that his "biggest surprise" was "how few inside Yoknapatawpha locations are mentioned" ("Appendix Location"). In the same email, Railton suggested that perhaps the "recent trauma of WORLD War has made Faulkner acutely aware" that his county is part of a "much larger world." For all that Faulkner affirmed Cowley's sense of a Faulknerian "whole," his actions attested to the variability of that vision, as he adapted his view to the influence of Cowley and created a recent history that pushed his narrative well beyond the bounds of Yoknapatawpha, thanks not least to World War II. When selecting an excerpt from *Light in August*, Cowley considered the characters Joe Christmas or Lena Grove, but "found that they were too closely interwoven with the others. . . . So there's nothing to do but take Warren Grimm, who really comes out all of a piece" (28–29). The suggestion that Warren Grimm—or rather, Percy Grimm, as he is named in Faulkner's novel—could be used to represent *Light in August* indicates the extent to which "extractability" threatened to become the primary measure of selection for the *Portable Faulkner*. Making "wholeness" the ultimate good is a particularly frightening consideration when the ideologies of the Second World War linger in the background. Faulkner noted that in Grimm he had created "a Nazi" before Hitler's time, but, surprisingly, concurred with Cowley: "Warren Grimm does hold together, whole" (32).[6]

Cowley could only achieve his vision of Faulkner's work by breaking the dominance of the novel form. He argued to readers, "Faulkner's genius was not primarily novelistic" (30). He exulted to the editors at Viking Press, "I am very pleased with the volume as it now stands. Every story in it is (1) complete in itself, no matter how long or short; and (2) contributes to the history of Yoknapatawpha County, so that the volume as a whole is close to being a novel in itself" (62). Long fiction stumped Cowley because it insists on change as an integral feature of its narrative, even as he attempted to prove the stability of Faulkner's world. Both he and Faulkner struggled to establish relationships among the various pieces of Faulkner's oeuvre. Their challenges are familiar to Faulkner readers: If two characters in two stories, one a novel and one a short story, share a name, basic storyline, and character traits, are they the same? Even if so, does the characterization in one genre take priority over another, or is authority established by the one with the earlier or later publication date? How editor and author grappled with such inconsistencies—or, as Faulkner put it, "liberties" (Cowley 53)—speaks volumes about their priorities and offers a means of appreciating the ways in which contributors to DY negotiate such complexities. Although early DY work focused on drawing out the idiosyncrasies of each character in each text, new work on the project allows editors to create composite profiles of Faulkner's characters and outline discrepancies among the various texts in which the character appears.

Faulkner's "Appendix" introduced significant complications for Cowley, to the extent that both men showed frustration at points in their correspondence. What emerged from Faulkner, however, was a statement defending creative development that he later honed for the Snopes trilogy:

> The inconsistencies in the appendix prove that to me the book is still alive after 15 years, and being still alive is growing, changing; the appendix was done at the same heat as the book, even though 15 years later, and so it is the book itself which is inconsistent: not the appendix. That is, at the age of 30 I did not know these people as at 45 I now do; that I was even wrong

now and then in the very conclusion I drew from watching them, and the information I once believed. (I believe I was 28 when I first wrote the book. That's almost 20 years.) (90)

In the very act of declaring artistic freedom, Faulkner imposed another evaluative system on his work. Why is the later work the "right" one? Could this be an overcorrection on his part: running from the trap of nostalgia only to overstate the value of the present? Critics have occasionally followed Faulkner's logic. Stacy Burton pointedly critiques studies that hew too closely to Faulkner's own views, but then claims, "The later texts undoubtedly claim an authoritative status: the Appendix offers an encyclopedic format with clear-cut characterizations" (612). The "Appendix" entries themselves, however, undercut their taxonomic form.

Stephen Railton seems to delight in the sprawl of Digital Yoknapatawpha, however much he desires that particular components reach a stage of relative completion. He knows that much of the value of the project lies in its readiness to tackle elements that are ill-defined, innumerable, and often overlooked: "Already, for example, we are able to capture the full range of Faulkner's characters in a way that eluded the best efforts of print scholarship. This is particularly conspicuous in the case of his black characters, a great many (perhaps most) of whom are never named, and thus seldom appear in the previous inventories" ("Digital Yoknapatawpha" 458). This is an achievement that Faulkner himself would seem to approve, given his penchant for using the named entries in the "Appendix" as opportunities for introducing further stories that give rise to new, often unnamed, characters. Quantification and organization inevitably lead to further invention. The "Appendix" entry on Jason Lycurgus does not linger on that character, but rather moves to the governor and the general who appear after him in the Compson line, and who signal the peak and the beginning of the fall, respectively, of the Compson claim to land.

The editors of DY are relieved of the burden of establishing unity in Faulkner's work. Not only have critical trends changed, but the veracity of their work is demonstrated not by establishing that all pieces lead to the same end, but rather through the data collection process. The editors' methods reflect the critical values of the scholarly field: peer review, consultation of other experts in the event of a conflict, and careful documentation of the methods by which we arrive at editorial decisions. The transparency of the DY methodology is key to its success, as is the transparency of its results; by offering users the raw data it has gathered, DY ensures that they can assess the value of the collected data directly, and not solely through the curated visualizations and search tools created by the DY technical contributors. The recent work of the DY editors to offer curated keywords is one way to bridge Faulkner's language and concepts and our own. The keywords are ours, flagging topics of significance to contemporary readers and ensuring that things do not get lost simply because Faulkner's language does not match our current discussion. Even the keywords option, however, enables later editors to tag issues of critical interest as they emerge.

DY offers far more than the curated presentation the majority of users seek. Constructing the digital archive requires a great deal of epistemological humility, and a willingness to serve as the basis for more ambitious projects and uses at a later time. With each year, more and more data-interpretation models are developed to ensure that potential users who are new to Faulkner or to digital tools such as this one are invited in. But the integrity and the underlying viability of the project lie in its maintaining methodological transparency, and on contributors' willingness to make data available for uses and users far beyond what we have imagined thus far.

Part of what makes DY so very unlike Cowley's unified vision is its interest in helping users view Faulkner's world from a variety of perspectives. Johannes H. Burgers discusses this feature through a technical lens: "It is possible to look at the same data through any number of different perspectives, and reveal sophisticated relationships and connections between locations, characters, and events" (467). The goal is not a data point, but rather a link between, say, characters and the locations in which they appear, or the presence of a same-named character in different texts. The latter, of course, distinguishes DY from Faulkner, who remained as uninterested in cross-textual comparison as he was cross-textual consistency. By attesting to the need for characters to "grow," he erected significant artistic defenses against editorial and readerly intrusions. But to celebrate the growth and change of a character over time and texts, one does need to establish whether it is to be read as the "same" character.

When Faulkner wrote the Compson "Appendix" in 1945, he returned to material he had not, Quentin Compson excepted, touched since the publication of *The Sound and the Fury* in 1929. But though some critics, such as Mary Jane Dickerson, claim that the "Appendix" attests to "the enduring role of the Compson material in the shaping of his art" (317), most agree he was influenced by his recent work on *Go Down, Moses* (1942).[7] Faulkner seems to have been under the sway of the sprawling McCaslin genealogy when he returned to the Compsons, or more particularly the McCaslin ledgers, which contain traces of the stories of the McCaslins' black relatives, slaves, and sharecroppers.[8] The ledgers, which reduce slaves to a list of the materials their masters buy (bodies, clothing, etc.), put pressure on Faulkner's attempts to sum up the Compson family in an "Appendix" without dehumanizing or diminishing his characters. How well, in effect, could Faulkner "account" for his fictional property? Could he do so without reducing his characters' stories to mere evidence of ownership? Jason Compson IV is aligned with ledgers once in *The Sound and the Fury* and twice in the "Appendix." That link could be seen as a caution for Faulkner, as he attempted to capture the value of each named character in the "Appendix" without reducing any one to his or her commercial value.

Faulkner first insisted on the "endurance" of African Americans in *Go Down, Moses*, but the language of endurance reappears in the "Appendix" in reference to Dilsey. Her entry is brief and elides her surname, obscuring her relationship to the other members of her family. These features suggest a return to the conditions of the plantation ledger, in which black figures appear primarily in reference to the white family for which they work. The ledger-like distance from Dilsey's lived experience indicates that Faulkner is all too aware of the way the "Appendix," and American life, remains bounded by race relations, eighty years after Emancipation.

Faulkner's system of categorization in the "Appendix" both prefigures and challenges the DY editors' approach to character data analysis. In his selection of characters to include in the "Appendix" and in the story he spins for each, Faulkner stretches the boundaries of a standard reference work. Faulkner's entries in the "Appendix" enable his characters to evade categorization as he creates intertextual discrepancies, opens new stories within character entries, and undercuts familial and even racial inheritance by showing similar patterns of escape and acquisition across Native American and European family lines. By including a description of a photograph that *may* be of Caddy Compson under the heading "Candace Compson," is Faulkner confirming her identity in that picture? By recording this information in Caddy's character biography, do the DY editors lend credence to that identification? Faulkner's "Appendix" entries and those of the DY project struggle to accommodate the slippery ontological status of rumor.

One of the great points of consistency between *The Sound and the Fury* and the "Appendix" is Faulkner's emphasis on Caddy Compson's unchanging nature, at least as it appears to others. The "Appendix" labels her as "doomed," one who "accepted the doom without either seeking or fleeing it" (332). A brief description of her movement from state to state, and from marriage to marriage, is juxtaposed with a frozen image, a photograph from a "slick magazine" in which the woman who might be Caddy stands "ageless and beautiful, cold serene and damned" (334). Despite her ceaseless movement, she remains unchanged. Indeed, it is precisely because she appears unchanged that Jason Compson declares that Caddy is not the woman in the picture that Melissa Meek proffers: "'That Candace?' he said. 'Dont make me laugh. This bitch aint thirty yet. The other one's fifty now'" (336). In his denial, Jason challenges the literary convention of maintaining a fixed character across different appearances and even different texts. Through Jason, Faulkner reminds readers that real people do indeed grow and change, however fixed fictional characters remain in readers' minds. The centrality and length of the Caddy Compson entry in the "Appendix" echo Caddy's "central, othered presence" in *The Sound and the Fury* (Davis 245), but Caddy's entry is largely concerned with the new story of a new character, the town librarian Melissa Meek. The magazine image Meek carries may well, as she believes, capture the Caddy Compson she once knew, but Meek herself is transformed by the process of attempting to prove Caddy's identity.

The Jefferson Library of the "Appendix" is shrouded in hoary caricature, as is the librarian herself: Melissa Meek is "a mouse-sized and -colored woman who had never married" (333). Her childlike stature is cited at several points, aligning her with the character Rosa Coldfield, whose feet are "clear of the floor with that air of impotent and static rage like children's feet," and who maintains in her old age the air of a "crucified child" (*Absalom, Absalom!* 3–4). Faulkner has deployed the trope of the withered librarian before: in *The Sound and the Fury*, Quentin Compson thinks the woman in the bakery "looked like a librarian. Something among dusty shelves of ordered certitudes long divorced from reality, desiccating peacefully, as if a breath of that air which sees injustice done"

(125). If, as John T. Matthews argues, such passages sketch a world that is unwilling to confront the "history of injustice" (67), then the librarian of the "Appendix" becomes a much more radical figure over the course of her brief sketch. Melissa Meek is more than an exaggerated trope of female impotence. She becomes an activist who seeks to right wrongs, armed with her research.

In Meek, Faulkner introduces a new character with ties to the Compsons' world but also possessed of other methods of evaluating information and uncovering the truth. The Lafayette County and Oxford Public Library did not open until 1930, so it comes as no surprise that the public library is a late addition to Faulkner's Compson narrative, a new site for working through the relationship between research and local knowledge. In his earlier work, the libraries of plantation homes serve as settings for dramatic confrontation (such as the imagined one between Henry and Thomas Sutpen in *Absalom, Absalom!*) or storytelling (as in "Lion"). There, the term "library" is less a description of the room's contents than it is an indication of the social ambitions of those who refer to it. The young narrator of *The Unvanquished* explains that both his father and "the negroes" refer to a room in the plantation house as "the Office," since it is filled with agricultural implements, dogs, and men, but Bayard notes that his grandmother insists the room is "the library," "because there was one bookcase in it" that contained a smattering of volumes (15–16). The linguistic disagreement is not over the contents of the room, since it contains both books and seed, but rather over whether to acknowledge the labor of the plantation within the space of the plantation house. Is the room for physical or intellectual work? In Bayard's elaborate description of the battle over the name of the study/library, Faulkner makes clear that gentility is at stake.

Books, however, carry great potential for power in Faulkner's world. In *Light in August*, Byron Bunch thinks of the gossip about Gail Hightower that the people of Jefferson have gathered over the decades, and yet Byron knows something they do not: "Hightower read a great deal. That is, Byron had examined with a kind of musing and respectful consternation the books which lined the study walls" (73). What Hightower reads in a book equips him to save a mother during childbirth; there is a link between books and the world outside them, despite the stereotype of libraries as a retreat from reality. The reinterpretation of books and libraries that is suggested by Hightower's character comes to fruition in Melissa Meek and the Jefferson public library in which she appears, which echoes the civic role of Faulkner's own hometown library. The Oxford Public Library, sponsored by the Oxford Business and Professional Women's Club, was originally housed in the witness room of the courthouse (Vinson), and it gained a part-time librarian in 1931. It was also, as the library proudly announces, the first municipal building to be integrated in Oxford, although that only occurred after Faulkner's death.

Melissa Meek is not attached to any major Yoknapatawpha family, and yet she identifies familial attachments where others would deny them. She is, like the narrator of the "Appendix," and like Faulkner himself, a cataloger, one who seeks to categorize the image of Caddy and thus "save" her, but that quest seems doomed to failure. Again like Faulkner, however, Meek accomplishes a very different task in the course of her failure. In seeking to "save" Caddy, she revitalizes her own character, moving to the foreground of the narrative, seeking testimony from both black and white members of the Compson household, braving crowds of soldiers in Memphis, and abandoning the censure of high school students and the deathly tidiness of her library for something grander. That pursuit, Faulkner suggests, is worth narrating.

Much rides on Meek's quest, including the opportunity for Faulkner to offer a somewhat lengthy tribute to the throngs of soldiers Meek encounters in Memphis: "soldiers and sailors enroute either to leave or to death and the homeless young women, their companions, who for two years now had lived from day to day in pullmans and hotels when they were lucky and in daycoaches and buses and stations and lobbies and public restrooms when not, pausing only long enough to drop their foals in charity wards or policestations [sic] and then move on again" (337). Through Meek, Faulkner introduces more figures who were neither present in *The Sound and the Fury* nor imaginable at that point in time. He also moves quickly from the soldiers to the women they leave behind, lingering on figures who do not make the newspapers. The generosity of the narrative as experienced through Meek demonstrates the significance of Faulkner's insistence that his fiction will grow with each step. Meek does more than any other character in the "Appendix" to expand Faulkner's fictional world, and she does so by locking her library and venturing into the public. Jason Compson IV, for all his worldly business dealings, does little to expand Faulkner's world. His repeated turns to his niece, to the police, and to Dilsey demonstrate that he is not, as he claims, an "emancipated" man (340).

It is no accident that Jason Compson's perspective dominates the "Appendix" from his entry onward. He is responding to a new threat to his way of life, one that comes from the unlikeliest of directions. The old plantation ways may be under threat by the "new South," in which Jason plays a significant role, but Melissa Meek invades his store and challenges his narrative. When he denies her interpretation of his sister's fate, Meek seeks the testimony of a black member of Jason's former household. Jason's perspective may permeate the final entries of the "Appendix," but the text concludes with the character that Melissa Meek sought as the figure of authority.

DY's cataloging method ensures that the Jason Compsons will not limit what information is available to Faulkner's reader. Just as Ike McCaslin is conscious of how the lives of McCaslin slaves are circumscribed by the (often cramped) handwriting of his predecessors in the plantation ledgers, so, too, should readers take note of how the lives sketched in the "Appendix" are bound within headings that purport to maintain the Compsons' narrative prominence. There is more that DY could do to flag tone and focalization in each text, but by recording each character who appears, and the relationship of each character to the events of the narrative, it highlights Melissa Meek's capacity for "opening up" the story. By attending to what the text offers rather than what social and narrative conventions indicate about a character's prominence, DY makes clear the project's usefulness in engaging the conventions of literary criticism. Importantly, it does so by using the tools of traditional literary criticism. The project does not, as Timothy Brennan suggests of many digital humanities efforts, surrender discipline-specific tools in favor of new ones. If, as he argues, "data are 'curated' rather than assessed; information is 'leveraged'; facts are 'aggregated' rather than interrogated" (B13), DY is successful primarily in drawing together the efforts of dozens of scholars in a field that is known for its solitary work, and in relying on those scholars to ensure that the database includes only information that has been assessed, argued over, and interpreted.

As the project editors are aware, digital tools may enable scholars to count the number of appearances of the word "Caddy" in the text of *The Sound and the Fury*, but only readers of Faulkner will know to draw in references to the slipper that once belonged to Caddy Compson, and negotiate Benjy's complicated relationship with golf caddies. What is being created in Digital Yoknapatawpha is what I would call a digital manifestation of the work of the humanities, which can then play a role in shaping the goals and methods of the digital humanities. Brennan argues that too often the digital humanities only reveal scholars' starting assumptions—as in, they reflect only what scholars relied on other evidence to know already. But revealing assumptions is a significant contribution to the work of the humanities. Articulating methods, priorities, categorization, and discipline-specific knowledge is key to ensuring that the work of modern Faulkner scholars avoids the perils to which Cowley was subject. He found unity when he began by assuming it.

Attempting to "save" Caddy enables Melissa Meek to transcend the characterization suggested by her name, her profession, and her lifelong habits (335). Although she begins by attempting to keep racy literature out of the hands of her patrons, she allows the library to become disorderly in her distraction over Caddy. She bears "two feverish spots of determination in her ordinarily colorless cheeks," enters the feedstore where Jason IV works and where "only men ever entered," and she speaks to him, despite having refused to do so for many years (333). She also makes a determined trip to Memphis, despite being easily overwhelmed by crowds (337). Meek's quest ends with a sense of failure, as the testimony of those closest to Caddy makes Meek unsuccessful in establishing the identity of the woman in the picture. She admits that "saving" Caddy is a futile endeavor. For one whose profession is that of the labeler, cataloger, and researcher, this is indeed a failure. But if, in the process, Faulkner has reopened the life of a woman whom both society and the narrative had "doomed" to close-minded spinsterhood, then a different quest may have been achieved. The goal is not to recover Caddy, but rather to discover Meek. In Meek's curation of Caddy's legacy, and Cowley's curation of Faulkner's, there is evidence of a generous impulse at work. If the "Garter King-at-Arms" is a caricature of Cowley or the literary critic, through Faulkner's portrayal of the county librarian he has reclaimed the potential of such roles. Though in attempting to keep *Forever Amber* from her patrons' hands Melissa Meek demonstrates her own predilections for control, she quickly moves beyond censorship.

The "Appendix" responds to the haunting imagery of the plantation ledger, and DY responds to both, creating an opportunity for more than the cataloging of artistic endeavor. Faulkner may have declared himself the "proprietor" of a fictional county, but he also envisioned significant movement in that landscape. Although he struggled when he saw others, such as Cowley, refashion what he had constructed, within his fiction he celebrated when Yoknapatawpha land changed hands. He resented that slave plantations were equated with the dawn of Southern history and culture: "The elegance of the colonial plantation didn't exist in my country. My country was still frontier.... The common picture of the South is all magnolias and crinoline and Grecian portals and things like that, which was true only around the fringes of the South. Not in the interior, the back wood" (Gwynn and Blotner 113). Faulkner's "back wood" conception of Yoknapatawpha shapes the "Appendix," which creates—under the pretense of exhuming—the history of those who preceded the Compsons and the other plantation families of Yoknapatawpha. Long before the Compson and McCaslin and Sartoris family lines run dry, Faulkner undermines the primacy and the inevitability of Yoknapatawpha's property owners, himself included.

A fixed view of the Yoknapatawpha landscape would favor characters of higher social classes, whose plantations dominate the landscape. But Faulkner's emphasis on movement draws readers' eyes to those figures who do not have prominent names, genealogies, or property; their movement within Yoknapatawpha attests to the passing of time and the efforts of individuals to carve out their own narratives within a seemingly static landscape. Through his emphasis on the history of a place, rather than the place itself, Faulkner draws attention to characters of lower socioeconomic status, even when his narratives reflect the social hierarchies that dominate his world. By tracking movement, DY has helped make visible the characters who are present in Faulkner's narratives but erased from his maps. In DY, the relentless work of data entry illuminates a facet of Faulkner's creation that tends to go unnoticed in traditional criticism: the near-innumerable unnamed characters who appear in his novels, but who will get no appendix entry to call their own. DY can also help make those characters comprehensible as groups and families, even when characters must remain nameless and unnumbered. His narratives include masses of agricultural workers who labor on plantations that carry another man's name, and townspeople who occasionally surge to the foreground as volatile crowds. Through DY, readers can trace the growth of the mob of *Intruder in the Dust*, recognizing in it not an alien intrusion on the narrative, but rather a compilation of town and country characters, men, women, and children that have been present in the narrative all along. Readers can also appreciate how frequently Faulkner uses unnamed characters to delineate the complex interactions of race and class, such as when in *The Sound and the Fury* Dilsey sniffs at what she terms the "white trash" churchgoers who would deny Benjy a place in their white church and yet be aghast at his welcome in the black one. Perhaps most importantly, readers can draw out of the background the innumerable black agricultural workers whose positions change subtly over the course of Faulkner's fiction. Field slaves become sharecroppers and tenant farmers, some of whom are still referred to in the language of slavery by Faulkner's white narrating characters. DY enables readers to appreciate the economic changes endured by those who cannot or will not join the Great Migration.

In the "Appendix," Faulkner may not create an entry for the soldiers and lovers and children who fill Memphis the day Melissa Meek visits, but he certainly registers their presence as she "fought her way through the crowded bus terminal . . . and fought her way into the bus" (337). She cannot see, much less name, the "shape," whom the narrator identifies as a "man in khaki" who installs Meek in a seat and makes space for her small body on the crowded bus. And yet Faulkner's insistence on the crowd of bodies, and the influence of such bodies on Meek's story, is a reminder of the many bodies needed to account for the Yoknapatawpha he created. In a character catalog like the one the "Appendix" purports to be, or a map of land that is carved up into plantations, these figures would recede from view. But DY's insistence on accounting for all those drawn by Faulkner enables readers to see that background movement and the press of bodies. Digital humanities tools for gathering what may seem "mere" data points ensure that such individuals are identified and enumerated in Faulkner's fiction. The DY data enables us to suggest tensions among presence, narration, and social status—all tools of the literary trade—but also allows us to recognize characters through their movement, so that we can better determine which is prompted by their own ambition and which reflects their socioeconomic vulnerability. For Faulkner to make a contribution to the digital world, we must allow him to once again be a voice of the "interior, the back wood," challenging the order and elegance that readers expect. Faulkner's "Appendix" is therefore not merely supplementary, but inherently creative.

Notes

1. Faulkner included the phrase on a map he supplied to accompany *Absalom, Absalom!* for publication in 1936. In Digital Yoknapatawpha, Stephen Railton and Christopher Rieger provide an extended analysis of Faulkner's maps alongside images drawn from the collections at Southeast Missouri State University and the University of Virginia.
2. Cowley repeatedly referred to a "rainspout" (42, 46, 64, 162), even though that is not a word Faulkner used in correspondence with Cowley. My own wording of the title of Faulkner's "Appendix" follows his instructions regarding the publication of the 1946 Modern Library edition of *The Sound and the Fury* and *As I Lay Dying*.
3. Cowley opened his letter by declaring that "the reason the book pleases me is that it gives me a chance to present your work as a whole.... [T]he reader will have a picture of Yocknapatawpha [*sic*] county . . . from Indian times down to World War II" (22). As he outlined the pieces to be included in the volume, he admitted, "The big objection to this scheme is that it has nothing from 'The Sound and the Fury,' which is a unit in itself, and too big a unit for a 600-page book that tries to present your work as a whole.... But in spite of this objection, I think that a better picture of your work as a whole could be given in this fashion. You know my theory . . .— that you are at your best on two levels, either in long stories that can be written in one burst of energy, like 'The Bear' and 'Spotted Horses' and 'Old Man,' or (and) in the Yocknapatawpha [*sic*] cycle as a whole" (23). Even in the initial pitch, Cowley expressed reservations about some of the "factual discrepancies" in Faulkner's work, but hastily added, "But what to [*sic*] hell, those inconsistencies aren't important—the chief thing is that your Mississippi work hangs together beautifully as a whole—as an entire creation there is nothing like it in American literature" (23–24). Cowley did, however, write repeatedly of the "problems" and "difficulties" of grappling with such inconsistencies in his subsequent letters to Faulkner, and to readers of *The Faulkner-Cowley File* (27).
4. As Susan Donaldson notes, Cowley encouraged critics to read Faulkner's world as a "parable" for the South (27).
5. See Howard Horsford for an analysis of Faulkner's representation of the Native American presence in northern Mississippi, and Melanie Benson Taylor for an analysis of Faulkner's Native American stories and his influence on Native American writing.
6. Cowley, followed by Faulkner, appears to have confused Faulkner's character Percy Grimm with a character from John Dos Passos's *1919*, as Don Graham and Barbara Shaw suggest (331).

7. See Davis for an extended discussion of the links between the Beauchamp family of *Go Down, Moses* and the black characters of the "Appendix" (238).
8. Ben Robbins also argues for the influence of Faulkner's work in Hollywood, which immediately preceded his writing of the "Appendix." Robbins argues that the cinematic trope of the femme fatale is evident in Faulkner's entry on Caddy Compson.

Works Cited

Brennan, Timothy. "The Digital-Humanities Bust." *Chronicle Review*, 20 Oct. 2017, B12–B14.
Burgers, Johannes H. "Using the *Digital Yoknapatawpha* Database for Research." *Mississippi Quarterly*, vol. 68, nos. 3–4, 2015, pp. 466–69.
Burton, Stacy. "Rereading Faulkner: Authority, Criticism, and *The Sound and the Fury*." *Modern Philology*, vol. 98, no. 4, 2001, pp. 604–28.
Cowley, Malcolm. *The Faulkner-Cowley File: Letters and Memories, 1944–1962*. Viking, 1966.
Davis, Thadious. *Games of Property: Law, Race, Gender, and Faulkner's* Go Down, Moses. Duke UP, 2003.
Dickerson, Mary Jane. "'The Magician's Wand': Faulkner's Compson Appendix." *Mississippi Quarterly*, vol. 28, 1975, pp. 317–37.
Donaldson, Susan V. "Reading Faulkner Reading Cowley Reading Faulkner: Authority and Gender in the Compson Appendix." *Faulkner Journal*, vol. 7, nos. 1–2, 1991–92, pp. 27–41.
Faulkner, William. *Absalom, Absalom!* 1936. Vintage International, 1990.
———. "Appendix." *The Sound and the Fury*. Vintage International, 1990, pp. 325–43.
———. *Light in August*. 1932. Vintage International, 1990.
———. *The Sound and the Fury*. 1929. Vintage International, 1990.
———. *The Unvanquished*. 1938. Vintage International, 1990.
Graham, Don, and Barbara Shaw. "Faulkner's Small Debt to Dos Passos: A Source for the Percy Grimm Episode." *Mississippi Quarterly*, vol. 27, no. 3, 1974, pp. 327–31.
Gwynn, Frederick L., and Joseph L. Blotner. *Faulkner in the University: Class Conferences at the University of Virginia, 1957–1958*. Vintage, 1959.
Horsford, Howard C. "Faulkner's (Mostly) Unreal Indians in Early Mississippi History." *American Literature*, vol. 64, no. 2, 1992, pp. 311–30.
Lester, Cheryl. "To Market, to Market: *The Portable Faulkner*." *Criticism*, vol. 29, no. 3, 1987, pp. 371–92.

Matthews, John T. "The Rhetoric of Containment in Faulkner." *Faulkner's Discourse,* edited by Lothar Hönnighausen, Niemeyer, 1989, pp. 55–67.

Meriwether, James B. "The Novel Faulkner Never Wrote: His Golden Book or Doomsday Book." *American Literature,* vol. 42, no. 1, 1970, pp. 93–96.

Railton, Stephen. "Digital Yoknapatawpha: A Written Roundtable." *Mississippi Quarterly,* vol. 68, nos. 3–4, 2015, pp. 457–59.

———. "Re: Appendix Location and Character Lists—and Questions!" Email received by Erin Penner, 2 Feb. 2018.

Railton, Stephen, and Christopher Rieger. "Faulkner Mapping|Mapping Faulkner." Added to the project: 2017. Digital Yoknapatawpha, University of Virginia, http://faulkner.iath.virginia.edu/media/resources/DISPLAYS/FaulknerMapsHP.html.

Robbins, Ben. "Inscrutable Images and Cultural Migrations: Wartime Noir and the Compson Appendix." *Faulkner Journal,* vol. 28, no. 1, 2014, pp. 55–77.

Taylor, Melanie Benson. *Reconstructing the Native South: American Indian Literature and the Lost Cause.* U of Georgia P, 2011.

Urgo, Joseph R. *Faulkner's Apocrypha: A Fable, Snopes, and the Spirit of Human Rebellion.* UP of Mississippi, 1989.

Vinson, Thomas Corey. "The Lafayette County & Oxford Public Library: Historical Study." 2009. Unpublished manuscript. Author's personal collection.

Faulkner's Human Hive
COMPLEX SYSTEMS IN *THE HAMLET*

John Michael Corrigan

As ONE way to apply the technological concepts underlying the Digital Yoknapatawpha Project, this essay provides the reader with an interpretative architecture for using systems theory and the concept of complexity to understand Faulkner's representation of the social body in *The Hamlet* (1940). The novel, I contend, is a depiction of the community as a distributed process of self-organizing relationships—that is, interaction networks that systems theory represents in terms of nodes and edges. In this context, Faulkner represents the ways in which a network of social relationships is composed of interrelated nodes with the likelihood that one node will come to predominate and acquire centrality. In this increasing hierarchal process, resources and information no longer flow through open distributed processes but tend to cohere in a centralizing locality, so that one node of social space serves as the conductor for the flow of resources and information to the wider community. These hubs of information and resources are in themselves neither negative nor positive; rather, they can be expected in the emergence of any complex system. In *The Hamlet,* Faulkner repeatedly represents the pattern of human movement and behavior across time as a concentric clustering in which one node of social space among many takes prominence.

I proceed in three sections. I first argue that DY's methodology of data curation, while individually tailored to the unique literary qualities of Faulkner's fictional county, features the underlying epistemology of networked systems—namely, the supposition that individual movements in social space and the pattern this behavior assumes across time can be cartographically and graphically visualized and that these visualizations provide a necessary interpretative framework with which to assess Faulkner's artistic accomplishment. To do this, I contextualize DY in terms of the study of networks and in relation to complex systems theory, which is a distinct, but overlapping, field of inquiry. I briefly introduce the history of the study of networks, define some of its primary terms and concepts, and provide eight primary features of complexity. Secondly, I proceed to close textual examinations of the ways in which Faulkner repeatedly demonstrates how individual interactions tend to cluster concentrically in social space, producing, as a result, weighted and thereby hierarchal nodes of social relation. In the second section, I show this pattern of clustering by means of three examples: the behavior of Eula's suitors, Lump Snopes's financial exploitation of his cousin's obsession with Jack Houston's cow, and Mink Snopes's botched concealment of Houston's body. Finally, I apply my analysis to what is perhaps Faulkner's most complicated narrative sequence, the horse auction, in which systems complexity involves the simultaneous emergence of hierarchy and its destabilization in the chaotic, but still coherent, pattern of the social body of Frenchman's Bend and, beyond it, the contours of Yoknapatawpha County.

Complex Systems and the Interaction Networks That Compose Them

Digital Yoknapatawpha involves a systematic approach to the data curation of Faulkner's Yoknapatawpha canon and suggests a far-reaching epistemology that allows us to see his artistic project in a new light. The project's editors have created a database of this by identifying and then encoding, first, all the locations; second, the characters that appear in these locations; and third, the events linked to locations and the characters either involved or mentioned within them. The methodological premise of this data acquisition rests upon the supposition that human beings interact in social space and that the pattern of their behavior can be at once visualized and interpreted. In this respect, DY interpretatively curates Faulkner's narratives into visualizations of interaction that leave users free to draw their own conclusions.

Rafael Alvarado, a senior technologist with the project, emphasizes the open-ended nature of this inquiry in his introduction to another set of visualizations that the project offers, known as force-directed graphs. These particular graphs "are intended to make visible the implicit structures of social space encoded in [Faulkner's] works" (Alvarado). Elaborating on the network theory that underpins the group's data curation, he explains that "an algorithm models a graph as a physical system with forces of attraction and repulsion exerted between nodes, in this case, between a text's Characters and the Locations at which they appear." What the graphs show, therefore, are networks in which characters cluster around locations, with lines that connect them not only to these locations but also, through these nodes of social space, to each other. The more events that take place in a location, the more the graph centralizes that node with the diameter of the location node growing accordingly. By way of explanation, Alvarado compares the "composite or synchronic" nature of the graph to "what an archaeologist finds in a settlement pattern: she sees the tracks of generations of people and animals, all superimposed onto a village plan, which show the inhabitants' recurring pathways of movement." While these computational visualizations "show structure," Alvarado concludes, the "information does not show process—a limitation to be sure." The humanistic scholar is thereby invited to find a way to address this "limitation"—to expand the focus of inquiry by analyzing the "process" of individual interaction to elucidate the significance of such interaction within the "recurring pathways of movements" in the larger scope of Faulkner's canon.

The study of networks makes visible the individual interactions that constitute group behavior and thereby gives visual and statistical shape to datasets too large for any one consciousness to intuit and comprehend. When applying network theory to Faulkner's representation of the community in *The Hamlet*, one must acknowledge that the suppositions and methodology of the interpreter are paramount. Simply to say that Frenchman's Bend is composed of many overlapping interaction networks that together compose a complex system may sound impressive rhetorically to the layperson or to the scholar uninitiated in such terminology, but it does not convey very much about Faulkner's art or the fictional world he populated. First of all, interaction networks can take many different forms—and they also express themselves at different scales ranging from microbiology all the way up to ecosystems and beyond, from the neurons in brains to the individual relationships that constitute a larger community of people. Before I proceed to a close reading of *The Hamlet*, I must first define the character of interaction networks in the context of complex systems more broadly, beginning with some historical context and definitions of a number of key terms and concepts.

In large part, systems theory rose to prominence because of rapid advances in computer science, and it has become indispensable to the study of myriad natural and human-made systems, whether these involve large communication systems, biological systems, social interaction systems, or transportation infrastructures (Barrat et al. 3747–52). In fact, the formal study of networks is quite a bit older than one might suppose, since it dates back to 1735 when "Swiss-born mathematician Leonhard Euler ... invented network theory" with the "basic units of graph theory—which he originally called the 'geometry of position'—nodes (or vertices) and edges (or links)" (Ferguson 24–25). "Nineteenth-century scientists applied [Euler's] framework to everything from cartography to electrical circuits to isomers of organic components. That there might also be *social* networks certainly occurred to some of the great political thinkers of that age," but no investigator attempted "to formalize this insight" until the turn of the twentieth century (25–26), when Euler's geometry of position came to underline the study of networks and the distinct, but overlapping, field of complex systems.[1] Mark Newman provides a simple definition by which we can orient ourselves: the "pattern of connections in a given system can be represented as a network, the components of the system being the network vertices and the connections the edges" (2). More simply, we can visualize a network as a graph where each vertex or node represents an object, and the edge or link is the connection between objects. However, imagining a network in this way is not an end in itself. A visualization in which all nodes and edges are equal reveals little to nothing about how real-world systems actually work. If one assigns value to the nodes and directionality to the edges, this basic structure begins to take many forms, which we can simplify by identifying the following features: 1) a weighted or unweighted network (the weight representing specific values given to the nodes that, in turn, indicate the degree of centrality each node takes in any given network); and 2) a directed or nondirected graph, which denotes the direction of movement from one node to the next or, by contrast, the cessation of movement (Sedgewick 566). The layperson can imagine the direction in which information or resources flow through a network. These flows constitute a pattern of behavior—and the more weighted a system, the more such flows favor certain nodes, thereby indicating the centrality of different nodes in the network.

The epistemological shift from analyzing the essential properties of things to investigating the pattern that objects make in the world may appear subtle, but it marks a key distinction that informs systems theory. In *Gödel, Escher, Bach*, Douglas R. Hofstadter was one of the first to popularize the shift from an intrinsic view of matter to one that emphasizes pattern and configuration. The "key is not the *stuff* out of which brains are made," he writes in the opening of the book, "but the *patterns* that can come to exist inside the stuff of a brain" (4). "This is a liberating shift," he continues, "because it allows one to move to a different level of considering what brains are: as media that support complex patterns that mirror, albeit far from perfectly, the world, of which, needless to say, those brains are themselves denizens—that is in the inevitable self-mirroring that arises, however partial or imperfect it may be, that the strange loops of consciousness start to swirl" (4). Hofstadter insists, moreover, that one attends to the pattern of individual interactions in order to comprehend the larger aggregate behavior of a system while these interactions, no matter how small, must be imagined as a form of language and communication. Indeed, these interactions exist everywhere, in minds as well as in every other biological network.

Hofstadter famously parallels the movement of individual ants within a colony to "the composition of a human brain out of neurons. Certainly no one would insist that individual brain cells have to be intelligent beings on their own, in order to explain the fact that a person can have an intelligent conversation" (320). The analogy between brains and ant colonies may seem commonplace today, but in the late seventies, such a position met with opposition. As with many elegant ways of seeing the world, Hofstadter's depiction of brains and ant hills—where higher-order behavior emerges out of but cannot be reduced to lower-level interactions—has become a standard way of visualizing the world in the twenty-first century. By way of evidence, consider Deborah Gordon's critically acclaimed book on ant colonies as interaction networks. Thirty-one years after Hofstadter, she similarly dissuades the reader from imagining a "hidden program" within the colony and urges the reader to accept the seemingly counterintuitive supposition that individual ant interactions with their noise, randomness, and variability produce larger "patterns of regularities" (47). Gordon conveys a now-elementary tenet of system structure. Even though disordered movement may characterize many of the interactions within the ant colony, the aggregate self-organizes, which means that it produces spontaneous pattern formation; or, to use another description, it creates "dynamic patterns synchronized in time and extending over large distances of space many orders of magnitude bigger than a [single] interaction" (Kelso 8).

Gordon's description of the ant colony arises out of the application of network theory to biological systems—systems so large and robust that one may speak of system complexity. Indeed, complexity describes a system that resists simple characterization and thus requires an examination of the myriad connections that compose it. In *Diversity and Complexity*, Scott E. Page provides this rather general definition, by arguing that "systems that produce complexity consist of *diverse* rule-following entities whose behaviors are *interdependent*. Those entities interact over a contact structure or network," and these "entities often *adapt*" (17). It is important to add that the study of complexity does not yet possess a uniform methodology, for there is much disagreement among scholars concerning the application of basic terminology. Renate Sitte, for instance, writes that there is still "no unanimous consensus as to what complexity is" (22), while describing qualities that are generally accepted across disciplines. "Systems are complex," Sitte affirms, "when they undergo changes in structure, changes in functioning, when they have adaptive feedback, are evolving, or simply when they have a large number of components or relations" (25).

Scholars thus agree upon a number of the "strongest characteristics of a complex system": "1) intricate interdependencies among many parts; 2) many variables operating simultaneously; 3) generally nonlinear; 4) cause and effect are not close in time and space; 5) intuitive interventions do not produce the expected outcome; 6) reductionist analysis fails or is misleading; 7) emergence; and 8) self-organization" (Sitte 26; adapted). If one employs these characteristics in an analysis of Faulkner's representation of Yoknapatawpha, it becomes clear that the writer's fictional world is not just complex in the general literary usage of the term, including such features as multiple levels of meaning, nonlinear structure, and intertextuality. Faulkner also presents Frenchman's Bend as a dynamic network of social space in which distributed patterns of human movement spontaneously produce emergent and adaptive behavior. In *The Hamlet*, as I show below, the community exhibits the features of complex systems outlined above, especially in the case of the horse auction, where all these characteristics are active. One may plausibly suggest, therefore, that Faulkner was already discovering the epistemology of systems complexity in the creation and populating of his own imagined landscape.

Concentric Clustering of the Social Body

Scholars in Faulkner studies have only just begun to apply various aspects of network theory. Charles Hannon argues persuasively that "a model of network expansion—one that trades local control for *the benefits of a distributed network*—... can serve as a grid for understanding Faulkner's modernizing of narrative form" (94; emphasis added). Hannon's terminology comes from computer science. "Distributed" processing occurs when more than one processor runs a computer application; instead of one computer processing information, a network of computers takes on the task. The advantages to this can be intuitively gleaned by the layperson: not only is this process more efficient (one can potentially increase the processing power by orders of magnitude), but the application can become more robust and resilient, since it no longer relies upon one node in the network and can continue indefinitely even if a particular node or nodes fail. Consequently, Hannon charts the transition in Faulkner's narrative form from *Flags in the Dust* to *Absalom, Absalom!* as a proliferation of information networks expanding beyond an original centralized node of exchange (94–95). Hannon's insight identifies not only an emerging mode of narrative discourse in Faulkner's writing, but also, I argue here, the dynamic and adaptive structure that the social body acquires across time.

The Hamlet represents how historical transitions take place through distributed processes in which every action, no matter how seemingly trivial or small, can affect the behavior of the social body. Thus, Faulkner opens the novel by establishing an overarching chronology for the community, emphasizing its distributed processes, not dependent wholly on any particular site of social space, no matter how centralized this site once was. In the first two paragraphs, over a hundred years are compressed to portray the changing social structure of a north Mississippi community. Frenchman's Bend, we read, "was a section of rich river-bottom country" that became the "site of a tremendous pre-Civil War plantation" (3) that was "parceled out now into small shiftless mortgaged farms" (4). Here, we see the transition from the wilderness to the various organizations of the plantation economy—first slave and then tenant, as the land of Frenchman's Bend, once dominated by an elite planter class, is now subject to the crop-lien system of the New South. Even with this larger historical overview, Faulkner provides much detail about the new economic conditions in which a banking industry sells the mortgages to the landowner Will Varner, who rents these mortgages out to various sharecroppers. In these opening pages, these socioeconomic transitions are writ large and presented as one complex and changing system in which individuals participate in such a way that no one person or authority determines the outcome. At the same time, Frenchman's Bend retains its hierarchal structure with social status and material wealth conferring varying degrees of power and, in turn, producing inequalities that determine the destinies of whole social groups, not simply the fate of individuals.[2] Thus, Faulkner presents, for both good and ill, the resilience of this plantation economy even when the Frenchman's original plantation dream, most visibly figured in the decaying Frenchman's Place, is replaced by a new centralized node of social space.

On the *DY* site, the force-directed graph of *The Hamlet* captures a feature of the systemic inequality of Frenchman's Bend and, more generally, of the New South. Although the graph is a nondeterministic visualization, processing the novel's data each time it is rendered, the location nodes with the most weight always appear centrally. Varner's store emerges as the node that possesses by far the most weight, signifying that it is a centralized hub around which all other nodes, both locations and characters, cluster. On the one hand, this is a rather obvious representation of how many more events take place at the store than at any other location during the course of the narrative. On the other hand, the graph dynamically captures the central role these furnish stores possessed in the social organization of the New South. Whereas the Frenchman's manor was once, during slavery, the central hub of social space, the furnish store replaced it because of the emergence of the crop-lien system. The substitution does not erase economic and social inequality, since these furnish stores were largely run on credit and often charged high interest to the sharecropper. Faulkner establishes this early on in *The Hamlet* when Ab Snopes inquires about tenanting land. "What do you rent for?" Ab asks, with Jody Varner replying, "Furnish out of the store here. No cash" (9). While the type of currency/credit and interest rate could vary, the system that emerged made these furnish stores centers of social space; it was through them that information and resources flowed to the community and back again in a feedback loop that primarily enriched the landowner or, as the historian Gavin Wright termed these New South landowners, the "laborlord" (18).

Faulkner was increasingly cognizant of the ways in which the crop-lien economy operated, and his novels reflect this awareness. In works like *The Hamlet* and *Go Down, Moses,* the furnish store emerges prominently as a hub of social space around which people concentrically cluster and through which flows of information and resources are centralized. Faulkner imagined this clustering by means of a visual language that strikingly resembles DY's own force-directed graphs with characters connected to and grouping around primary hubs of social space. In *Go Down, Moses,* for instance, Faulkner depicts the two lien ledgers that are kept in the most privileged—that is, highest—place within the McCaslin furnish store, exerting an invisible but powerful force that binds across time the black laborers' movements to the store: "two threads frail as truth and impalpable as equators yet cable-strong to bind for life" (228). If these graphs of Digital Yoknapatawpha show networks with lines that connect characters to locations and to each other, we actually see these threads of relation embedded in the pages of Faulkner's novel, where people cluster around the furnish store which they frequent and which also controls them. Such depictions are not infrequent in the Yoknapatawpha canon. Faulkner repeatedly narrativizes the emergence of these clusters and their adaptation to new circumstances. The white population of *The Hamlet,* for instance, possesses a greater degree of freedom than that of the black laborers of the McCaslin place, yet the pattern of their behavior is the same. Under certain conditions, the individuals of *The Hamlet* group around one spatial node of exchange, while in other circumstances, they select new centers around which to move—and these patterns of movement over long periods of time lead to the emergence of new social and cultural behavior, even while constituting the overarching hierarchal dimensions of Frenchman's Bend with the furnish store at its center.

What becomes clear by using this approach to the novel is that Frenchman's Bend is composed of many interacting and overlapping networks, some of which emerge only to die out, but all of which are dynamically linked to, affect, and are affected by the aggregate behavior of the whole. While, as noted above, Faulkner opens the narrative with a temporal compression of movement in physical space, he also slows the narrative pace in order to present the individual interactions that constitute this evolving social body. The most obvious interaction network that emerges early on is Eula Varner and the suitors that besiege her once she reaches puberty. Faulkner indicates that this pattern of social behavior arises without the express intentionality on the part of any one agent; he emphasizes an instinctual clustering across time around the young girl who does nothing actively to provoke the activity: "She would take no part in them, yet she would dominate them. Sitting beside the stove exactly as she had sat during the hours of school, inattentive and serene amid the uproar of squeals and trampling feet, she would be assaulted simultaneously beneath a dozen simultaneous shadowy nooks and corners" (127). Even when Faulkner limits the narrative purview to focus on a single interaction network, we find that he represents not merely one event, not one "assault," but a cluster of events that together constitute a dynamic interaction network of interrelations that expresses itself in a dozen similar "nooks and corners" and thus becomes more than one action among many, but a predictable pattern played out across time and extended over physical space.

In the passage above, Eula sits "amid the uproar of squeals and trampling feet" of the children and youths, and this description of relatively free movement serves as fitting prelude for a more intricate consideration of how beings—both human and nonhuman—cluster in social space and produce, as a result, spontaneous order. The uproarious movement of the children is not a one-time phenomenon, but recurrent behavior that, while appearing chaotic, self-organizes and overlaps with the varying assaults of the suitors. Faulkner soon articulates a grander figuration by means of which an interaction network unfolds across time so as to produce a centralized node of social space. In anticipation of his later representation of nonhuman beings in the novel, Faulkner tropes the young suitors as a swarm of insects whose movement and behavior self-organizes concentrically around Eula: "It would have but one point, like a swarm of bees, and she would be that point, that center, swarmed over and importuned yet serene and intact apparently even oblivious, tranquilly abrogating the whole long sum of human thinking and suffering which is called knowledge, education, wisdom, at once supremely unchaste and inviolable: the queen, the matrix" (127). The imagery of bees and their queen in their center articulates the manner in which this structure of social space is predicated upon the aggregate movement of the social body. Eula does not direct the individuals around her; no one individual directs them. Nonetheless, the pattern has a center around which individuals cluster, a vertex simultaneously privileged and desired by the swarm of young men, but this center does not administer the activity around it. Instead, the "sum" of the individual interactions spontaneously self-organizes without direction or guidance from any one governing will or agency, and Eula continues to be profoundly unaware of the suitors as well as of "the sum of human thinking and suffering" to which their movements are related.

We can observe a number of the strongest qualities of systems complexity in the swarming pattern of the suitors. Faulkner does not simply describe suitors attacking Eula; he establishes the collective behavior of all the children as a chaotic uproar out of which an assault organizes, emerging in different locations and over an extended period of time. Faulkner also continues to trope this swarming or clustering activity as insect behavior: "Through that spring and through the long succeeding summer of her fourteenth year, the youths of fifteen and sixteen and seventeen who had been in school with her and others who had, swarmed like wasps about the ripe peach which her full damp mouth resembled" (141). No longer bees, but now wasps, this imagery provides a variable articulation of the cluster pattern as it seeks a source of sustenance that Faulkner interweaves with the imagery of Eula's mouth. Yet again, Faulkner emphasizes no one individual, but the "dozen" suitors who "form a group, close, homogeneous, and loud, of which she was the serene and usually steadily and constantly eating axis, center" (141). In these depictions, we find a hierarchal grouping in which value and weight are given to one node of social space—Eula, the "constantly eating axis"—but without any top-down governance. Eula's profound disinterest is equally matched with the persistent lack of planning on the part of her suitors: "One night they charged the moving buggy from the roadside shadows and were driven off by the whip because they had no concerted plan but were moved by a spontaneous combustion of rage and grief" (152).

Faulkner thereby develops Eula's section by depicting this interaction network as one that produces predictable results across time, while remaining nonlinear and highly variable. The suitors cluster in different locations—and Eula is similarly mobile. There is an express lack of individuality in this behavior: these young men may as well be iterations of the same person. The schoolteacher Labove, however, is the exception. Despite his misanthropic nature, he is also a suitor, moved by the faceless instinct that pervades the group of young men. And while his behavior may differ from the others, his movements similarly cluster about Eula through that year and into the next. Labove may be a "militant fanatic" ready to turn his "uncompromising back upon the world" (117), but he only differs in degree, not in kind, from the group of which he is a member. Labove's inclusion in the group reinforces the fact that the behavior of the interaction network in question is not simply the repetition of the same pattern *ad nauseam,* but a more spontaneous and varied pattern produced by individuals of differing personalities and motivations.

Faulkner's ingenuity in his characterization of Labove lies in the fact that variables cannot escape the overarching complex system, even while they continue to create new clusters of behavior. Labove is part of the interaction network that groups around Eula, but his own behavior inadvertently serves as a catalyst for new configurations of spontaneous order. Thus, Faulkner describes in detail Labove moving into an "unheated lean-to room in Frenchman's Bend" (122), while also portraying how the community adapts to the strange young man in its midst. The description is worth quoting in full, since it indicates how thoroughly Faulkner interweaves the idea of interaction networks into his narrative technique and content:

> It was in the house of a widow who lived near the school. He owned a razor, the unmatching coat and trousers he stood in, two shirts, the coach's overcoat, a Coke, a Blackstone, a volume of Mississippi Reports, an original Horace and a Thucydides which the classics professor, in whose home he had built the morning fires, had given him at Christmas, and the brightest lamp the village had ever seen. It was nickel, with valves and pistons and gauges; as it sat on his plank table it obviously cost more than everything else he owned lumped together and people would come in from miles away at night to see the fierce still glare it made. (122)

Due to the fact that Labove must study at night to juggle his work responsibilities with his obligations at the University of Mississippi, the young man possesses "the brightest lamp" the community has ever seen. Although he does not care about the community, the "fierce glare" of his lamp assumes a quasi-religious value among the members of the community who repeatedly come moth-like "from miles away at night" to see it. We can thereby observe a new concentric clustering in social space, one that is unintended but ritualistically manifest in the people's movements around the lamp.

This description of Labove indicates that one's position in the community—indeed the very way that a person comes to live among others—depends upon multiple interacting nodes of agency that give rise to unexpected, self-organizing outcomes. In the examples above, we see the emergence of one interaction network in time as well as the way that one network conjoins or overlaps with others, composing in their interrelation the greater structure of social space and the movements of the social body within it. Another striking example of this clustering pattern within Frenchman's Bend is Lump Snopes's financial manipulation of Ike, his cousin, which mirrors Flem Snopes's ability to manipulate any financial transaction to his own advantage. While the mentally disabled Ike knows little beyond his instinctual desire for the cow, Lump builds a business model that involves the recurrent movement of the community's men, which establishes, however briefly, a new center of social space. Moreover, Faulkner's description of V. K. Ratliff's discovery of the business echoes the earlier clustering behavior of Eula's suitors. Instead of any moralizing condemnation of either Ike's bestiality or Lump's exploitation of his cousin's obsession, Faulkner emphasizes emergent pathways of movement:

> That lot was beyond the house from the road; the rear wall of the stable was not in sight from either. It was not directly in view from anywhere in the village proper, and on this September forenoon Ratliff realized that it did not need to be. Because he was walking a path, a path which he had not seen before, which had not been there in May. Then that rear wall came into his view, the planks nailed horizontally upon it, that plank at head-height prized off and leaning, the projecting nails faced carefully inward, against the wall and no more motionless than the row of backs, the row of heads which filled the gap. (216–17)

The stable in which Ike copulates with the cow "was not directly in view from anywhere in the village proper," but has become visibly linked to the village by a newly emergent "path" and, as Ratliff follows it, he comes to join "the row of heads" that habitually group around the spectacle. Just as the suitors concentrically crowded around Eula's mouth, here, the townsfolk cluster about another "orifice" (217). Ratliff's humanity becomes apparent in this case, but not because he deviates from the movements of the community. He too walks the freshly formed path and, unlike his friend Bookwright, he looks at the sight. When he looks, however, he projects himself into the consciousness of Ike: Ratliff "did look, leaning his face in between two other heads; and it was though it were himself inside the stall with the cow, himself looking out of the blasted tongueless face at the row of faces watching him" (217). Lump's business effectively ends in this moment—and the reader learns that although some nodes of social space may take prominence, the centrality of one gathering location cannot be sustained indefinitely. Indeed, a cluster pattern can be disrupted by even one small change in group behavior. In this case, Ratliff's ability to see through the eyes of another is enough to disturb the centrality of the stable.

Where *The Hamlet* unquestionably emphasizes network centrality, it just as powerfully values individual behavior as a wellspring of novelty and change. Indeed, network centrality and novelty form an interlocking pattern: individual expressions of novelty, moral or otherwise, may evoke change for the better, but like any other behavior, these expressions are subject to the unexpected pattern formations within complex systems. One of the most telling examples of this is Mink Snopes's tragic bungling of Houston's murder. Mink's own enmity with Houston arises in no small part because of his cousin Ike's affair with the cow. Again, the sequence of cause and effect is separated over space and time, another feature, we recall, of complex systems. To be sure, Mink does not kill Houston on behalf of Ike, but the cow affair leads, through a complex web of events, to Mink committing the violent act; and in his attempt to conceal Houston's body, Mink finds himself a victim of the clustering behavior of social groups. As in earlier passages, the new pattern that unveils itself involves the clustering of animals—bees and buzzards. Mink chooses a hollow tree in which to conceal Houston's body, not fully appreciating that this node once served as a center around which other beings clustered and could very well do so again:

> He seemed to know exactly where he was, he did not even look over his shoulder until he released the body at last and stood erect and laid his hand upon what he sought—the shell of a once-tremendous pin oak, topless and bout ten feet tall, standing in the clearing which the lightning bolt of age or decay or whatever it had been, had created. Two

years ago he had lined a wild bee into it; the sapling which he had cut and propped against the shell to reach the honey was still in place. (249–50)

Once, the activity of the wild bees produced a vertex around which beings—both human and nonhuman—grouped. With this architecture "still in place," the oak serves again as a center of activity. Three days after Mink disposes of the corpse, he wakes to see a new assemblage of movement. Much like the suitors who swarmed about Eula or the townsfolk who nightly gravitate toward Labove's bright lamp, the buzzards circle Houston's dead body in the dead hollow of the oak, thwarting Mink's laborious efforts to conceal his crime: "He just watched the black concentric spiraling as if [the buzzards] followed an invisible funnel, disappearing one by one below the trees" (257). Despite his intentions, then, Mink's actions have created yet another coordinated social ritual in nature. The "limitless freedom of the sunny sky" is thereby filled with "black concentric spiraling," a visualization that underscores how unintended patterns of behavior can self-organize and concentrically cluster anywhere.

Horses, Hives, and Human Hierarchies

Faulkner composed much of the novel's final section "two years before he returned to the material which was to become *The Hamlet*" (Greiner 1133). As much of *The Hamlet*'s concluding section that emerged first in the story "Spotted Horses" indicates, Faulkner's initial vision for the novel was on a scale that dwarfs even the interaction behavior we have seen thus far. With virtually the whole of Frenchman's Bend engaged in the buying and selling of spotted ponies, the fourth section achieves something far more difficult than representing individual exchange or concentric rituals: it narrates how many interacting nodes, each with different motivations and interests, can produce a widespread aggregate pattern of nonlinear behavior that temporarily groups in social space. The crowd behavior may suggest uniformity, but Faulkner concentrates on the intricate interdependencies among the many parts of the crowd, emphasizing that its variables operate simultaneously and independently—two strong characteristics, I may add, of complexity as outlined above following Sitte. Indeed, Faulkner emphasizes the roiling chaos within the social body that continually threatens to break free. This technique underscores another feature of complexity—namely, chaotic systems that are extremely sensitive to each of the variables that compose them. This context also helps to explain why Faulkner blurs any firm distinction between so-called natural and human systems. *The Hamlet* involves the bustling activity of beehives, the menacing concentration of wasps, the circling movement of buzzards, and, in section 4, the frenetic behavior of wild horses—all of which not only mirror the behavior of their human counterparts, but also serve as selfsame expressions of how the social body moves, behaves, and thinks in social space.

On one level of analysis, there is a clear dialectical tension between humans and horses. From the opening of the section, coercion and restraint are decisive parts of this process of assemblage. Flem Snopes and Buck Hipps arrive at the store with the ponies "shackled to one another and to the wagon itself with sections of barbed wire" (300). Despite the normalizing imposition of their shackles, Faulkner emphasizes the behavioral diversity of the animals. As their "mismatched eyes rolled wild and subdued, they huddled, gaudy motionless and alert, wild as deer, deadly as rattlesnakes, quiet as doves" (300). The description of the herd appears incongruous, encompassing wild and deadly animals as well as creatures often considered peaceful. With its amalgamation of varying, even contradictory characteristics, the herd's quivering energy expresses itself fluidly as surges or waves of movement: "the movement of its surge against the wire which held it travelling backward among the rest of the band in a wave of thuds and lunges" (300). Here, Faulkner captures the modus operandi of an interaction network; the horses' undulating motion, their surging and wavelike tactile interaction, transmits its energy pattern throughout the group: "The Texan grasped the wire and began to draw the first horse up to the wagon, the animal plunging and surging back against the wire as though trying to hang itself, the contagion passing back through the herd from animal to animal until they were rearing and plunging against the wire" (303). A "contagion" moves "from animal to animal," inciting the beings assembled to act in ways they might not otherwise do. As we saw in Hofstadter's theory of the self-mirroring that occurs in brains and ant colonies, the interaction pattern Faulkner depicts constitutes a form of communication that travels through an extensive network to produce self-organization. Importantly, it is not the surging of the horses alone that evokes this behavior, but also the coercive actions of Buck that also come to be mirrored by the community of Frenchman's Bend.

Here, in the self-mirroring activity of horses and humans, we can discern yet another feature of system complexity in which the tense dynamic between humans and horses gives way to larger, more all-encompassing behavior. Like the one-on-one interaction of the horses, the men of Frenchman's Bend begin to imitate the activity of Buck Hipps, whose pattern of behavior therefore corrals not simply the horses, but also the men. It takes just a few participating nodes to spark such a surge through the social body. Flem may have introduced the Texan by arriving with him, but it is another man of influence, Jody Varner, who gives Buck his first participant (302). With Jody's acquiescence, Eck Snopes "grasped the wire also" (303) and, within a twenty-four-hour period, virtually the whole community of men have adopted his movements by employing "wire," "stakes" (310), and "plow-line" (331) to subdue the wild ponies and cluster them into a vertex of social space. One must note that this emergent aggregate pattern is not without opposing variables. Ratliff, who as we saw exercised great social influence before, warns the men assembled at Varner's store of Flem's hidden hand in the swindle afoot. Even as he countered Lump's ability to manipulate a centralized node of social space, this last section narrates the failure of Ratliff's influence. Not heeding his warning, the men succumb to the advantages of paying less for a team of horses, and the emerging pattern of self-mirroring propels them toward a fateful decision. As the horses communicated with each other by rubbing bodily against each other and producing a collective wave of motion, so the men converse and their verbal exchange produces "something stubborn, convinced, and passive" (306) in them. As the men speak, moreover, they are no longer visualized as agents, but as "silhouettes" in darkness, whose language is immediately echoed by a "bird, a shadow, fleet and dark and swift, [which] curved across the moonlight, upward into the pear tree and began to sing" (306). Faulkner's symbolic logic may be difficult initially to tease out, but it clearly identifies a mimetic, imitative, or self-mirroring pattern transposed from the shadowy men to the "shadow" of a "mockingbird."

As the mockingbird echoes the men from a prominently placed pear tree across the lane from the store, Faulkner introduces an imagistic touchstone or objective correlative, to use T. S. Eliot's term, that he develops in the depiction of the entire event. The bird replicates the language of the men, and the tree on which it sits is also no casual image; it is a type of *axis mundi* through which seeming opposites and unrelated occurrences are connected: "The pear tree across the road opposite was now in full and frosty bloom, the twigs and branches springing not outward from the limbs but standing motionless and perpendicular above the horizontal boughs like the separate and upstreaming hair of a drowned woman sleeping upon the uttermost floor of the windless and tideless sea" (306). There is clearly a variety of ways to interpret such a condensed symbolism; one key to the pattern in question is Faulkner's insistence that the tree is composed by an alignment of the vertical "twigs and branches" that "stand" above the "horizontal boughs." In this configuration of the vertical and the horizontal, the above and the below, we have an imagistic parallel for the alignment of the clustering of the social body around a vertex and the simultaneous urge for flight, to break free from the wire bonds, as the horses ceaselessly attempt to do. As much as these two principles—vertical assemblage and horizontal flight—are at odds with each other, they are nonetheless part of an interlocking and evolving whole.

With this imagistic alignment of opposites, all beings—horses, mockingbirds, and men—come to resemble each other: the horses as phantoms, the mockingbirds as shadows, and the men as silhouettes (305, 311, 312, 331, 333). And Faulkner represents how these beings concentrically cluster, while employing the pear tree as a symbolic touchstone for the way that these interaction networks align into one complex system of behavior. Thus, where the tree is initially imagined as a "drowned woman" (306) or "drowned silver" (331) and the wild horses are similarly submerged as "phantom fish" (304, 331), the pattern self-organizes and, in doing so, arises out of the depths: "Then the pear tree came into sight. It rose in mazed and silver immobility like exploding snow; the mockingbird still sang in it" (339). The tree that appears in the night as a drowned woman explodes, like snow in all directions—aligning with a greater transition from night to day, from below to above, from within to without. Whether or not one interprets this as the emergence and self-expression of an immanent principle in being—an *élan vital,* to use Henri Bergson's term—this behavior is clearly portrayed in terms of emergence, or what complex systems theory describes as the self-organizing of higher-order behavior that arises from, but cannot be reduced to, its lower-level constituent parts. In *The Hamlet*, this emergence, ascent, bursting forth—whatever figurative variation we wish to use—is unmistakable and provides a symbolic paradigm that directly corresponds with the individuals clustering at the auction lot. Gradually increasing in size from "six men" in Mrs. Littlejohn's lane (308) to "more than fifty men standing along the fence" (314), the crowd thereby comes from miles around to see the Texas horses up for auction. Some of these men speak, although, like many of the men at Varner's store, they are largely described as "one of the others" (309, 311, 313, 332) or "a second," "third," or "newcomer" (309, 320, 322) without individual characteristics.

The changing pear tree also foreshadows the calamitous conclusion of the horse auction for the men and women of Frenchman's Bend. With the pear tree rising out of the depths like "exploding snow," we see the prefigurement of the wild horses bursting free from their barbed-wire confinement in the lot. After all, the auction is built upon containing a wild and irrepressible energy and is highly sensitive to small changes that can disrupt its aggregate behavior. Buck Hipps's departure may be one of these factors, although Lon Quick's forgetting to close the lot gate (333, 364) clearly operates as the decisive and unintended action that decenters the behavioral cluster. Whatever the case, the freedom of the horses is, on one level at least, a victory against confinement that any reader is likely to appreciate. And its power is subtly established by a reversal or chiasmus of the earlier models of swarm behavior that we have seen so far: the suitors clustering about Eula's mouth (141), the men looking through a hole at Ike and the cow (217), and Mink thrusting Houston's body "into the growing orifice" of an oak (281). In these later scenes both before and after the auction, Faulkner intimates that this center will not hold; indeed, its energy will push back against confinement. The horses are thus repeatedly troped with interior metaphors, both mouth and orifices that are by no means placid. In the barn, for instance, the "entire interior exploded into mad tossing shapes like a down-rush of flames" (312), and the horses become a "towering parti-colored wave full of feet and glaring eyes and wild teeth, which overtopping, burst into scattered units, revealing at last the gaping orifice and the little boy still standing in it, unscathed, his eye still leaning to the vanished knothole" (312). Here, the horses rise, jumping through the doorway back into the lot and eviscerating the knothole or "orifice" through which Wallstreet Snopes peers. This pattern comes to a finale when the horses are once again pinned into the shadow of the barn, forced as it were into mimetic confinement, only to explode outward like "a gaudy vomit of long wild faces and splotched chests" (333) that "crash through the gate" and pour outward toward their freedom.

We can identify a residual Romanticism in Faulkner's narrative that resonates powerfully with our own present inclinations and values in humanistic discourse. The narrative fulfills the audience's own predilections for flight and novelty, reflecting undoubtedly a hunger for interior authenticity—an underlying modernist disenchantment with bureaucratic or industrial mechanization. Indeed, Faulkner persistently questions the mechanisms of control that operate in human systems and affirms the lived, material worlds of those—both animal and human—that populate his fiction. In the words of Christina Colvin, "Faulkner's effort to represent animals . . . as members of lived, material worlds invites an interrogation of the ways Faulkner's animals resist human systems of discourse" (95). Yet this perspective is by no means univocal, since he also provides his readers with a means of eschewing such distinctions between human and nonhuman. In *The Hamlet,* all beings concentrically cluster and produce vertices of social space—and while Faulkner invites us to question the structures they make or, more appropriately, that we make, there is nonetheless an open-endedness that persistently relies on the reader's response to the patterns in question. Part of grappling with this open-endedness is the realization that nothing is final in Faulkner's Yoknapatawpha. Just as Flem secures his victories in Frenchman's Bend, obtaining control over the principal vertex of social space in the community and achieving the ability to manipulate the social body—its movements, behavior and thinking—to his advantage, he joins the wagon trains that take him and his family to Jefferson. Flem's departure implicitly signals a new dispersal and clustering pattern that occurred en masse in the South, the flight from rural to urban life and, with it, the rise of big industrial agriculture and the decline of sharecropping.

With the perspectives offered by complex systems theory, we are better equipped to visualize this conflictual and interlocking relationship between vertical control and horizontal flight as they compose the changing face of Yoknapatawpha. The larger narrative of the Snopes trilogy suggests that, on some basic level, any system of complexity requires both principles. Faulkner certainly upholds the two, visualizing, on the one hand, the greater concentric clustering of Yoknapatawpha's social body in very similar terms to the horse auction with its centralizing push for control and the wire ties that hold its disparate parts in place. In perhaps the most iconic scene in *The Town,* this is what Gavin Stevens sees with "Jefferson, the center, radiating weakly its puny glow into space; beyond it, enclosing it, spreads the County, tied by the diverging roads to that center as is the rim to the hub by its spokes" (331). Like the barbed wire or plow lines of the auction, the diverging roads "tie" the diffuse rural land to the center and thereby bind a "living water" into "concentric rings" (331). From this God-eye view, Frenchman's Bend, an "ant-heap" (332), is similarly secured to the road-spokes that arc at once to the center and outward "to the world" (330). Yet, as every reader of Faulkner knows, this God-eye view is not the sole or even most important measure of hierarchies in his fiction. These invocations of complex order may overwhelm individual consciousness, as happens with Mink Snopes in *The Mansion,* who sees Memphis upon his release from Parchman penitentiary and is "engulfed" by "the gravity or suction" of the city, which "stooped soaring down, bearing down upon him like breathing the vast concrete mass and weight until he himself was breathless, having to pant for air" (313). But such invocations also pose a moral quandary about our age of networks, persistently imagined from the individual's perspective. As Ratliff looks through the eyes of Ike Snopes, so Faulkner asks his readers to do the same, not to disavow the broader system of complexity, but to see through all its nodes, all of which are living subjects in their own right.

Within the concentric clustering and dispersal of the social body, we confront the suffering and endurance of individuals, whether they be Mink, who is bound lifelong to a series of small plots of land, or Mrs. Armstid, the person most disadvantaged by Flem's auction scheme. Carolyn Porter addresses the "distinctively dark side" of *The Hamlet*'s final section by noting the "inevitable rise of the cash nexus as the central locus of power in the novel's world" and, more viscerally, in "Mrs. Armstid's plight" that "remain[s] to haunt us" (178). Porter does not identify, however, why Mrs. Armstid's plight serves as the measure for the unjust "cash nexus" that Flem controls in the community. Readers may well feel the smart of the blows that her husband rains down upon her or lament the loss of the money over which she has labored. Faulkner also forces his readers to see through Mrs. Armstid's eyes, to perceive an invocation of complex order that, though beautiful in its vastness and interconnection of parts, is still the system that binds and holds this woman in place:

> After a time Mrs Armstid raised her head and looked up the road where it went on, mild with spring dust, past Mrs Littlejohn's, beginning to rise, on past the not-yet-bloomed (that would be in June) locust grove across the way, on past the schoolhouse, the weathered roof of which, rising beyond an orchard of peach and pear trees, resembled a hive swarmed about by a cloud of pink-and-white bees, ascending, mounting toward the crest of the hill where the church stood among its sparse gleam of marble headstones in the somber cedar grove where during the long afternoons of summer the constant mourning doves called back and forth. (349)

Mrs. Armstid has just asked Flem Snopes for the return of her money as she was promised by Buck Hipps. Flem's refusal is taken as a victory: "By God," Lump laughs, "you cant beat him" (351). Mrs. Armstid herself does not argue, not in this node of social space that Flem has so clearly secured for himself. But, on the threshold of Varner's store, she sees the greater pattern of which she is a part "rising" with one level stacked upon another and the trees resembling a hive of bees that ascend further toward the highest promontory of the community. Just like Mink in *The Mansion*, she is mastered by this aggregate pattern, but her suffering is nonetheless implicitly manifest in its very organization, from her position below as well as in the "back and forth" communication of "the mourning doves" above. Here again, we see the self-mirroring that can spread through an aggregate pattern of behavior. Like the mockingbirds that repeat the language of the men, the doves residing above the community echo the pattern of suffering below, suggesting that no part is too small to affect the life of the whole.

As all beings cluster and disperse in social space, the rub, Faulkner implies, is individual in nature. Thus, Flem, moving to Jefferson, may repeat in stages what he has achieved in Frenchman's Bend, beginning with a side-street restaurant and gradually appropriating the central hubs through which resources flow into the wider community, first the power plant and then his final victory, the Sartoris bank. But there is a symmetry to the complex design of the social body suggesting that, while nothing is final, the life of the whole rests at last upon the individual self. T. S. Eliot captures this poetically in "Preludes" when he confesses that even though our individual experiences are replicated in "a thousand furnished rooms," his mind still curls round and clings to the "notion of some infinitely gentle / Infinitely suffering thing" (24–25). In *The Hamlet*, this idea is poignantly realized in Faulkner's affirmation of Mrs. Armstid, for after Flem's refusal, the woman "descends the steps" of Varner's store, and it becomes clear that she is the "drowned woman" that we saw figured initially and powerfully in the pear tree: "[T]he gray folds of the garment once more lost all inference and intimation of locomotion, so that she seemed to progress without motion like a figure on a retreating and diminishing float; a gray and blasted tree-trunk moving, somehow intact and upright, upon an unhurried flood" (351).[3] The whole pattern rising from the depths is reenacted as Mrs. Armstid appears "a gray and blasted tree-trunk" moving above the water, just as the "the upstreaming hair of the drowned woman" rose above to become "exploding snow." The horses are one facet of this emergence and their escape is some small victory against constraint, but Mrs. Armstid is that member of the system who is most damaged by their flight. In stark contrast to, and as a result of, their explosive flight, she is left as a "blasted tree-trunk moving . . . without motion" (351), thereby fulfilling the initial imagistic insistence that this tree appears locked in place, as "motionless" above as she was below at the bottom of a "windless and tideless sea" (306).[4] The imagery is certainly intricate, but this is the point of humanistic inquiry, that visualizing structure alone "does not show process," as we saw in Rafael Alvarado's assessment of DY's graphs. Faulkner's process invariably involves our participation—not simply to see through the eyes of the other, but to affirm that other as a measure of ourselves. Mrs. Armstid's plight so poignantly haunts us because she is the means through which we come to understand the complex system in which we are nestled as well as to address the injustices that threaten to overwhelm it.

DY's CARTOGRAPHIC visualizations of Faulkner's county help to strengthen new spatial interpretations of his fiction. The site offers maps and graphs that illuminate Faulkner's own symbolic representations of the increasingly complex social structures of modernity. Besides the visual maps that are a mainstay of the site, DY provides a variety of additional features from the location-character graphs that we originally analyzed to heatmaps and to a forthcoming demographic toolkit that lets users slice through the data to quantify the racial and gender makeup of a particular novel or the entirety of the Yoknapatawpha fiction. These features are not a replacement for humanistic inquiry; rather, they allow users to grapple more reliably with complexity. In this context, I have paid particular attention to the life of the social body as it moves, behaves, and thinks in social space, and I have argued that this way of imagining Faulkner's community is not a theoretic imposition of our own time, but a vital lens that allows us to understand the ways in which Faulkner anticipated our own information age with its sprawling networks and hyper-connectivity.

While *The Hamlet* presents a relatively small network of individuals, the novel emphatically departs from any traditional hero-centric conception of narrative form by presenting an evolving community without clear-cut protagonists and antagonists. Alex Woloch has called this type of narrative a "character-system" in his effort to understand the "inherently social dimension [of] narrative form" (17). "For the character-system," he elaborates, "offers not simply many *interacting* individuals but many *intersecting* character-spaces, each of which encompasses an *embedded* interaction between the discretely implied person and the dynamically elaborated narrative form" (17–18). Characters do not need to form any immediately observable bond to be dynamically interlinked; rather, they share space, and their behavior informs each other even if they are long separated in time. Franco Moretti makes a very similar point in pursuing a network analysis of Shakespeare's *Hamlet*. "Making the past just as visible as the present," he argues, "is one major change introduced by the use of networks. Then, they make visible specific 'regions' within the plot as a whole: sub-systems, that share some significant property" (84). Digital Yoknapatawpha immediately presents its users with such a network visualization of Faulkner's narratives, permitting the user to see the broader contours of Faulkner's county with its interlinking networks—families, farms, plantations, hamlets, and towns—as they dynamically form complex assemblages of modernity. This is not to say that there are no moral agents in such a novelistic discourse, but that Faulkner's morality is realized in the dynamic interaction of individuals as they cluster in social space to form and deform hierarchies of power, privilege, and belief.

Notes

1. For a brief analysis of the relationship between network and complexity theory, see Richardson 75–79.
2. For an analysis of how cultural codes define social hierarchy in the Snopes trilogy, see Schreiber 459–76.

3. See Hodge, who addresses how the wood metaphor functions in Faulkner's *As I Lay Dying* and how it is relates particularly to gender (13–24).
4. Germane to this analysis is Lorie Watkins's contention that female mobility in Faulkner's fiction is the means to escape "social and spatial strictures," "restrictions that most of his female characters can escape only briefly in flight or totally in death" (170). I would add that by contrasting the immobility of Mrs. Armstid with the flight of horses, Faulkner implicitly indicates that "patriarchal culture limits female mobility as a spatial/social [form of] control" (164).

Works Cited

Alvarado, Rafael. "Visualizing Character and Location in Faulkner." Unpublished manuscript.

Alvarado, R. C., Robbie Bingler, Worthy Martin, and Stephen Railton, "About Force-Directed Graphs." Added to the project: 2018. Digital Yoknapatawpha, University of Virginia, http://faulkner.drupal.shanti.virginia.edu/node/17681?canvas.

Barrat, A., M. Barthélemy, R. Pastor-Satorras, and A. Vespignani. "The Architecture of Complex Weighted Networks." *PNAS*, vol. 101, no. 11, 2004, pp. 3747–52.

Colvin, Christina M. "'His Guts Are All Out of Him': Faulkner's Eruptive Animals." *Journal of Modern Literature*, vol. 38, no. 1, 2014, pp. 94–106.

Corrigan, John Michael. "Encoding Yoknapatawpha: Considering Faulkner in the Information Age." *Mississippi Quarterly*, vol. 68, nos. 3–4, 2015, pp. 470–73.

Eliot, T. S. *Collected Poems: 1909–1962*. Faber & Faber, 2002.

Faulkner, William. *Go Down, Moses*. 1942. Vintage International, 1990.

———. *The Hamlet*. 1940. Vintage International, 1991.

———. *The Mansion*. 1959. Vintage International, 2011.

———. *The Town*. 1957. Vintage International, 2011.

Ferguson, Niall. *The Square and the Tower: Networks and Power, from the Freemasons to Facebook*. Penguin, 2018.

Gordon, Deborah M. *Ant Encounters: Interaction Networks and Colony Behavior*. Princeton UP, 2010.

Greiner, Donald J. "Universal Snopesism: The Significance of 'Spotted Horses.'" *English Journal*, vol. 57, no. 8, 1968, pp. 1133–37.

Hannon, Charles. "Topologies of Discourse in Faulkner." *Faulkner in Context*, edited by John T. Matthews, Cambridge UP, 2015, pp. 91–99.

Hodge, Amber. "The Casket in the Corpse: The Wooden (Wo)man and Corporeal Impermanence in *As I Lay Dying*." *Southern Quarterly*, vol. 53, no. 1, 2015, pp. 13–24.

Hofstadter, Douglas R. *Gödel, Escher, Bach: An Eternal Golden Braid*. 1979. Penguin, 1994.
Kelso, J. A. Scott. *Dynamic Patterns: The Self-Organization of Brain and Behavior*. MIT Press, 1995.
Moretti, Franco. "Network Theory, Plot Analysis." *New Left Review*, vol. 68, 2011, pp. 80–102.
Newman, Mark. *Networks: An Introduction*. Oxford UP, 2010.
Page, Scott E. *Diversity and Complexity*. Princeton UP, 2011.
Porter, Carolyn. *William Faulkner: Lives and Legacies*. Oxford UP, 2007.
Richardson, Kurt A. "Systems Theory and Complexity: Part 1." *E:CO*, vol. 6, no. 3, 2004, pp. 75–79.
Schreiber, Evelyn Jaffe. "'The Cradle of Your Nativity': Codes of Class Culture and Southern Desire in Faulkner's Snopes Trilogy." *A Companion to William Faulkner*, edited by Richard Moreland, Wiley-Blackwell, 2007, pp. 459–76.
Sedgewick, Robert, and Kevin Wayne. *Algorithms*. 4th ed., Pearson Education, 2011.
Sitte, Renate. "About the Predictability and Complexity of Complex Systems." *From System Complexity to Emergent Properties*, edited by Moulay Aziz-Alaoui and Cyrille Bertelle, Springer, 2009, pp. 23–48.
Watkins, Lorie. "Women in Motion: Escaping Yoknapatawpha." *Faulkner's Geographies*, edited by Jay Watson and Ann J. Abadie, UP of Mississippi, 2011, pp. 163–74.
Woloch, Alex. *The One vs. the Many: Minor Characters and the Space of the Protagonist in the Novel*. Princeton UP, 2003.
Wright, Gavin. *Old South, New South: Revolutions in the Southern Economy since the Civil War*. Basic Books, 1986.

Digital *Yaakni Patafa*
PLOTTING INDIGENOUS SPACE AND RACE

MELANIE BENSON TAYLOR

> We have a few old mouth-to-mouth tales; we exhume from old trunks and boxes and drawers letters without salutation or signature, in which men and women who once lived and breathed are now merely initials or nicknames out of some now incomprehensible affection which sound to us like Sanskrit or Choctaw; we see dimly people, the people in whose living blood and seed we ourselves lay dormant and waiting, in this shadowy attenuation of time possessing now heroic proportions, performing their acts of simple passion and simple violence, impervious to time and inexplicable.
>
> —Faulkner, *Absalom, Absalom!* (1936)

ON THE surface, the goals of the Digital Yoknapatawpha Project seem to contradict nearly every tenet of indigenous wisdom and practice. Over and against the perceived fluidity and circularity of Native time are the Digital Yoknapatawpha (DY) team's meticulous, linear plottings of time, space, event, and character in motley permutations and precision. Add to this the uncomfortable fact that Yoknapatawpha itself is, explicitly, a palimpsest reinscribing indigenous space with settler colonial cartographies, with Faulkner himself serving as the "sole owner and proprietor" of an imaginative landscape seized from its original inhabitants. The very name Faulkner chose for his "postage stamp of *native* soil" (my emphasis) elides two Chickasaw words—*yaakni* (land or earth) and *pataffi/patafa* (to cut open or disembowel).[1] "Yoknapatawpha" thus invokes an unquietly "split" or "furrowed" space, although Faulkner interpreted it more generously and gently as "water flowing slow through the flat land" (Gwynn and Blotner 74). And finally, the choice to represent Indian heritage as a race—demarcated by a colored icon like those used to classify white, black, and mixed characters—subsumes the more accurate cultural and legal rubrics for indigenous identity. And yet, while all of these choices may prompt conceptual and ethical challenges for scholars of indigenous cultures, they may nonetheless have uncanny and compelling pertinence for Faulkner's post-plantation, U.S. southern context in particular. DY is, in fact, uniquely poised to force uncomfortable but necessary conversations about the complexities of indigenous identity as *both* a phenomenon inextricable (if extirpated) from land and territory *and* a racial conceit spawned by the very settlement of that land—twin disgraces elided permanently in the American narrative, which Faulkner captured with unmatched nuance and horror.

Once Removed: Manifesting an Indian Progenitor

It is not just President Donald Trump and the Republicans who sneered at Massachusetts Senator Elizabeth Warren in 2018 for resorting to a DNA test to authenticate her claims to Cherokee ancestry. For different reasons, Native Americans have frequently objected to the reliance on genetic markers as definitive measures of indigenous heritage. "In turning to the burgeoning, for-profit DNA industry," Aviva Chomsky and others have observed, Warren "implicitly lent her progressive weight to claims about race and identity that go hand in hand with moves to undermine Native sovereignty" (Chomsky). Such arguments correctly identify the slippery slope by which reducing Indian identity to a genetic trait directly undermines the treaty and land rights of sovereign tribal nations. Historian Jean O'Brien explains that any "insistence on 'blood purity' as a central criterion of 'authentic' Indianness" in fact revives the antiquated scientific racism of the nineteenth century, where Indians' intermarriage with other racial groups (particularly African Americans) became grounds for a narrative of "disappearance" and the justification for their dispossession (quoted in Chomsky). Moreover, these trendy new DNA tests tend to correlate geography with ethnicity, producing "racial" demographics that can be traced to mapped regions of the globe.

These DNA profiles can be seen as something of a bellwether in current attitudes about race, which tends in the U.S. context to overwhelm more nuanced narratives of cultural heritage. In the U.S. South particularly, race is largely processed through the black-white prism of slavery; these are identities that rely symbiotically on one another, poised in dialectical,

Hegelian duality. As Nell Irvin Painter puts it in her *History of White People,* "Race is an idea, not a fact" (ix). This logic further disassembles the "truth" of indigenous identity, lost particularly in the southern vortex of place-based race where Indians are ghostly progenitors. The fiction of complete Removal is, of course, just that; many southeastern Indian tribes and individuals did remain after the sweeping Removal policies of the 1830s, but they have tended to fly low on the popular radar. Recently, a "Native South" both past and present—pre- and post-plantation—has been excavated by literary critics Eric Gary Anderson, Annette Trefzer, Gina Caison, and Kirstin Squint and historians Theda Perdue, Mike Green, Malinda Maynor Lowery, Robbie Etheridge, James Taylor Carson, and Greg O'Brien. In numerous books, articles, and a flagship journal (*Native South*) devoted to building a scholarly archive about Indian histories, economies, governance structures, foodways, language revitalization efforts, literature, and art in the Southeast, these scholars have diligently uncovered the Native traces plowed under by the chronicles of chattel slavery, Reconstruction, and Jim Crow. Most aim to "insert" or "embed" Native cultures within a predominantly biracial discourse (Frank and Ray viii, xi); others seek to establish altogether through-lines that emphasize Indian irrelevance to Western systems and resistance to settlement culture.

More complicated is the acknowledgement that what is being remembered is, in many cases, also a chimera divorced from landed occupancy; still, the primacy of an embodied homeland is nonetheless burnished continually. According to Cherokee writer Cynthia Kasee—who grew up not in her once-native South but in Cincinnati—"to understand the 'race memory' of the Indian removals, if you're not Indian, try picturing yourself as a Jew visiting Auschwitz or a Cambodian survivor returning to Pol Pot's killing fields.... To be a descendant of a removed tribe is to be homesick for a place you've never been" (180, 182). Echoing N. Scott Momaday's concept of an indigenous "memory in the blood,"[2] Kasee and others deploy tropes hinged on simultaneous absence and inaccessibility; this remembering "blood" is not tangible but aspirational, in most cases. As North Carolina Cherokee poet MariJo Moore puts it in a poem about her Appalachian home, "Memories unfold from around these / glorious ancestral mountains /... close enough to smell / but not close enough to touch / just close enough to taste / but never close enough to touch" (177). As Alabama Creek poet Janet McAdams styles it, the "land called 'indigenous'" may exist only "on the map of my body," a place "where Indianness is simultaneously sentimentalized and ignored": "this is real life," she concludes, "which is inexact, messy" (256). Such "messy" terrain may be the best approximation of what Chadwick Allen calls an "authenticating genealogy" for contemporary Native peoples ("Blood" 94)—a layered "blood/land/memory complex" that trumps institutionalized forms of race (and racism) for indigenous peoples.[3]

Land and no land; embodied culture and cathected knowing. Contemporary indigeneity exists in just such a paradoxical, dialectical borderland. So, too, does the South—a space no longer delineated strictly by the borders of traditional territories but, in the wake of progressive movements in the New Southern Studies and American Studies more broadly, a fluid, leaky state of mind and economies of being. Indeed, the best new work in southern literary and critical studies alike attempts, in many ways, to flee its moorings. Leigh Anne Duck's now-famous call for a "Southern studies without 'The South'" has charged a new generation of scholars with the challenge of circumventing "the realm of our most basic assumptions" seated in both geographic and conceptual containers that have exposed their artifice (329). Similarly, Scott Romine and Jennifer Greeson, editors of a recent *Keywords in Southern Studies* volume, claim that conducting southern studies in the twenty-first century requires new and revisionary forms of "thinking geographically, thinking historically, thinking relationally, thinking about power, thinking about justice, thinking back" (4). In areas of local and global intersectionality, one contributor suggests, we may better "glean from the history of colonization and slavery the means by which the colonized and enslaved have improvised alternative visions of freedom and justice" (Thompson 153).

For both Indians and southerners, such "alternative visions" do not emerge easily; in the literature of both groups, some of the most frequently deployed tropes return to the wellsprings of tradition, history, and place, often depicted as paradisiacal conceits undone by invasive, extractive economies and regulations. Such preoccupations tend to reinvigorate a focus on tenancy as a precursor to belonging, and for either regional or tribal integrity. As Pamunkey/Tauxenent artist Rose Powhatan puts it, "I'm living in a country with the curious distinction that your tribe can be changed and you can be erased from the Book of Life when you change your address. Move off the reservation and you cease to be Indian. You're dead. You never existed" (23–24). One must exercise "constant vigilance,"

Powhatan laments, "if you intend to be a survivor" (24–25). In indigenous conversations, survival is consonant with sovereignty; and unfortunately, the will to self-determination generally subsists as intellectual, artistic, and aspirational rather than material. Confronting the ponderous roadblocks of sovereignty has led some scholars of race and settler colonialism to call for a reflexive interrogation of indigenous politics. As Jared Sexton puts it, "The indigenous relation to land precedes and exceeds any regime of property" and "the slave's inhabitation of the earth precedes and exceeds any prior relation to land—landlessness. And selflessness is the correlate." The end point of such logic is, Sexton tells us, a landless and selfless place, one with literally "no ground for identity," and we must change the stakes of our scholarship in order to find space for reclamation: "The flesh of the earth demands it: the landless inhabitation of selfless existence" (593).

But we are, of course, not quite there yet, either in our scholarship or our lived convictions. As an acknowledgment of the anxieties of being in an unsettled space like the South—a land that, in historian James Taylor Carson's phrase, "sits on piles of bones"—the Indian as a structuring device lurks everywhere and nowhere in the southern narrative, a haunting signifier of human fragility and historical trauma that would precipitate such landless, selfless nightmares. Especially for white southerners, indigenous ancestors have served as handy tropes to legitimize settlement claims and suppress regional or material complicity along the way. In a Southern Focus Poll conducted in 1996, Theda Perdue and Michael Green reported that "40 percent of Southerners claimed Native ancestry . . . [, which is] considerably more than the 22 percent who claim descent from a Confederate soldier" (147). Take, for instance, the so-called First Families of Virginia—an elite community that claims direct descent from Pocahontas and John Smith/Rolfe, a mythological lifeline that nourishes the imperative of indigeneity as a "race" that would, paradoxically, substantiate whiteness and white privilege. As Mick and Ben Gidley put it, "As long as they have been in the Americas, white people have been escaping the mapped and policed world of the European empires, 'running to the hills,' 'going Indian'" (171).

Faulkner was in robust company when he manufactured his own fictional Indian archetypes, although his would be distinctly less alluring ancestors. Well into the twentieth century, writers such as Stark Young, Allen Tate, Eudora Welty, Caroline Gordon, and others used indigenous characters and themes to bolster their anti-modern, anti-capitalist agendas.[4] *I'll Take My Stand,* the 1930 collection of essays by Nashville or Vanderbilt Agrarians, frequently depicts an indigenous kinship with a preindustrial world and a noble attachment to the gnawed land; in such dramas, the white southerner frequently plays the role of "native" and the northern carpetbagger the "invader."[5] Perhaps unexpectedly, African Americans in the South have often been drawn to their own archives of indigeneity as well, sometimes through traceable ancestries and other times in spiritual or conceptual chests of lore. When Patrick Minges assembled a trove of WPA interviews with former slaves, he discovered a recurring focus on Native kinship ties, one which often endowed its recipients with seemingly supernatural capacities to withstand the trials of slavery and Jim Crow. Indeed, there exists an identifiable category of the "Black Indian" as a direct product of the plantation complex, where African American slaves mixed commonly with the indigenous peoples who were sometimes their peers and sometimes their masters.[6] African American scholar Willard Johnson observes that "the majority of African American families I know, or that I have come into contact with and have worked with, claim to have an Indian connection. A majority, by far," and he cites a statistic that perhaps three-quarters of black Americans may have some Native ancestry. Yet few of these confront explicitly the chattel slave context for such bequests, preferring instead to romanticize a "fuzzy" history. We know, to be sure, that African American–Indian intimacy in the Old South has given way to rivalry in the New, and what William Loren Katz once deemed a "hidden heritage" has been uncovered and explored in the complex scholarship of both African and indigenous studies (whose key figures include Jack Forbes, Kim Tallbear, Tiya Miles, Christina Snyder, Shona Jackson, Gabrielle Tayac, Keely Byars-Nichols, Sharon Holland, and others). In the end, it's not just that race in the South is complicated; it is, by turns, convoluted, suppressed, competitive, and mystified.

There is no shortage of criticism exploring Faulkner's own racial attitudes and ambivalences, both in his life and in his art. Scholarship on Faulkner's Indians constitutes a more slender archive, but what exists tends to collapse the author's indigenous fantasies into these broader rubrics of historical haunting and regional race-making. Yet the Indians in both his fiction and his South demand a different kind of witness. In many ways alert to the tremendous complications of the Indian mytheme, Faulkner's answer to the problem of how to represent them was to eschew "facts" and history altogether. Indeed, he wrote about Indians more extensively than many of his literary peers: altogether he left six stories, written in the 1930s and '40s, which chronicle the clans of Ikkemotubbe (Doom) and the Weddels;[7] a suggestive trinity of mixed- and full-blooded Indians (Sam Fathers, Jobaker, and Boon Hogganbeck) in *Go Down, Moses;* key figures in the Appendix to *The Sound and the Fury;* the doomed Trail walkers in the prologues to *Requiem for a Nun;* and the essay "Mississippi." When asked about the sources for his Indian characters, he famously claimed that he had "made them up" (Dabney 11). While this profession has earned from critics both admonishment and absolution—that is, Faulkner becomes either a reckless appropriator or a typical American seduced by an Indian archetype, depending on whom you ask—the most compelling critiques attempt to appreciate and unravel the sources of his misprision rather than simply castigate his mistakes.

Indeed, it turns out that Faulkner knew more than he let on, even if his knowledge was filtered through the needs of a charged and dissembling racial and economic perplexity. Faulkner once admitted that he had "known some of [the Indians'] descendants. They have mixed with white people or with Negroes—are still in my country. And I don't think that—that people are all that different no matter what color they are. That people are different more because of the pressure of their environment than because of their blood."[8] While many critics have thus chosen to reject Faulkner's Indians as Indians at all, seeing them instead as postcolonial anxieties in redface,[9] others have focused on liberating his Indians from their stereotypical guises. Lewis Dabney's pioneering work, *The Indians of Yoknapatawpha,* meticulously measured Faulkner's errors—both willed and unwitting—against local indigenous histories and cultures. Other critics, including Howard Horsford, Arthur Kinney, Lothar Hönnighausen, and Robert Dale Parker, have followed suit in various ways. Still other critics have attempted to demonstrate just how much Faulkner actually knew and got right: as Don Doyle redirects us, "There is too much correspondence between the dates, events and people of his fictional Yoknapatawpha and the actual Lafayette County to believe that he was not a diligent student of Mississippi history" ("Mississippi" 145–46). Like Doyle, Patricia Galloway uncovers moments when Faulkner reinvents documented individuals and incidents, producing not a faithful record of the region's histories but something more of "an amalgam, in space and time, of features of the Chickasaws, Choctaws, and Natchez of Mississippi" (28). Even the presumption of absence is itself a fiction: Faulkner repeatedly burnished the "vanishing Indian" myth, and even some of his critics have agreed that "there were no Indians in the country during Faulkner's time, nor had been for almost a hundred years" (Howell 386). But, as I have also detailed more extensively elsewhere, Faulkner ran frequently into reminders that Indians were very much present in his South, albeit in diminished numbers and forms.[10] He had other motivations for treating his Indians as caricatures, altering their tribes from one text to another, bungling their genealogies, and rendering them more like the Hollywood, Plains, or southwestern warriors that he encountered in theaters, books, and sometimes real life.[11]

Put simply, Faulkner's Indians were not Indians at all, but white and black recipients of a regional experience: mausoleums, if you will, of an unsettled history and the extraordinary ambivalences and alliances it bequeathed. Despite their more evident association with slavery, as in his relatively complex character of Sam Fathers (not just Indian but also a part-black, emancipated slave), Indians in Faulkner's work most often resemble white southerners affronted by the decadence and degeneracy of Euramerican "civilization," as critics such as Walter Benn Michaels, Jay Winston, Robert Dale Parker, and Annette Trefzer have demonstrated.[12] As Doyle suggests, all of the Indian stories take place during the "twilight of their time in Mississippi. It is a doomed race of Natives who watch in amazement" as white settlers "exploit" and "swindle" them. The Indians submit to the boons of capitalism, most strikingly in their complicity in plantation slavery, as Faulkner depicts somewhat scathingly in his 1930 story "Red Leaves," where white culture's "corruptive influence is everywhere" (Doyle, "Mississippi" 47). While critics like Winston believe that Faulkner's indigenous subjects served as a vehicle to imaginatively "transcend" the burdens of history (129), it seems more clear that his Indians are meant to serve as warnings—literal embodiments of the "doom" of modern history and economic progress. A character like Sam Fathers is troublesome in this regard: he serves as a mentor and spiritual guide for Isaac McCaslin in *Go Down, Moses*, but the tools of transcendence he offers are ultimately useless. In one of the most fascinating readings to date, Michael D'Alessandro suggests that Faulkner was self-aware in his creation of this Plasticine and "performative" Indian, and that he actually "seeks to draw readers' attention to, and not distract notice from" the fact that Sam is finally a "sham": "Faulkner implies that white descendants' overeagerness to believe such a theatrical version of race constitutes perhaps the most dangerous quality of a South rushing toward modernization in the late nineteenth century. Tragically, this false South becomes the inheritance of those who, as represented by Ike and his descendants, remain incapable of reading history and irresponsible in trying to preserve it" (376).

While it is unclear how purposefully Faulkner worked to draw out such a message, it is repeatedly and abundantly obvious that such Indian depictions are mere levers—if loaded and revelatory ones—for the complexities of race born from colonial trauma and nourished by the capitalist energies of the new century. These visions increasingly include Indians as a feature of primal hope and resounding absence, both a haunting and a harbinger. In his 1954 essay "Mississippi," Faulkner attempts to chart the convergences between the "real" and fictional histories in his work. It is clear that Indians as such are utterly "vanished" from his world, leaving behind only traces of weaponry and biology: "Except for looking occasionally out from behind the face of a white man or a Negro, the Chickasaws and Choctaws and Natchez and Yazoos were as gone as the predecessors; and the people the boy crept with were the descendants of the Sartorises and De Spains and Compsons who had commanded the Manassas and Sharpsburg and Shiloh and Chickamauga regiments, and the McCaslins and Ewells and Holstons and Hogganbecks whose fathers and grandfathers had manned them, and now and then a Snopes too because by the beginning of the twentieth century Snopeses were everywhere" (12). Indeed, it is the "Snopeses" and their imbrication in the artless, heartless voids of modernity that overwhelm the world Faulkner knew and created. It seems no mistake, then, when Faulkner chooses to end one of his last novels, *The Town* (the second in the Snopes trilogy), by deporting a tribe of half-breed Snopes Indians. Byron Snopes fathers four "waifs" with a "Jicarilla Apache squaw in Old Mexico" (379), producing abominations that Michael Wainwright deems "*malevolent aliens*" to the "uneasy Yoknapatawphians" (178). Embodiments of both Snopes materialism and enigmatic Indian silence, the children become violent terrors, lashing out at their benefactors (and a rich woman's dog) while devouring Coca-Cola and candy. John T. Matthews calls the little Indians' corruption an example of "Third World consumption with a vengeance," and a signifier of the infectious "global framework of Snopesism" (18). The waifs are loaded onto a train and mailed back to Byron Snopes, while the entire town "watched them mount and vanish one by one" (*The Town* 390).

But like all ghosts, these Indian wraiths do not disappear. I have written elsewhere about Faulkner's "secret" Indians—the characters who are marked only textually, and admittedly subtly (perhaps even unwittingly) as indigenous. They do not self-identify as Natives, and neither their fictional colleagues nor their creator designates or suspects them as such. Instead, textual clues accrete in ways that become difficult to ignore, such as Jewel Bundren's repeated characterization as a "wooden," highblooded, cigar store Indian in *As I Lay Dying*; Thomas Sutpen's affinity for the "wild men" that he imports from Haiti, and perhaps from the woods of Virginia in *Absalom, Absalom!*; or the suggestively named, silent, alluring, and exceedingly American "Red" of *Sanctuary*.[13] Positing these characters as subterranean Indians depends on elaborate close reading, to be sure, but the payoff of such alternative narratives is the production of a complex historiography that both hinges on and repudiates Indigenous precedence. As Aude Lalande has argued, Indians are "almost always at the margin of the narrative, a silent or evanescent presence, but one which occupies a central place symbolically" (1). Such symbology centers on concerns about "origin, roots, and settlement." Although they are "slowly disappearing," she suggests, Indians "offer, from the opposite side . . . a broad anthropological reflection on the idea of foundation and the relationships it imposes in order to be established, perpetuated, and preserved . . . relationships with the land itself, the men that inhabit it, the wilderness, and the elements that make up its vastness" (2). Native peoples are always, stereotypically, yoked to the diminishing "wilderness": "the death pangs of the Indians are the death pangs of nature," Lalande concludes (27). Similarly, Benjamin Wilson argues that "Native American identity in Faulkner is necessarily tied to the land, and vice versa" (180).

Faulkner is certainly aware of this immense graveyard of debt, centered on but by no means limited to the trauma of Indian Removal, which he explored most forthrightly near the end of his career—most elaborately in *Requiem for a Nun*, a hybrid (part-drama, part-prose) narrative set in 1939–40. during the trial of Nancy Mannigoe, a black woman accused of killing the infant daughter of Temple Drake Stevens. Interspersed within the contemporary dramatic scenes are prose sections articulating the genealogies of Jefferson's civic structure—the courthouse, statehouse, and jail, respectively. The modern horrors of the novel's present are thus intricately sited atop the ruins of a civilization always already ruined, as the lawyer Gavin Stevens famously intones: "The past is never dead. It's not even past" (73).[14] We first encounter Jefferson as a rural, Chickasaw trading post and agency store run by Ratcliffe—the apparent progenitor to the sewing machine salesman "V. K. Ratliff" of Faulkner's earlier narratives (where he appears as "Suratt") and most extensively in the Snopes trilogy. Ratcliffe becomes embroiled in a plot by Jefferson's town founders to acquire a lock for the county jail from the mail pouch of a mail-rider named Thomas Jefferson Pettigrew. But the lock goes missing, and Pettigrew and the founders hatch a plot to register its loss on the Chickasaw accounts at the agency store: "You could call that lock 'axle grease' on that Indian account," Pettigrew suggests, "to grease the wagons for Oklahoma" (24). Ratcliffe sanctions the ruse: "Put it on the Book," he says, and the narrator emphasizes: "the Book: not a ledger, but *the* ledger" (17).

Literally locked together and recorded fatally in the Book—the holy ledger of the colonial-plantation complex—are the dialectical tropes of freedom and imprisonment, removal and settlement, which constitute the bedrock of the American narrative and southern world-building. Pettigrew manages to dissuade the founders from going through with their plot, but his ethical grandstanding is ultimately self-serving: the town is named "Jefferson" after him, a silent nod to the real-life Jefferson who underwrote the South's Indian Removal legislation enacted by Andrew Jackson. The man's actual surname, "Pettigrew," is common among the Chickasaw, a likely testament to the confluence of settler and indigenous cultures in the early Southeast; but it was the name of both a school and a creek in Chickasaw County, Mississippi, a reference that suggestively collapses indigeneity, geography, and pedagogy in the instantiation of southern place-making—the former quotients relegated to invisibility beneath the more overt patriotic narrative.

While Pettigrew is thus elevated to Jefferson, or transformed from Indian to American, Ratcliffe and the founders are needled by what might have been: "That lock," Ratcliffe laments. "That Indian axle grease." They "knew, understood.... It was neither the lock nor axle grease; it was the fifteen dollars which could have been charged to the Indian Department on Ratcliffe's books and nobody would ever have found it, noticed it, missed it" (28). The transaction would not have been a function of "greed," the narrator assures us, but a redundancy of settlement's petty thefts: it was, in fact, "the United States itself which had voluntarily offered to show them how to transmute the inevitable lock into proofless and ephemeral axle grease" (28–29). In other words, the United States supplies its citizens with the tools for the nation's own defrauding—a slippery accounting that relies centrally on the transubstantiation of indigenous land and bodies into developed farms, crops, and railroads. Freedom, or the absence of a lock, slides unseen into the mechanisms of Removal. Importantly, it is not the fraudulent plot itself but its abortion that haunts Ratcliffe: he believes the missed opportunity will leave "the whole race of man, as long as it endured, forever and irrevocably fifteen dollars deficit, fifteen dollars *in the red*" (29, emphasis added). An obvious pun on both debt and indigeneity, the fate of being "in the red" suggests that indigenous priority can be neither erased nor absorbed—a terrible "red" vacancy marks the ledger, a flaw in the books that leaves the "whole race of man" in permanent arrears.

Working In and Out of the Red: Digital Yoknapatawpha Logic and Limits

To be sure, Faulkner here and elsewhere wants to make clear that the South is but an episteme for the rapacious mechanisms of progress that are not simply national but global. The trope of debt thus conjures what David Graeber has termed the "secret scandal" of modern capitalism: the troubling fact that it is a system made possible not by free labor or fair exchange but, first and foremost, by aggressive dispossession.[15] As Wendy Warren's recent history *New England Bound* has emphasized, slavery in the United States uncannily predated the country's independence, and that the economy was sited early and deeply in a vast network that vitally included New England. New scholarship on the history of U.S. political economy has turned increasingly to the study of capitalism as "a concept [that] can structure investigations of the history of the United States" and of the concomitant "emergence and fragmentation of identities" dependent on these systems (slavery, Reconstruction, sharecropping, wage labor, to name a few), according to Sven Beckert and Christine Desan. Their project, emerging from a decade-long workshop among top economic scholars at Harvard, has succeeded in drawing new cartographies of influence and demolishing "one of the deepest dividing lines of American historiography, between Southern and Northern history." Most importantly, they turn attention to the central role of "violence and coercion" in the twin development of capitalism and racism (1, 3, 11). Typically, Indians are left out of this conversation almost entirely, perceived to be both predecessors to an alien regime and naturally inimical to the principles of capitalism. Indeed, while "beleaguered Native Americans" are included briefly in Beckert and Desan's introduction as a potential "point of departure" from the "master narrative," none of the essays they collect chooses to follow this trail to see where it might lead (4).

These are ponderous omissions in our national historiography, but they track closely with national perceptions, processes, and priorities. The brilliance of Faulkner's work, of course, has always been his ability to register the buried complexities of historical and racial consciousness in the white South with uncommon nuance, empathy, concern, and bemusement by turns. But there were obvious limits to both his knowledge and his capacity to transmute what he knew into the language of modern southern witness and race relations. His deterritorialization of southern conceptual space in favor of global histories and marketplaces is not meant finally to honor, recognize, or absolve the Indians sacrificed to make way for it all, but in some ways to indict them as part of a larger human condition that exploded the boundaries of Removal, slavery, and the South itself. In *Requiem,* he presages an American future of homogenous enterprise: "one vast single net of commerce webbed and veined," northern and southern cities made "suburbs one to the other, inextricable in destiny," and men's voices univocally "round with the sound of money; one unanimous golden affirmation[,] . . . that Idea risen now, suspended like a balloon or a portent or a thundercloud above what used to be wilderness" (83). The "wilderness" belongs to the white South and the Indians simultaneously, and the defeat of the latter predicts that of their conquerors *because* neither was innocent or immune from the start. In Faulkner's permutation, Ikkemotubbe "sold" what was not his to sell—the involuntary seizures of land collapsed utterly into "transactions," the tragedies of dispossession displaced by the more compelling and disturbing narratives of Indian slavery and profit that mar the record.

But these are harsh indictments, and unpopular ones. While scholarship on the Native South is increasingly metered about Indians' early implications in chattel slavery, a powerful rhetoric of indigenous exceptionalism continues to offer an ethical reprieve. Before we can rightfully assess DY's responsibility for representing (or, perhaps, rectifying) the indigenous casualties of the South, it is important to agree soberly upon exactly what is both feasible and desirable in the broader conversation about Faulkner's appropriative mythologies. When he chooses to imaginatively settle Choctaw and Chickasaw soil with the residues of a composite colonial history, what is left to rescue? Some indigenous scholars, most notably Patrick Carroll Morgan and Jodi Byrd, believe that any and all traces of indigenous precedence in the dominant record can be grounds for strategic recuperation: "The power, and further, the very materiality, of [Yoknapatawpha] continues to disrupt the structural colonial and racial patterns that seek to first remove and then obscure indigenous presences in the South, no matter how such a region is geographically constituted," Byrd claims (618). In place of colonial cartographies, Kirstin Squint further advocates instead a "furrowed land hermeneutics" driven by indigenous epistemologies. Squint and Byrd are not recommending merely symbolic moves; both believe firmly in the critic's capacity to decolonize and reterritorialize spaces like the South by first disassembling our conceptual frameworks and then engaging in new and attentive kinds of indigenous knowledge-making. From there, Byrd muses, "What if Indians were able to return to these spaces as agentic participants capable of determining their own pasts and futures beyond those of the vested and occupying nation states?" (619).

It is a good question, but perhaps one that exceeds the power of the critic, or the Digital Yoknapatawpha Project. Certainly, the motivations and commitments of our scholarship matter and can have transformative effects. But we must ask—not just of projects like DY, but of the literary critical enterprise more generally—whether our objectives are (and should be) documentary or revisionary. A key feature of many indigenous critical strategies in the field of Native southern historiography involves rebuilding a more "accurate" picture of southeastern Indian history and culture—a rescue operation, of sorts, meant to destabilize the authority of mainstream, "settler" texts. Does Faulkner's cosmos merit the same kind of rehabilitative retooling? When we map the plots, patterns, and characters that populate his world, should we be compelled to represent indigenous actors and territories as they would like to be represented, or how Faulkner actually saw (and did not see) them?

This is, finally, a bit of a trick question that requires us to contend with the optics of race in America, and in the southern context in particular, and to reckon with the fact that Indians simply do not fit into the containers that have been constructed to contain them. It is a tautology, finally: it is clear that Faulkner's Indians are not raced beings unto themselves, but that they have been permanently rendered as such by their detention within the broader race dramas and anxieties of the post-plantation, modernizing South. Consequently, DY's choice to represent these Native figures in starkly color-coded terms—not only in the demographic data, but visually in the small red, black, white, gray, or sometimes striped figures on the maps—turns out to be more apt than we might otherwise admit. These colored figures, even the appropriately striped (that is, mixed) ones, affirm that for Faulkner—indeed, for the majority of Americans even now—race as a rubric is both viable and visible, on the surface of both body and text. Such demands are often resoundingly and violently operative in Faulkner's texts, as in the fatal regard of a populace determined to see, place, and *race* an indeterminate character like Joe Christmas in *Light in August* (whose murky lineage is aptly rendered gray in DY's graphic lexicon). A more explicitly mixed—black, white, and Indian—character like Sam Fathers is represented as a striped figure composed of all three colors. Such depictions do raise the question of whether race is in the eye of the beholder—or in such cases, the reductive gaze of apartheid—or if it is instead a matter of more fluid and unmappable criteria. It is, of course, both simultaneously, according to the divergent rules of race-making and being.

The more imposing question becomes whether DY has either the duty or (more practically) the capability to represent at once a social imperative and a more nuanced truth, especially when the two conflict. In some small way, perhaps, DY leans toward this complexity in its composite vocabularies of space and being. Its land/map and race/demographics are layered painstakingly, capturing the complexities of indigenous history as it appears, and disappears, in Faulkner's South. Repeatedly removed and yet perennially latent, Faulkner's Indians are recursively made present by mechanisms specific to the plantation order and the biracial economy that supplanted them. Perhaps the most compelling way to conceive of Faulkner's Indians, ultimately, is in the form of a meticulously presenced absence—a potent paradox that captures, in all its contortions, the ambivalence, repression, and horror of a region structured on concentric removals and appropriations. The power of DY is its capacity to lay bare these patterns in raw details and reductive tones, striking forms of settler presencing that might offend indigenous sensibilities and inhibit the kinds of dramatic reterritorializations that critics like Byrd would want. But perhaps we simply need to rethink the terms and stakes of what such projects are intended to accomplish—to think beyond the page and screen to new, nuanced permutations of race, place, and belonging. What gets unsettled in the process is not the indigenous, once again and always, but the white southern matrix constructed precariously upon it—the murmuring space that bubbles up in so many of Faulkner's texts, and from the southern landscape itself.

Notes

1. See Don Doyle, who explains that Faulkner seemed "only vaguely aware" of the Chickasaw source words for "Yoknapatawpha" (*Faulkner's County* 387). Doyle provides a full breakdown of the etymology, according to both local lore and Chickasaw dictionaries (*Faulkner's County* 24–25).
2. Momaday first deploys the concept in his award-winning novel *House Made of Dawn* and returns to it in later works, such as "The Man Made of Words."
3. See Allen, *Blood Narrative*.
4. By far the most thorough study of the Native traces in modern southern fiction, Annette Trefzer's *Disturbing Indians* examines how Faulkner, Caroline Gordon, Andrew Lytle, and Eudora Welty responded to indigenous histories in order to better understand their identities as both southerners and Americans.
5. See Twelve Southerners, *I'll Take My Stand:* John Crowe Ransom, "Reconstructed but Unregenerate" 20, 23; John Gould Fletcher, "Education, Past and Present" 99–100; and Herman Clarence Nixon, "Whither Southern Economy?" 183.
6. See, for example, Minges.
7. These stories are "Red Leaves" (1930), "A Justice" (1931), "Lo!" (1934), "Mountain Victory" (1932), "A Bear Hunt" (1934), and "A Courtship" (1948).
8. Faulkner, "Frederick Gwynn's Undergraduate Class," 2 May 1958.
9. See, for instance, the special issue of the *Faulkner Journal* (vol. 18, nos. 1/2, 2002/2003) devoted to "Faulkner's Indians," edited by Gene Moore; these essays seek to reevaluate the function of Faulkner's Native American

themes through the lens of postcolonial theory, particularly Homi Bhabha's notion of the "third space," as a useful corrective to the persistent biracial codes of southern culture and criticism. Annette Trefzer's *Disturbing Indians* was the first scholarly work to examine the broader use of Indian tropes in a specifically southern, modern, literary context.
10. See Taylor, *Indian* 59–61.
11. According to Faulkner's younger brother Murry, the Falkner boys would spend countless childhood hours watching silent films, and especially westerns (particularly those of Broncho Billy Anderson): "The opening scene in the westerns never varied. There would be, in the distance, an enormous cloud of dust. The dimensions of the cloud may have changed from picture to picture, but the background—never. . . . The dust cloud held to its size and volume and soon we could make out the first of the fleeing Indians, lying flat on the backs of their ponies, whose flying hoofs were keeping perfect time with the piano player, or perhaps the other way around. My brothers and I used to wonder what would have happened to us and the rest of the enchanted audience if the movie folks had gotten mixed up one time and let the cowboys blast out of the dust cloud first with the Indians chasing them. Probably we would have run out of the Opera House" (50). We know also that Faulkner read about Indians in anthropological works like James Frazer's *Golden Bough*. And in life, he reportedly once witnessed a group of forlorn Indians with pity during a car ride with Ben Wasson from California back to Mississippi. Somewhere in the Arizona desert, according to Wasson, they passed a group of "blank-faced Indians sitting by the highway"; Faulkner, affected by the "monotony and heat" of their trip and the "persistent sorrow" of his time spent in Hollywood, "mused on their griefs. 'This was theirs,' he said to Ben, 'all of it. This whole country. We took it from them and shoved them off onto reservations. I reckon it's bad enough the way we treat the black folks. But they're like children and need looking after, expect to be looked after. Oh, hell, I don't know any answers for other people. I can't take care of my own problems'" (Blotner 383).
12. These pieces, along with more recent investigations by Trefzer and a handful of others, have broken fertile ground in their nuanced treatments of Faulkner's "postcolonial" depictions, figuring the Indian as a disruptive kind of "third space," after Bhabha, to complicate in useful ways the biracial narrative that has long dominated southern culture and criticism.
13. See Taylor, *Indian* 56–111.
14. Critics such as John T. Matthews and Spencer Morrison have argued that Faulkner's late novels register distinct Cold War anxieties about the

influence of a U.S. military-industrial complex yoked dangerously to unfettered market capitalism. See Matthews, "Many Mansions"; Matthews, *Seeing*; and Morrison. With *Requiem* in particular, Matthews sees Faulkner "diagnosing . . . the unhealed trauma of the plantation South's violent origins in New World colonialism" as a direct response to the mid-century emergence of "imperial democracy—a paradoxical creature, for sure" (*Seeing* 226).

15. See also Huato.

Works Cited

Allen, Chadwick. "Blood (and) Memory." *American Literature*, vol. 71, no. 1, 1999, pp. 93–116.

———. *Blood Narrative: Indigenous Identity in American Indian and Maori Literary and Activist Texts*. Duke UP, 2002.

Beckert, Sven, and Christine Desan, editors. *American Capitalism: New Histories*. Columbia UP, 2018.

Blotner, Joseph L. *Faulkner: A Biography*. UP of Mississippi, 2005.

Byrd, Jodi A. "A Return to the South." *American Quarterly*, vol. 66, no. 3, 2014, pp. 609–20.

Chomsky, Aviva. "Strangers in Their Own Land," *Nation*, 29 Nov. 2018, https://www.thenation.com/article/dna-tests-elizabeth-warren-native-american-race-science.

Dabney, Lewis M. *The Indians of Yoknapatawpha: A Study in Literature and History*. Louisiana State UP, 1974.

D'Alessandro, Michael. "Childless 'Fathers,' Native Sons: Mississippi Tribal Histories and Performing the Indian in Faulkner's *Go Down, Moses*." *Mississippi Quarterly*, vol. 67, no. 3, July 2014, pp. 375–401.

Doyle, Don H. *Faulkner's County: The Historical Roots of Yoknapatawpha*. U of North Carolina P, 2001.

———. "The Mississippi Frontier in Faulkner's Fiction and in Fact," *Southern Quarterly*, vol. 29, no. 4, 1991, pp. 145–46.

Duck, Leigh Anne. "Southern Nonidentity." *Safundi*, vol. 9, no. 3, 2008, pp. 319–30.

Falkner, Murry C. *The Falkners of Mississippi: A Memoir*. Louisiana State UP, 1967.

Faulkner, William. "Frederick Gwynn's Undergraduate Class, May 2, 1958." Faulkner at Virginia, https://faulkner.lib.virginia.edu/display/wfaudio26_2.html#wfaudio26_2.11.

———. "Mississippi." *Essays, Speeches and Public Letters*, edited by James B. Meriwether. New York: Modern Library, 2004, pp. 11–43.

———. *Requiem for a Nun.* 1951. Vintage International, 2012.

———. *The Town.* 1957. Vintage International, 2011.

Fletcher, John Gould. "Education, Past and Present." *I'll Take My Stand: The South and the Agrarian Tradition,* edited by Louis D. Rubin Jr., Louisiana State UP, 1978, pp. 92–121.

Frank, Andrew K., and Kristofer Ray. "Guest Editors' Introduction: Indians as Southerners; Southerners as Indians: Rethinking the History of a Region." *Native South,* vol. 10, 2017, pp. vii–xiv.

Galloway, Patricia. "The Construction of Faulkner's Indians." *Faulkner Journal,* vol. 18, no. 1–2, 2002–3, pp. 9–31.

Gidley, Mick, and Ben Gidley. "The Native-American South." *A Companion to the Literature and Culture of the American South,* edited by Richard Gray and Owen Robinson, Blackwell, 2004, pp. 166–84.

Howell, Elmo. "William Faulkner and the Mississippi Indians." *Georgia Review,* vol. 21, no. 3, 1967, pp. 386–96.

Huato, Julio. "Graeber's *Debt:* When a Wealth of Facts Confronts a Poverty of Theory." *Science and Society,* vol. 79, no. 2, 2015, pp. 318–25.

Kasee, Cynthia. "Homecoming." *The People Who Stayed: Southeastern Indian Writing after Removal,* edited by Geary Hobson et al., U of Oklahoma P, 2010, pp. 180–82.

Katz, William Loren. *Black Indians: A Hidden Heritage.* Atheneum, 2012.

Lalande, Aude. "The Impossibility of Foundation: The Indians of William Faulkner," *L'Homme,* vol. 166, no. 2, 2003, pp. 31–58.

Matthews, John T. "Many Mansions: Faulkner's Cold War Conflicts." *Global Faulkner: Faulkner and Yoknapatawpha, 2006,* edited by Annette Trefzer and Ann J. Abadie, UP of Mississippi, 2009, pp. 3–23.

———. *William Faulkner: Seeing through the South.* Wiley-Blackwell, 2009.

McAdams, Janet. "From *Betty Creek.*" *The People Who Stayed: Southeastern Indian Writing after Removal,* edited by Geary Hobson et al., U of Oklahoma P, 2010, pp. 251–55.

Minges, Patrick, ed. *Black Indian Slave Narratives.* John F. Blair, 2004.

Momaday, N. Scott. *House Made of Dawn.* 1968. Perennial Classics, 1999.

———. "The Man Made of Words." *Indian Voices: The First Convocation of American Indian Scholars.* Indian Historian Press, 1970, pp. 49–84.

Moore, Gene, ed. *Faulkner's Indians.* Special issue of *Faulkner Journal,* vol.18, nos. 1–2, Fall 2002–Spring 2003.

Moore, MariJo. "In these Mountains." *The People Who Stayed: Southeastern Indian Writing after Removal,* edited by Geary Hobson et al., U of Oklahoma P, 2010, p. 177.

Morrison, Spencer. "*Requiem*'s Ruins: Unmaking and Making in Cold War Faulkner." *American Literature,* vol. 85, no. 2, June 2013, pp. 303–31.

Nixon, Herman Clarence. "Whither Southern Economy?" *I'll Take My Stand: The South and the Agrarian Tradition*, edited by Louis D. Rubin Jr., Louisiana State UP, 1978, pp. 176–200.

Painter, Nell Irvin. *The History of White People*. W. W. Norton, 2010.

Perdue, Theda, and Michael D. Green. *The Columbia Guide to American Indians of the Southeast*. Columbia UP, 2001.

Powhatan, Rose. "Surviving Document Genocide." *The People Who Stayed: Southeastern Indian Writing after Removal*, edited by Geary Hobson et al., U of Oklahoma P, 2010, pp. 23–28.

Ransom, John Crowe. "Reconstructed but Unregenerate." *I'll Take My Stand: The South and the Agrarian Tradition*, edited by Louis D. Rubin Jr., Louisiana State UP, 1978, pp. 1–27.

Romine, Scott, and Jennifer Rae Greeson, editors. *Keywords for Southern Studies*. U of Georgia P, 2016.

Sexton, Jared. "The Vel of Slavery: Tracking the Figure of the Unsovereign." *Critical Sociology*, vol. 42, nos. 4–5, July 2016, pp. 583–97.

Squint, Kirstin L. *LeAnne Howe at the Intersection of Southern and Native American Literature*. Louisiana State UP, 2018.

Taylor, Melanie Benson. *The Indian in American Southern Literature*. Cambridge UP, 2020.

Thompson, Shirley Elizabeth. "Creole/Creolization." *Keywords for Southern Studies*, edited by Scott Romine and Jennifer Rae Greeson, U of Georgia P, 2016, pp. 141–54.

Trefzer, Annette. *Disturbing Indians*. U of Alabama P, 2009.

Wainwright, Michael. *Darwin and Faulkner's Novels: Evolution and Southern Fiction*. Palgrave Macmillan, 2008.

Warren, Wendy. *New England Bound: Slavery and Colonization in Early America*. Liveright, 2016.

Wilson, Benjamin J. "Approaching the Other through Aesthetics: Faulkner, Warren, Native Americans, and Modernism." *Faulkner and Warren*, edited by Christopher Rieger and Robert W. Hamblin, Southeast Missouri State UP, 2015, pp. 178–93.

Winston, Jay S. "Going Native in Yoknapatawpha: Faulkner's Fragmented America and 'the Indian.'" *Faulkner Journal*, vol. 18, nos. 1–2, Fall 2002–Spring 2003, pp. 129–42.

Digital Yoknapatawpha
PEDAGOGICAL PRACTICES AND THE POLITICS OF
DIGITAL HUMANITIES IN THE TWENTY-FIRST-CENTURY
CLASSROOM

Ren Denton

Pedagogy is political. Whether one subscribes to critical, culturally responsive, social, or Socratic pedagogy, the style one chooses to engage students with information is an act that proposes a political vision, according to Roger Simon (371). How teaching practices and curriculum content are integrated and how classroom strategies and evaluation methods are used reflect what the teacher values as having the most worth to the students and their social and political environments (Simon 371). In other words, one's pedagogy is formed in the intersection between one's beliefs about learning techniques and one's social ideology. Thus, any critical discussions about pedagogy, as Henry Giroux claims, raise "questions not simply about how students learn but also about how educators (in the broad sense of the term) construct the ideological and political positions from which they speak" (45). To strengthen the connection between the politics of pedagogy and research, Brett Hirsch has issued a call for digital humanities, as a field, "to start thinking critically not only about what we teach under the banner of 'digital humanities' and how we teach it, but also to consider the broader institutional implications and political consequences of doing so" (13). In the interest of critically thinking about Digital Yoknapatawpha (DY) as a digital humanities project, this essay examines DY's functioning within institutions where there is increasing public pressure to shift from foundational knowledge pedagogies to pedagogies that induce activity-centered learning. However, I do not position digital humanities at odds with foundational learning; I argue that DY's resources offer pedogeological versatility that blends both foundational knowledge learning and activity-centered learning that can be primed to meet the criteria for critical, culturally responsive, social, or Socratic pedagogy.

Arguably, English courses have come under greater institutional scrutiny than most college courses because of their unique role as "gatekeeper courses" and their ongoing challenge to increase literacy and communication skills—skills that are declining on a national level. Consequently, national and state teaching and learning initiatives have prompted institutions to reevaluate the function of English professors and call upon these professors to expand their role from transmitter of knowledge to facilitator of learning so that students become active participants, co-inquirers and co-learners. Hirsch argues that "digital humanities is in a better position to undertake this transition" because the field encourages students to build their knowledge structures through making or doing (15). Olin Bjork discusses the shift to digital sources in English composition courses, pointing to the fact that as composition studies maintain focus on rhetorical strategies found in both print and electronic sources, they build essential college-level skills in understanding all communication modes. However, the shift to digital humanities presents a challenge in that English composition instructors now have the task of teaching multi-literacies, Bjork asserts. In meeting this challenge, we may align our approach to digital humanities with the rhetorical studies already used in the English classroom, and, in so doing, we may teach students to be "engaged producers and not merely informed consumers of digital culture" (100).

Before we bring our students to the resources of DY, we need to understand that the goal of digital humanists is not unlike that of traditional humanists. Just as those who study Faulkner expose the underpinnings of power dynamics, digital humanists use their technical expertise to show how digital systems sustain inequalities (Gold and Klein). For example, Safiya Noble "reveals the racist assumptions planted in the algorithms that power Google searches" (Gold and Klein xi). Thus, just as literary scholars show how literature perpetuates or confronts cultural biases, digital humanists expose how those "social and cultural biases pervade our technologies, infrastructures, platforms, and devices" (Gold and Klein xi). We will be more effective and purposeful in our pedagogy if we recognize a crucial fact: as we bring our students to a space that is dedicated to expanding Faulkner studies that engage the social and political, we also bring them into a space that is social and political, so we should interrogate the project as much as we interrogate Faulkner's texts.

Digital humanities, Noble argues, comes out of neoliberal and neocolonial investments in knowledge infrastructures that mirror our colonial past and present. She claims that digital humanities "exacerbates existing patterns of exploitation and at times even creates new ones" (27). As digital projects archive black cultural productions, they neutralize the critiques found in those productions, allowing digital humanities to "digitize Black culture, but not to use it in the service of dismantling racist systems that contain and constrain freedom for Black bodies" (29). She calls for digital humanities to "turn toward deeper engagements with social transformation" because we are "living in a moment where Black people's lives can be documented and digitalized, but cannot be empowered or respected in society" (30). Thus, my interrogation of DY as a teaching tool also looks for moments where the site could be used to produce transformations within individual students, even as they examine how the DY editors and collaborators chose to represent race and class and compare those representations to how Faulkner presents them on the printed page.

For example, students have an opportunity to interrogate DY as a space that speaks to the #MeToo movement. "That Evening Sun" opens with a description of laundrywomen gathering laundry from the white families they service. The story narrows its focus to Nancy, a laundrywoman who sometimes helps the Compson family with the children. She is described as "tall, with a high, sad face sunken a little where her teeth were missing" (353). Nancy's teeth were kicked out when she confronted a white man for not paying her for the sex he solicited. The man, Mr. Stovall, is a deacon in the Baptist church and a banker. Nancy's public confrontation embarrasses him so much that he knocks her to the ground and kicks her in the mouth (354). There is no reason to believe that Nancy is lying about the money she is owed, primarily since Mr. Compson blames her marital troubles on her involvement with white men (295), and she is pregnant with what might be a white man's baby—perhaps even Mr. Stovall's. A rhetorical interrogation of the scene in the text opens a rich vein flowing with questions about the intersection of race and gender. DY describes the confrontation as Nancy "accusing" Mr. Stovall (Mr. Stovall's Biography, DY), since there is no stated proof in the story that Mr. Stovall had sex with Nancy under the pretense that he would pay for it. This legally objective description gives students a rhetorical window to discuss what is implied with "accusing" versus "confronting" or "exposing." Such implications speak to a long history of white rape of black women and women not being believed when they report sexual abuse. Thus, as students examine the way DY represents a profound scene that speaks to sexual exploitation and violence, they might claim the neutralization is the kind of silencing technique Noble discusses (27–35), which, in turn, may force some critical recognition of how much of society neutralizes black protest against state-induced violence to the black body. In this example, critical pedagogy emerges to foster critical awareness, as the interrogation of language draws parallels between Nancy's situation and the students' political and social environments, illustrating language's role in shaping the social realities of race and gender. Teaching students to connect literature to their social and political lives transforms a literature course from forms and genres into a course that produces critically thinking citizens ready for the social challenges of the twenty-first century.

James Bellanca and Ron Brandt argue that if we are going to be successful in cultivating wise citizens, we must look at our desired outcomes before we build the learning models that we need. In other words, before we transform our learning models to produce critically thinking citizens, we must ask ourselves what we want our students to know or do five years after taking our courses. I want students to have strong close-reading skills that allow them to recognize often-unstated messages in a text (printed, digital, social, or environmental) so that as they interpret and analyze information, they can apply that information to problem-solving.

My most difficult challenge in facilitating my students' development of close reading skills is overcoming their apathy toward reading. I have even resorted to having students read aloud in class, revealing that students are reading, but they are not paying attention to the words. Many students confess that they are reading word-for-word, but, at the end of the text, they cannot tell me what they have read. As a result, I now search for ways to make reading interactive. DY transforms Faulkner's texts (texts that are known for provoking critical examinations of oppression) into an interactive experience that helps students visualize the spaces they are interrogating. For example, when I teach "That Evening Sun," some students miss the question on the reading quiz that asks what location separates the Compsons' house from Nancy's house. However, when we look at DY's location map for the story, we see the two houses directly opposite each other with a ditch between them. The rhetorical visual argues that Nancy and the Compsons are equal on an existential level but opposite on a social scale. The text's location description emphasizes the equality when Quentin, down in the ditch, "couldn't see where the moonlight and the shadows tangled" (309). In other words, the light and dark being indistinguishable represents how white and black humanity are indistinguishable, but both are tangled in the superficial racial division that governs the Compsons' world as well as our own. Once students see the ditch as the marker that separates the Compsons from Nancy, DY's location description draws attention to the fear of violence in "Negro Hollow," as Quentin explains how they were usually not allowed to cross the ditch because Nancy's husband, Jesus, was violent. Thus, the visualization opens up discussions about cultural assumptions and representations about black men and communities and how residential segregation, redlining, ghettoization, and suburbanization perpetuate these assumptions. In this vein, DY's interactive quality opens up to critical pedagogy, as students can see and challenge the legal segregation practices that dominate Quentin's society.

Interrogating racial assumptions about people and spaces, whether they are in Faulkner's texts or DY, cultivates an inclusive classroom and is a good practice for culturally responsive teaching. Students recognizing or identifying with Quentin's fear must turn toward their own ideas about racism and bias, even as they listen to their classmates' experiences that align more closely to Nancy's than Quentin's. Not only are such interrogations appropriate for college classrooms, but they also have practical value. As institutions expand with a multicultural student body, many of them have made diversity and inclusivity part of their mission statements. Thus, allowing for course materials and conversations that critically examine fields of oppression effectively promotes diversity awareness and offers departments the assessment data they need to track the institution's fulfillment of their diversity goals.

DY fosters inclusivity more effectively when instructors use the site as a collaborative learning experience. Barbara Gross Davis states, "Group work can reduce prejudice and bias by giving students opportunities to interact with others from different backgrounds" (63). The small group activity draws from social pedagogy in that activities can be designed to include everyone, as each individual is a resource for learning. As small groups work together interpreting the texts and the site's representations of those interpretations, the various perspectives and experiences a diverse group collectively brings to the task lead to lines of inquiry that may have been overlooked by those working singly. For example, breaking students into groups for deeper exploration of "That Evening Sun" allows opportunities for them to be exposed to perhaps-unfamiliar cultural phenomena, such as the blues. When students click on "Manuscripts," they can read about the story's history of rejection and revision. Upon reading the history, students can make the connection between the story's title and W. C. Handy's "St. Louis Blues," which contains the line "I hate to see that evening sun go down." Identifying this fact helps students connect Nancy's "not singing but not unsinging" to the sounds of the blues—and all of the cultural implications associated with the blues. Furthermore, students then see how Faulkner was forced to change Jesus's name if he wanted the story to be printed in H. L. Mencken's *American Mercury*. Because not everyone might be familiar with Christian symbolism or biblical references, a larger group of students can work to identify the religious undertones in a story with a black man named "Jesus" and consider how changing his name changes something in the text. Thus, in this group exercise, students have the opportunity to learn about and consider religious and cultural perspectives that they might not share.

Of course, instructors may also choose to have students privately experience DY for individual projects that may or may not be presented to the class. Such activities invoke a synthesis of one's own reflections and the texts, as students may examine their own assumptions about a character's social status and race, for example, even as they explore the site's representation of those characters. Whether students work in groups or individually, instructors will find that DY augments the inquiry process with new reading strategies and critical discussions that improve critical thinking skills.

Furthermore, the activity-centered learning DY affords adapts well to national or state initiatives that target first-generation college students and marginalized populations. Many universities nationwide currently promote state initiatives focused on encouraging a shift from the traditional lecture to activities that promote problem-solving and practical application. Teachers are encouraged to think about blending their lectures with active learning trends that can sustain long-term learning.

DY is an active-learning tool that makes lectures interactive or functions well in interdisciplinary student learning communities and other student-centered learning methods. Returning to our example of "That Evening Sun," if we go to the character-character visualization graphing tool, we get an image that allows a Socratic approach to transform lectures into active investigations into the periphery of power dynamics. In the graph, we see a visual marker of "Unnamed Bad Man." The man in question is referenced in the story Nancy tells the children about a queen who has to cross the ditch where the bad man is before she can get home. DY speculates that the Bad Man is Jesus, since the story parallels Nancy's life. If the bad man is Jesus, then what does it mean that Jesus is outside of society? How does this serve discussions about economies of sacrifice? How does it illustrate the invisibility of black men that have also been marked as "bad" as a justification for pushing them to the periphery of society? These questions adapt well to large class, small group, or individual investigations. More importantly, questions about how to apply the knowledge they acquire to solve societal problems lead to a plethora of possibilities for essays or thesis projects that produce new knowledge.

Digital humanities' goal is to help students produce new knowledge instead of passively consuming digital or media representation. To do that, students need to learn to be critical of what they are consuming. Corey Seemiller and Meghan Grace discuss how Generation Z is digitally connected to copious amounts of information at all times—more information "than the instructor could ever know and teach in class" (26). For this reason, students need to learn the difference between academically sound or credible sites and sites that feed misinformation to the public, because for Generation Z, research is "less about the process of knowledge acquisition and more about quickly finding answers needed for an assignment" (174). It can therefore be difficult to encourage Generation Z to produce new knowledge, as they have become accustomed to finding answers and solutions online. Thus, to further demonstrate DY's usefulness in such a learning culture, I examine my DY-centered activities to determine if they meet common learning outcomes for the standard college English or literature course. In other words, I will contextualize DY within a course that emphasizes interpretation, analysis, and evaluation while incorporating advanced research methods. L. Dee Fink asks, "What kinds of learning can be said to constitute significant learning?" After reviewing descriptions of quality teaching and learning, she has created a taxonomy that changes the learner: Foundational Knowledge, Application, Integration, Human Dimension, Caring, and Learning How to Learn (35). As I contextualize DY within a course that develops critical thinking skills, I use Fink's taxonomy to illustrate DY as a worthy component of a literature or humanities course.

Foundational knowledge is the base that supports the students' ability to understand how facts fit together or how abstract concepts work. Yet, as James Lang points out, "some instructors believe that the learning of facts or concepts, or helping students remember facts and concepts—or even procedures or basic skills—falls beneath them" because we "are interested only in higher-order activities like critical thinking or making judgments or creating new knowledge" (13–14). DY can both fact-build and promote critical thinking, even as it helps students harvest the representations of the human experience in Faulkner's works. For example, Faulkner's novel *As I Lay Dying* is perhaps a quintessential representation of the human experience, as we watch Addie Bundren die while her family builds the coffin that will hold her body on the way to the burial place in Jefferson. However, the novel disorients readers because it is told from fifteen points of view. Students can use DY to understand the characters and orient themselves in time and space. For example, DY's biographies of Addie's children name the birth order and legitimacy while quoting the text's description of the characters in an arranged order that gives students a stronger sense of character so that they can discern what motivates specific characters. These details are often lost in Faulkner's prose, which unwinds a little information at a time as the storyline moves between past and present. Hence, DY provides students equitable access to the basics of the novel so that they may clarify plot, events, and points of view. With that understanding of life for the underclass in Mississippi, they may well examine the Bundrens' trip as a metaphor for the human experience.

Fink claims that once students have basic knowledge, they are ready for "some kind of action, which may be intellectual, physical, or social" (34). For Fink, that action is application learning or developing new learning skills. It is in the application stage that students can be made to think critically or creatively (34–35). As students learn about the text as a representation of the human experience, they are also learning in the field of "human dimension," which Fink defines as students learning "something about themselves or others," enabling them to "function and interact more effectively" (36). In this regard, DY meets the students on their level, even as it promotes integration of knowledge. Fink asserts that integration occurs when students can "see and understand the connections between different things" (36). Advanced students encountering *As I Lay Dying* for the first time can more easily connect their new understanding of the novel's events and characters to social theories, once they have an accessible source that clarifies the text's disorienting reading experience. The application of their foundational knowledge leads to a discussion of the themes extending beyond this one text. For instance, students may notice Faulkner's repeated interest in family dynamics at the time of death or destruction if they center their exploration of DY on "A Rose for Emily," "Barn Burning," and *As I Lay Dying*. The timeline and movement of events on the maps may prompt students to ask what Faulkner is saying about the inability to escape the past and death or destruction moving from South to North. Such inquiries enable students and scholars to interact with abstract ideas as well as physical spaces. When one juxtaposes the visuals for the three texts, one may ask specific research questions: What does it mean for the death of an upper-class relic (Miss Emily) to be contained to the center of town while the death of a lower-class member (Addie Bundren) is paraded through the countryside and into town? What are the similarities between the movement of the Snopeses and Bundrens where one marches through burning emblems of plantation power while the other escorts death and rot to town? How does Emily's motive for killing Homer contrast with Snopes's motive for burning barns? These questions can be discussed in class or become individual projects that help readers connect larger sociological issues to Faulkner's works while gaining an appreciation for the text as an expression of possibilities.

Students also have opportunities to compare manuscripts of the same story, leading to larger thematic research projects. For example, a student might compare the three manuscripts of Faulkner's short story "Wash" as an investigation of socioeconomic representations and poverty's complexities. DY gives access to Southeast Missouri State University's Center for Faulkner Studies' Brodsky Collection, which includes two manuscripts and a typescript of "Wash." Students can trace the changes in how Wash's life was first conceived before Faulkner wove the threads of a tapestry of destitution and desperation, revealing an ugly truth about the particular vulnerability of girls coming of age within a family suffering the dehumanization of chronic poverty.

As students seek to find answers to their research questions, they must look through the contextual clues left in the fictions, and DY can assist them with that search. Wash, for example, is from the underclass who later serves as a foil to Sutpen in Faulkner's novel *Absalom, Absalom!* Wash is described in DY's character description as a degraded individual driven to commit murder:

> Gaunt and malaria-ridden, Wash Jones emerges as a furious underdog figure. A poor and jobless squatter, he lives with his granddaughter Milly in Thomas Sutpen's "crazy shack" on a slough in the river bottom of Sutpen's land. During the Civil War, he was one of the few remaining white men in Yoknapatawpha between 18–50 who did not enlist in the war, and he was often teased because of it. When Sutpen returned from the war, Wash helped him manage a country store, which also meant Wash had to care for Sutpen when he was drunk. Wash's downtrodden condition factors into the emotion that causes him to commit multiple counts of homicide as a way to even the score.

The description focuses the students' attention on Wash's condition rather than on Wash's personality. By concentrating on that, we open a line of inquiry into the nature of poverty and its psychological effects on chronic sufferers.

Once students understand how chronic poverty may produce acute and chronic stress as well as cognitive lags, students can expand their research through DY's graphing tool that gives students a visualization to provoke epiphanies about sociological dynamics within the story. The location character graph gives the best context clues for the line of inquiry that we are following in this example. The locations appear in green while characters are represented in blue. We see three locations: Sutpen's plantation, Sutpen's store, and the fishing camp that Wash occupies. The characters are clustered around the sites where they appear most often. Thus, we may notice that Sutpen's plantation is isolated to a few slaves and Mrs. Sutpen, with General Sherman's appearance signifying the South's defeat, while Wash's quarters are subject to random trespassers. One implication of this is that those in poverty often are subject to surveillance. Moreover, we see the store as a private space in between the isolated plantation and Wash's place of residence. The store represents a shared space between the wealthy and the impoverished classes. When students visually see the store as a shared space, the activities that take place in that shared space take on numerous metaphors ready for exploration and interpretation. Through careful analysis of the text and DY's visual cues, students are guided into a research area that builds a solid foundation on which to build an interdisciplinary knowledge of sociology, psychology, and Faulkner's literary representations of America's darker secrets associated with the plantation's model of economics that continues to govern our brand of capitalism.

While there are many ways to help students build their knowledge base, my students, who are mostly first-generation college students from rural backgrounds, have informed me that they prefer directive modes of teaching such as guided worksheets or bulleted tasks that can be completed as a group or individually. The amount of information overwhelmed those who were lost in the free form of that learning style because they were used to having structure to their assignments. They have said they prefer the worksheets to an in-class experience because they can take their time, work at their own pace, and process the information that the activity seeks to impart.

However, before I created worksheets, I evaluated my previous experiences with students interacting with DY in the classroom. I originally introduced DY as an unstructured class activity. Students were overwhelmed by the breadth of the site and unsure what they were to learn from it. During my second attempt at teaching with DY, I assisted with the search of characters, locations, and events. The graphs were especially helpful for "A Rose for Emily." The location-character graph, which plots locations of characters' relation to each other, positions the Grierson House as the center of events in the story, so students saw how just how central Miss Emily was to the town. The observation led to a discussion about small-town gossip, illustrating how the town's constant discussion of Miss Emily could represent the South's obsession with southern aristocracy. Through discussing this representation, we saw how traditions, local economics, and social life revolve around "old money," serving as an obstacle to progression. As we questioned how a single narrator would know about the events told in the story, they realized that they had initially ignored the black servant Tobe's presence, opening a discussion about how race and socioeconomic class often renders one invisible (Denton).

In examining my students' initial responses, I realized that one value of the site was found in its ability to enhance close reading skills. One student said she did not realize that Miss Emily killed Homer Barron even after she read "A Rose for Emily" twice. She thought Homer died of natural causes and Emily kept the body, but when she read the description of the drugstore, she realized that a mystery surrounds Miss Emily's purchase of arsenic and the last time the townspeople saw Homer Barron. She represents how I imagined all my students reacting to DY. When I considered what I wanted my students to gain from the experience of using DY as a supplement to Faulkner's texts, which are a rich source of artistic representations of history and culture, I looked for an interactive workshop experience that could be used in small groups in person or by individual students in my online courses. I wanted students to make significant strides in close reading, critical thinking, analysis, interpretation, and evaluation while also learning about Faulkner's common themes. I also wanted to engage students with history as an interpretive lens that illuminates our current sociological conditions. James Berlin discusses the importance of English courses teaching students how to apply historical interpretations that go beyond our own cultural and political influences so that we can understand the different (and changing) assumptions "about the relative distribution of wealth and power within a society" (105). DY facilitates historical and cultural interpretations that contribute to foundational knowledge of Faulkner's era, especially if students have a structured activity to help them make connections.

Victoria Bryan, a DY teaching collaborator, designed the worksheet model that I used to teach students how to navigate the site and how to use the internet to build their knowledge. This model gives students specific tasks to help them navigate DY's website as well as exercises that blend information-gathering questions with critical-thinking questions. Worksheets can be created to address themes, history, and cultural context. For example, teachers can easily illustrate Faulkner's "the past is never dead" common theme by having students focus on the movement of the timeline—how it jumps back and forth between past and present in Faulkner's stories. Students can see the various forms of narrative movement, and when they realize that Faulkner links the past events to present events, they understand how time and action seem to merge in his narratives.

The worksheet I designed for "Barn Burning" asks specific questions that lead students to the movement of events and a consideration of the significance of those movements (see appendix). The worksheet focuses the student's attention on the collaborators' interpretation of Snopes's migration from south to north, so students use the map in DY as they consider how such a movement (a reversal of Sherman's fiery march) could be a critique of the New South's relationship to the North. To encourage a deeper probe of "Barning Burning," the worksheet prompts students to Google "hegemony" and "hierarchy," so that they can understand the structure of a traditional southern society and recognize the New South perpetuating that structure. As students read character biographies, they move through questions that yield critical thinking. For example, after reading the "Colonel John Sartoris" and "Sarty Snopes" biographies, students are asked to think through the southern inspirations and myths that are embodied in the figure of Colonel John Sartoris as well as any possible motivation or hopes Ab may have had for his son when he named his son after Colonel Sartoris (Denton). After students completed their worksheets, we held class discussions that demonstrated how DY's visualization of events and movements promotes analytical thinking that seeks to explain the many possible critiques about the meaning of Snopes's movement from North to South. Such inquiries enable students and scholars to examine abstract ideas as well as physical spaces in the narrative.

Student responses to the worksheet have revealed the effectiveness of DY's ability to build cultural knowledge. One student said that until he explored DY he didn't realize that Ab Snopes was a horse thief before he was a sharecropper; he lacked the cultural and historical knowledge that would allow him to remember and fully appreciate Snopes's shift from horse thief to sharecropper. He said DY gave him insight into the story's themes because he saw how the motivation for the barn burning was not completely different from the motivation to steal horses. To push his thinking, I asked how that information and comparison could be used to determine if Snopes's actions made a statement about what kind of south the "New South" should be if the south was going to reinvent itself. His statement has since led me to ask if we can view Ab as a type of tragic hero fighting for the underclass. Thus, in turn, his statement on "white sweat" pushes students back into Faulkner's texts to explore possible tragic hero figures for the underclass.

The "Barn Burning" exercise also goes beyond the socioeconomic class division to help students understand the racial implications that are latent in the text, even as the exercise introduces cultural theories to help students interpret the site. Students encounter important contextualized questions that stress racial themes in short stories like "Barn Burning" and "That Evening Sun." The worksheet introduces quotes from the works of literary theorists such as Thadious Davis and historians such as James Cobb. Students are asked to engage with this work, examine the information DY presents, and return to the text to speculate on the value of seeing the number of "unnamed Negroes" in Faulkner's texts, even as they consider Davis's claim about Faulkner using black characters to formulate an aesthetic sense. Students are asked to identify how unnamed black characters drive the plot, the recognition of which enriches the students' understanding of Snopes' motive for burning barns. One student said that after she read "Barn Burning," she was confused until she read the biographies. She stated in the discussion board, "Everything cleared up about the story. I didn't know what was going on besides a crazy man running around and burning barns down." Another student claimed that the experience helped her think more deeply than when she read the story on her own. She particularly recognized with more surety the power dynamics at play within "Barn Burning."

In addition to facilitating historical and cultural learning, humanities courses often produce learning outcomes associated with ethics and problem-solving. Literature, in particular, can help students discern the ethical issues present in our society, even as students become aware that art can shape or critique our culture's sense of ethics. Fortunately, learning that emphasizes ethics draws in Generation Z students, according to Seemiller and Grace, who claim, "Generation Z sees the world through multiple screens, but as evidenced by their we-centric attitudes, they recognize that societal issues are much larger than themselves. With their loyalty, determination, and responsibility as well as a realistic outlook on life inherited from Generation X, this generation is committed to those around them and motivated by making a difference. Add to that their characteristics of care and compassion, and you can expect Generation Z to use both their heads and hearts to solve the world's problems"

(17). If working toward a better society motivates Generation Z, then why not find ways to use DY to empower students to act, even as we get them to evaluate our society's shifting senses of ethics? If we can help students to think about solving an ethical problem, we are teaching within the "caring" domain that Fink claims motivates students to "have the energy they need for learning" (36).

If we use Faulkner's "Dry September," *Intruder in the Dust,* and/or *Light in August* to illustrate how Faulkner represents lynching, a cultural crisis in the South during his lifetime, we can provide opportunities for independent discovery that ensures students will play "an active role in creating their learning" (Seemiller and Grace 179). For example, when students first read any of these texts, they may miss the various narrative techniques and struggle to track the difference between the text's use of hypothesizing, remembering, flashbacks or flashforwards, stream-of-consciousness, or telling. DY's Narrative Structure Analysis graphs plot narrative techniques while including a pie chart showing the percentage of the text's use of each technique. By drawing students' attention to these various techniques, one may trace what social issues surface through flashbacks or flashforwards, stream-of-consciousness, hypothesizing, remembering, or telling. As students uncover the way information is transported to the reader, they may discern how each narrative technique works as a perpetuator of cultural assumptions or as a witness or critique of cultural wrongdoings in Faulkner's society as well as our own.

In my freshman composition course, I used "Dry September" as a rhetorical text that can investigate the need for the Black Lives Matter movement. My goal was to help students wade through cultural and historical narratives and counternarratives so that they could understand the racial and political climate of their current times and have enough information to draw educated conclusions and form their own opinions accordingly. After learning about America's lynching problem, students were asked whether Faulkner was responding to his culture or simply recording it. They were also asked to connect the story to the message that the Black Lives Matter movement promotes. We searched the text's rhetorical tools and DY to provide the evidence we needed to back our position. Students were inclined to claim that Faulkner was responding to the culture, and they learned how to point to judgments the text seems to make, as well as the manuscript changes that DY provides. For example, they noticed how Faulkner deliberately changed the focus from Minnie to the violence and brutality that white society inflicts upon black bodies and black communities. As students connected the way the story documents the violence that controls black communities to Black Lives Matter, students recognized themselves as participants in their culture and saw how their experiences and values have shaped their own reactions to the movement.

DY provides a similar opportunity with *Intruder in the Dust*, as students discover that the collaborators had to make a judgment call about the timing in Faulkner's novel. Because the year is not explicitly stated in the novel and the timelines are contradictory in places, it is not clear if the story takes place during the Great Depression or in the Forties. The collaborators settled on 1947, in effect setting it in the context of Truman's Committee on Civil Rights and Civil Rights political platforms that began to form in that era. As students interrogate DY's judgment for the novel's temporal setting, students have the opportunity to reconcile Faulkner's personal belief that the South should not be forced to reform with his illustrations of the horrors (and curses) of living in a bloody and violent South. As students examine Faulkner's works as responses to his culture, they also come to understand Faulkner's belief that change must be organic for it to be effective. It is in this space where students may be asked to reflect upon the kind of individual changes that need to occur and how Faulkner may have envisioned his art facilitating those organic changes.

Finally, instructors can be confident that DY cannot replace the reading experience or be used like SparkNotes. The editors carefully select the data so that students cannot use the site in lieu of reading the original text. In addition to creating the computer-generated maps and graphs, collaborators have linked supplementary materials such as manuscripts, audio recordings, interviews, and photographs. DY claims that it encourages students to build their own knowledge through encountering visuals and information that help them identify material that supplements their initial reading. DY meets that goal very well, according to my students' feedback. DY's various layers offer challenges no matter where the students stand in their intellectual development. As teachers decide if they want a structured or unstructured approach or a combination of the two, they should not be afraid to "fail" while experimenting. As I intentionally focused my students' concentration on specific themes, I witnessed how DY provides students opportunities to examine physical spaces while making abstract ideas more accessible. In short, as we consider our own pedagogical approaches and their politics, our course's learning objectives, and twenty-first-century needs before introducing our students to DY, then we may purposefully prepare DY activities that engage our students in the type of critical thinking that leads to learning, application, and problem-solving.

Appendix: Faulkner, the New South, and Modernism

DIGITAL YOKNAPATAWPHA

"Barn Burning"

PURPOSE

To lead students to new discoveries of textual meaning and to introduce students to digital humanities so that they are exposed to twenty-first-century job market skills.

SKILLS

Close reading skills
Critical thinking skills
Analytical skills
Evaluation skills
Interpretation skills
Problem-solving skills
Research skills

KNOWLEDGE

This assignment will also introduce important content knowledge in this discipline:

> Foundational knowledge of the text and story's era
> Faulkner's common themes connected to modernization of the South and the South's tendency to live in the past;
> How to connect the ideas of historians and social theorists to works of literature;
> A deeper understanding of the South's condition as a representation of the human condition.

TASKS

Go to the Digital Yoknapatawpha website at http://faulkner.iath.virginia.edu.

Scroll through the book images (the small squares at the bottom of the page) and click on "Barn Burning."

Explore the maps to answer the following questions.

GRADING

Excellent work demonstrates that the student read the story carefully and actively engaged with the site. Answers will include quoted and cited passages, critical thought, and analysis that interprets the significance of events.

TECHNOLOGY NEEDED

Internet access

RESOURCES

Story, Digital Yoknapatawpha, Campus Computer Labs, Library, Office Hours

1. Under "Map Controls: Show Characters," select "All." Run your cursor over the character representations on the map. Click on the names and read the biographies.

    - What character description most surprises you or helps you better understand the story? (Explain.)

2. Find Snopes's Farm and read the description.

    - What does this tell us about Snopes's socioeconomic status? His struggles?

3. Go to "Show Characters" and select "Major Characters." Find Ab Snopes, click on the representation, and read the biography.

    - What ironies do you see in Ab's naming his son "Sarty" (after Colonel John Sartoris)?
    - What may Sarty's name imply about the way Ab may have regarded his son from the moment of Sarty's birth?

4. Historian David R. Goldfield states that the New South "marched forward to modernity, while looking to the past for its inspiration." Play the events timeline movement and watch the time bar.

- Why does the story extend back to 1865? What does this backward movement have to do with the story?
- Find "Colonel John Sartoris" and read the biography. What southern inspirations and myths are embodied in the figure of Colonel John Sartoris?

5. Find "Sarty Snopes" and read the biography. Compare and contrast Sarty's description with that of Colonel John Sartoris.

- To outsiders, what might Sarty's name suggest about Ab's possible motivations or hopes he had for his son when he named his son after Colonel John Sartoris?

6. Many literary critics have argued that Faulkner's black characters are simply props that form the southern backdrop for Faulkner's stories. In response, Thadious Davis claims that Faulkner "is not so interested in blacks as individual characters as he is in formulating his aesthetic image and sense of 'Negro'" (*Faulkner's "Negro": Art and the Southern Context*).
   Think about the black characters in "Barn Burning." Go to "Map Controls: Show Characters" and select "All." The black characters appear in black on the map. Click on the black characters and read their biographies.

- In your opinion, why does Faulkner leave his black characters unnamed?
- What other unnamed characters are present?
- Which unnamed characters drive the plot and what is their racial identity? And does the racial identity of the unnamed characters who contribute to or drive the plot matter to the significance of the events? Explain.

7. Thadious Davis also argues that Faulkner does not use the "Negro" to create a mystique. She says, "All of the ingredients of a mystique are already entrenched in southern history and popular culture." What does she mean by that statement, and how does "Barn Burning" illustrate the veracity of it? (Draw your clues from the story and number 6. You will need to Google "Black Representation in the Media 1920" and research the topic.)

8. As whites regained their political power after Reconstruction, a "New South" emerged. The New South thought they could "out-Yankee the Yankee" by doing business like the North, but maintaining pastoral values (the

idealized version of country life). As the New South underwent industrialization, it restored Old South hegemonic and hierarchical ideas. Google "Hegemony" and "Hierarchy" and write the meaning here:

- Go to DY and play the events. Notice that the events move from south to north. Click on "North Road" (marked by a star). Read the information. Judging from the information provided in statement 8, what is the significance of Snopes's destructive movement north?

9. Historian James C. Cobb claims that "the New South would make southern society essentially impervious to Yankee interference in the conduct of its affairs while forcing northern whites to acknowledge the just and honorable nature of the white South's position in 1861" (*Away Down South: A History of Southern Identity*).

- Now study the above quote in relationship to the acts of Ab Snopes. What similarities can you draw between a fallen and defeated South and Ab Snopes?
- Study the quote again. Replace "northern whites" with "plantation owners" or "southern landowners" and "the South" with "poor whites." Now, why would Ab Snopes burn the barns of landowners?
- What symbolism may be found in the barn burning?
- How may one argue that Snopes's action symbolically prepares a way for the South to modernize?

Works Cited

Bellanca, James, and Ron Brandt. *21st Century Skills: Rethinking How Students Learn*. Solution Tree Press, 2010.

Berlin, James A. *Rhetorics, Poetics, and Culture: Refiguring College English Studies*. National Council of Teachers of English, 1996.

Bjork, Olin. "Digital Humanities and the First-Year Writing Course." *Digital Humanities Pedagogy: Practices, Principles, and Politics*. Open Book Publishers, 2012.

Bryan, Victoria, and Ren Denton. "Faulkner, Narration, and the New South: 'A Rose for Emily.'" *Teaching Faulkner: Teaching Faulkner Newsletter*, no. 34, Center for Faulkner Studies, Southeast Missouri State U, Fall 2016.

Burgers, Johannes H., and Elizabeth Cornell. "Faulkner's 'A Rose for Emily.'" Added to the project: 2012. Additional editing 2018: John Corrigan and

Jennie J. Joiner. Digital Yoknapatawpha, University of Virginia, http://faulkner.iath.virginia.edu/?text=RE.
Burgers, Johannes H., Steven Knepper, Cheryl Lester, Julie Napolin, and Theresa M. Towner. "Faulkner's 'That Evening Sun.'" Added to the project: 2014. Additional editing 2018: Johannes H. Burgers and Theresa M. Towner. Digital Yoknapatawpha. University of Virginia, http://faulkner.iath.virginia.edu/?text=TES.
Carothers, James B., Elizabeth Cornell, Chad Jewett, Cheryl Lester, John Padgett, and Theresa M. Towner. "Faulkner's *Light in August*." Added to the project: 2013. Digital Yoknapatawpha, University of Virginia, http://faulkner.iath.virginia.edu/?text=LA.
Cobb, James C. *Away Down South: A History of Southern Identity.* Oxford UP, 2005.
Corrigan, John, Dotty Dye, Jennie J. Joiner, Erin Kay Penner, and William Teem. "Faulkner's *As I Lay Dying*." Added to the project: 2014. Additional editing 2019–20: Erin Kay Penner. Digital Yoknapatawpha, University of Virginia, http://faulkner.iath.virginia.edu/?text=LD.
Davis, Barbara Gross. *Tools for Teaching.* 2nd ed., Jossey-Bass, 2009.
Davis, Thadious. *Faulkner's "Negro": Art and the Southern Context.* Louisiana State UP, 1983.
Denton, Ren. "Faulkner and Innovative Teaching: Using *Digital Yoknapatawpha* in the Classroom." *Teaching Faulkner: Teaching Faulkner Newsletter* no. 34, Center for Faulkner Studies, Southeast Missouri State U, Fall 2016.
Denton, Ren, Robert Coleman, and Taylor Hagood. "Faulkner's 'Wash.'" Added to the project: 2013. Additional editing 2019: Johannes H. Burgers and Erin Penner. Digital Yoknapatawpha, http://faulkner.iath.virginia.edu/?text=W.
Faulkner, William. *As I Lay Dying.* 1930. Vintage International, 1991.
———. "Barn Burning." *Collected Stories.* 1950. Vintage, 1995, pp. 3–25.
———. "Dry September." *Collected Stories.* 1950. Vintage, 1995, pp. 169–83.
———. *Intruder in the Dust.* 1948. Vintage International, 1991.
———. *Light in August.* 1932. Vintage International, 1991.
———. "A Rose for Emily." *Collected Stories.* 1950. Vintage, 1995, pp. 119–30.
———. "Wash." *Collected Stories.* 1950. Vintage, 1995, pp. 535–50.
Fink, L. Dee. *Creating Significant Learning Experiences: An Integrated Approach to Designing College Courses.* Jossey-Bass, 2013.
Gilbert, Sophie. "Learning to be Human." *Atlantic,* 30 June 2016, https://www.theatlantic.com/entertainment/archive/2016/06/learning-to-be-human/489659.
Giroux, Henry A. "Rethinking the Boundaries of Educational Discourse: Modernism, Postmodernism, and Feminism." *Margins in the Classroom: Teaching*

Literature, edited by Kostas Myrsiades and Linda S. Myrsiades, U of Minnesota P, 1994, pp. 1–51.

Gold, Matthew K., and Lauren F. Klein. *2019 Debates in the Digital Humanities.* U of Minnesota P, 2019.

Goldfield, David, R. *Still Fighting the Civil War: The American South and Southern History,* p. 21; quoted in James C. Cobb, *Away Down South: A History of Southern Identity,* Oxford UP, 2005, p. 68.

Hagood, Taylor, and Steven Knepper. "Faulkner's 'Barn Burning.'" Added to the project: 2012. Additional editing 2018: Erin Kay Penner and Christopher Rieger. Digital Yoknapatawpha, University of Virginia, http://faulkner.iath.virginia.edu/?text=BB.

Hirsch, Brett D. *Digital Humanities Pedagogy: Practices, Principles, and Politics.* Open Book Publishers, 2012.

Hunter, John. "The Digital Humanities and 'Critical Theory': An Institutional Cautionary Tale." *2019 Debates in the Digital Humanities,* edited by Matthew K. Gold and Lauren F. Klein, U of Minnesota P, 2019, pp. 188–94.

Lang, James. *Small Teaching: Everyday Lessons from the Science of Learning.* Jossey-Bass, 2016.

Noble, Safiya Umoja. "Toward a Critical Black Digital Humanities." *2019 Debates in the Digital Humanities,* edited by Matthew K. Gold and Lauren F. Klein, U of Minnesota P, 2019, pp. 27–35.

Seemiller, Corey, and Meghan Grace. *Generation Z Goes to College.* Jossey-Bass, 2016.

Simon, Roger. "Empowerment as a Pedagogy of Possibility." *Language Arts,* vol. 64, April 1987, pp. 370–82.

Winkelmes, Mary-Ann, et al. "A Teaching Intervention That Increases Underserved College Students' Success." *Peer Review,* AAC&U Study, vol. 18, nos. 1/2, Winter/Spring 2016, pp. 31–36.

Work in Progress

STEPHEN RAILTON

SNOW WAS falling outside the window of the E-Text Center on the December morning in 1996 when Director David Seaman taught me enough html tags to create my first web page, my first step on the digital path I'm still traveling. Meteorologically it was a good day to be indoors, but the more relevant environmental circumstances pushing me to take that step were personal and institutional. My kids, Ben and Annie, were introduced to computers at school before we ever had one at home, and their enthusiasm for those early educational programs like *The Oregon Trail* drew me along with them to Charlottesville's public library, where I sat beside them feeding disks into an Apple II that enabled them to bake virtual cakes or track down Carmen Sandiego. The way the technology allowed them to learn fractions or world geography while "playing" seemed full of potential for my own aspirations as a teacher. But what made it possible to imagine a path for me toward that new world was the institutional climate at the University of Virginia. The work that very early adopters like Alan Howard (a fellow Americanist) and Ed Ayers (a colleague in History) were already doing with the technology was inspiring. And the E-Text Center was only one of the commitments that UVA was making to this new mode of scholarship. Before I try to describe my own progress as a digital pilgrim, let me acknowledge the larger community of technologists at UVA, people like David and his staff in E-Text, and also the Institute for Advanced Technology in the Humanities, and the Digital Media and Music Center. Between 1996 and now, in 2020, that list grew a lot longer, and includes people at the Digital Media Lab; the Scholars' Lab; the Library's Digital Production Group; the Science, Humanities and Arts New Technology Initiative; the Geospatial and Statistical Data Center; and the Data Science Institute. As I recall the design of *The Oregon Trail*, users had to gather supplies to keep their journey moving. I didn't have anything to do with gathering together all the technical and human resources on which digital humanities depends and on which humanists at UVA can rely, but without them the journey I want to describe here could never have begun.

Part of my original attraction to DH (the shorthand I'll use for that journey throughout this essay) was the opportunity it offered to connect with a larger audience than I'd been able to reach in my published work as a scholar—the "world wide" part of "www" is very seductive—but at the start I was mainly thinking about the students in my own classrooms. That first web page was created for the project that became Mark Twain in His Times: An Electronic Archive (http://twain.lib.virginia.edu). A regular feature of the Twain seminar I'd been teaching off and on for years was a field trip across the grounds to the Special Collections Library, where students could see firsthand some of the wonderful Twain material that UVA is lucky enough to own. (That library, the richness of its holdings and the generosity of its staff, is another key part of the village that has made my DH work possible.) The students were impressed, I think, to see examples of Twain's manuscripts and letters and so on, but although I encouraged them to return to the archive on their own, and perhaps use something from the collections in their work for the class, the fact that most of them never did either was frustrating. When I put my children's enthusiasm for working on a computer together with the fact that college students were already on their PCs for a good part of every day even in those days before laptops and cell phones, I decided that if they wouldn't go to Special Collections, maybe the new technology would allow me to bring "Special Collections" to them. I was scheduled to teach the Twain seminar in fall of 1997. On that snowy day at the end of 1996, I was trying to make that idea a (virtual) reality.

Over the year that followed, I ended up learning a lot more than html. The first text on the reading list for that class was Twain's first book, *The Innocents Abroad*, which most students have never heard of but which was the bestselling of all Twain's books during his lifetime. It launched his career as a popular writer and defined the "Mark Twain" persona that accompanied Sam Clemens on the rest of his journey to fame and fortune, but from previous semesters I knew its 650 pages could get the seminar off to a rough start. On our trip to Special Collections, we always looked at examples of the sales prospectuses that Twain's publishers produced for the subscription agents, the door-to-door salespersons, from whom Twain's readers bought his books. The second edition of the prospectus for *Innocents* includes a large sampling of "Various Newspaper Notices" from around the country, all testifying explicitly or implicitly to the reasons why its first American readers loved the book. One of my first priorities for the website I envisioned was making a digital version of those "Notices," to help the students see not only who "Mark Twain" was "in his times" and what made the jokes they didn't get so hilarious to his contemporary audience, but also why I was making them read this long book before letting them play hooky with Tom Sawyer or get on the raft with Huck and Jim. As anyone who used the early versions of OCR technology to convert print into ASCII characters can appreciate, it took a lot of work to create http://twain.lib.virginia.edu/innocent/blurbs.html, but on the hot day at the end of August 1997, when I gave the Twain class their first reading assignment—to go online and read the "Notices" along with the first twenty or so of the book's chapters—I was confident that the E-Text Center and I had built a kind of time machine that would use the newest technology to take students back into the past, enabling them to see it in a transformative way.

The blank looks on most of the students' faces when at the next class meeting I asked them to discuss the online assignment shocked me back to nonvirtual reality. As we talked I realized that when they went to the web page, they had largely been alienated rather than enlightened by what they'd found there: a long scroll down an unbroken series of long lines of print—my html vocabulary at that stage didn't include "width='x pixels'" tags, so each line of text went right across the whole screen of their PC monitors, a common sight in those early days of the internet. My great mistake was that, focused on what I wanted to bring those students, I had entirely failed to consider the other half of the user-interface equation: the preconceptions that they brought to the internet as a medium. Twenty-something years later, students are much more experienced at reading prose on what amounts to a TV screen, but the fundamental lesson I learned in that seminar is still true: I was thinking of my website as a kind of higher-tech printing press, but the students sat down in front of their computers with a different set of expectations than when they open up a book. For starters, they expected images. The power of pictures was something Twain and his publishers already knew about readers in the nineteenth century, which is why (like all his subscription books) *Innocents Abroad* was advertised as "Profusely Adorned with 234 Beautiful, Spirited, and Appropriate Engravings." After that experience in the seminar, I made sure that my own web pages were adorned with enough illustrations to pull users' eyes into and down the e-pages; given how much "Mark Twain" and his work deployed images (it has been said that after Queen Victoria, he was the most photographed inhabitant of the era), those images were also "appropriate" and often vital parts of the story I was trying to tell. (For an example, see "Representing Jim, 1885–1985," http://twain.lib.virginia.edu/huckfinn/jiminpix.html.) The experience also brought home to me the significance of the "h" in the *Hyper*text Markup Language I was learning; online, students expect interactivity, nonlinear choices, ways to navigate a project's content for themselves. I'm still a fan of the logic of a printed text—that as a reader I am captive to the movement of the words from upper left to lower right, that as a writer I can expect my reader's sustained immersion in the rhythm of my syntax and the order of my ideas—but with the help of my students I've accepted the preconditions of DH, the interdependence of our message and our medium. We know about the potential downside of using visual enhancements and designing interactive pages—the shrinking of attention spans when readers become users—but as digital humanists we should also look for creative and illuminating ways to link the stories we are trying to tell to the expectations of users as well as the capabilities of electronic technology.

Over the years since that seminar, my students have repeatedly taught me how important it is to create DH projects with as much feedback as possible from the audience from whom they are being built. Three years into the development of the Twain site, a fellowship from UVA's Institute for Advanced Technology in the Humanities gave me a chance to start a new project. Hoping to take advantage of what I'd learned from the students, I asked myself which American author or text of all the ones I regularly teach would provide the richest occasion to test the possibilities of doing humanities digitally, of using this new set of tools to enrich appreciation and understanding of our literature and our culture. I confess that I kept hoping the answer would be something like *Moby-Dick*, but instead each time I considered the question, the answer was the same: Harriet Beecher Stowe's *Uncle Tom's Cabin*. The rhetorical brilliance of the novel is admirable on its own terms, but what really decided it for me was the complex and sustained afterlife of the book: in politics and history, but also in its many adaptations into songs, pictures, plays, movies, even children's toys. Language is only one of the many forms of discourse in which culture constructs itself. Its multimedia capabilities make DH particularly well-suited to the study of cultural history, and I couldn't think of any other work that could potentially reveal as much about both American culture and the potential of DH. The subtitle of *Uncle Tom's Cabin* & American Culture (http://utc.iath.virginia.edu)—"A Multi-Media Archive"—was the banner beneath which I set out toward a new pedagogical and scholarly future. There are thousands of texts in the archive, along with thousands of illustrations, but there are also as many examples as we could come up with of what print scholarship can't do: let users hear songs or view movie clips, for example, or rotate 3-D objects and play a Flash animation of *Uncle Tom's Cabin* as a magic lantern show. I was still hoping to build a time machine. Stowe's narrative lived and had its being in all these extra-textual forms for over three quarters of a century; the ability of electronic technology to provide at least a simulacrum of these various parts of the past that had once lived with all the cultural vitality of a blockbuster movie or an internet meme might allow that past to speak to the present with illuminating force.

Although it didn't occur to me at the outset, once we began building the project I discovered another virtue of working in virtual reality. As opposed to Mark Twain, the UVA library didn't already have a rich collection of material connected to Stowe's novel. The reasons for this are worth considering, as indices of Stowe's status as a Northerner and a woman, but what mattered to me at the time was that I would have to look elsewhere for what we would need to display the story of Stowe's story as a cultural phenomenon. The IATH fellowship came with some funding, enough to enable us to get started with that quest, but it soon became clear that we needed support on a larger scale. The National Endowment for the Arts and especially the National Endowment for the Humanities were essential partners over the years in which we developed the project. Doing DH requires not just a village, but in most cases a budget—in this case money to allow me to travel to archives and private collections around the country in which the pieces of the puzzle we were trying to put together were preserved, and to acquire digital reproductions of rare or unique materials like play posters and scripts. We don't dare claim that the result of this gathering has any kind of completeness—the hundreds of posters or the dozens of scripts in the site are a fraction of what was produced in the United States between 1852 and 1930, and no one will ever be able to say how big a fraction—but without money and the collaboration of many institutions and collectors, our attempt to re-present Stowe's story would have been stillborn. With that assistance, however, came the realization that virtual reality allowed us to draw together a vast amount of material from widely separated places into a digital archive that people anywhere in the world could visit without leaving their homes, and where scholars, teachers and students could study these often fragile historical artifacts without any danger of eroding the originals. Again, I wouldn't claim that rotating a statuette of Eva and Tom in VR can give anyone the same experience as seeing that object in person. Certainly more than a little is lost in the translation to bytes. But given the storage and display capacities of this new technology, it's still exciting to think of all the ways in which digitization may further research.

I suppose I felt something of a collector's passion as the amount and kinds of material in our database grew, though the goal of the quest was socialist—redistributing the wealth—rather than acquisitive. But in a sense I was still conceiving of the technology as an improved printing press, a "flash"ier mode of distribution. My favorite moments as we developed the project were achieved when the technology became something more like a mode of discovery. Such moments came when separate pieces of the puzzle could be linked together in virtual reality to provide new means of analysis that illuminated not just the separate parts of the story but the larger meaning of *Uncle Tom's Cabin* in American culture. The dozen canvas drops that the Harmount theatrical company carried on tour in the early twentieth century as they performed their version of the play, carefully preserved at the Jerome Lawrence & Robert E. Lee Theatre Research Institute at The Ohio State University, include a painted scene of a wharf complete with steamboats and bales of cotton, ambiguously labeled "AUCTION" on the side that faced away from the audience (http://utc.iath.virginia.edu/onstage/imagesosu/dropshp.html). Reconstructing what was enacted in front of that backdrop became possible when we could link it to a cluster of other items, including a colorful lithograph poster of African Americans performers dancing above the caption "On the Levee" (http://utc.iath.virginia.edu/interpret/exhibits/utconfilm/levee.html), part of the holdings of the Library Company of Philadelphia; the 1901 script of the Brady theatrical company's production, archived in the Museum of the City of New York (http://utc.iath.virginia.edu/onstage/scripts/osplglabIV1t.html); and the narrative description of scene 11, "The Auction of St. Clare's Slaves," prepared by the

Edison Company to accompany the release of their 1903 silent film version of the story, and part of the Thomas A. Edison Papers at Rutgers University (http://utc.iath.virginia.edu/onstage/films/ficattaeat.html). Each of these items helps contextualize the others, and together they can help a twenty-first-century audience of internet users "see" how, half a century after the novel was published, a quarter century after Reconstruction had been abandoned, how one of the most morally challenging scenes in the book—Tom and Emmeline being sold to Simon Legree to help cover the debt owed to a New York creditor—became a spectacle that let white American consciences off the hook. "Slavery Days"—the subtitle of Edison's film—became a source of entertainment. The technology even allows us to hear the soundtrack of this reassuring spectacle in songs like "At Uncle Tom's Cabin Door," released on one of those old, thick 78 rpm vinyls by the Victor Records company in 1913 and purchased on eBay (another scholarly resource made possible by computers and the internet) in 2001, then digitized by the Digital Media Center at UVA (http://utc.iath.virginia.edu/songs/utcdoorf.html). (I explore this part of the cultural afterlife of Stowe's novel more fully in "Uncle Tom's Cabin on Film 1: The Silent Era," http://utc.iath.virginia.edu/interpret/exhibits/utconfilm/utconfilm.html.)

This distinction between distribution and discovery modes, which I could not have consciously articulated while working on the Uncle Tom site, is now at the center of my thinking as a digital humanist. Consciously, however, I had no DH plans in mind at all when I began teaching Faulkner at about the same time as the *Uncle Tom's Cabin* project was running out of steam and money. It was intellectual and creative fun to take on the challenges involved with working in this electronic medium, but the "multimedia" aspects and large ambitions of the project were far beyond my limited command of coding, making me very dependent on the team of technologists at IATH. Every collaborator I've ever had will tell you that collaborating is hard for me. In the face of the delays, disagreements, and disappointments that inevitably arise from such a process, it was time, I thought, to return to the kinds of research and writing I'd been doing before 1996. Again I was wrong. And again it was environmental circumstances that led me back into virtual reality. After Doug Day retired from the English Department, taking with him the Faulkner classes he regularly taught, no one else wanted to take his place. It seemed wrong not to have any Faulkner courses here, where for two semesters in the 1950s Faulkner had met with undergraduate and graduate students in some of the same classrooms we still used, where the library housed the bulk of his papers. Though fully aware of my own inadequacies, including a midwestern accent that betrayed my non-southern background and a spotty acquaintance with the vast body of Faulkner criticism, I added "Faulkner" to my schedule of classes.

Halfway through that course, the blank looks on the faces of another set of students drove home a different kind of lesson: I learned that teaching Faulkner meant teaching *Absalom, Absalom!*—or rather, I learned what it meant to ask students to read *Absalom*. Faulkner's editor at Random House, Hal Smith, was probably the first to recognize the problem; in the margins of the first pages of an early manuscript titled "Faulkner's New Novel," he warns the author that, for example, "Almost anyone would get lost in this sentence," or that what gets vaguely introduced on page 14 doesn't get explained until page 24, "& that's too long for anyone to hang on" (see http://faulkner.iath.virginia.edu/media/resources/MANUSCRIPTS/AAMS14.html). Smith had almost no luck getting Faulkner to revise the novel's demanding prose, so he proposed that they add a "Chronology" as a kind of appendix when the novel was published to provide readers with an outline of the basic narrative events. Telling my students to use that "Chronology" as a guide, however, would have meant spoiling the whole design of the novel as a kind of postmodern detective fiction: Quentin and Shreve's ultimate discovery of Bon's "Negro blood" as the motive for his murder. I'm sure that over the decades good teachers have solved this problem in many creative ways, but from my vantage point in the early twenty-first century it seemed that here was another occasion where electronic technology might help. Instead of a static print chronology, we could design a digital one that would present the events of the story in narrative sequence as well as chronological order. Students at Virginia could discover the truth Faulkner is telling about the past and its legacy more or less as those two roommates at Harvard learn it in the novel. And so not long after stepping away from DH, I found myself sitting alongside Will Rourk, a programmer in the Digital Media Lab, as we built the Flash-based *Absalom, Absalom!* An Electronic Interactive Chronology.

It wasn't long after I began using that project in class that I learned that Adobe planned to stop supporting Flash. Adobe has just now—the end of 2020—made good on that threat; while you can still see the html pages that frame the electronic *Chronology* Will and I created (https://twain.lib.virginia.edu/absalom/index2.html), the chronologies themselves no longer display. This disappearance of Flash has been another teachable moment for me, revealing how the environmental nature of DH is subject to its own form of climate change. The shelf life of a book, that advanced technology of the fifteenth century, can be measured in centuries if not millennia. At least at this stage in the digital revolution, DHers know all too well how much work it can take to keep projects up to date as code standards, software programs, hardware platforms, and user habits keep coming and going "so quickly here" in the Oz-like land of virtual reality. I've had repeated opportunities to learn that lesson, but it hasn't brought an end to the journey. Before 1996 my associations with the term "user" were mainly linked to addictive drugs, but trying to walk away from the possibilities of electronic technology forced me to admit that I was hooked on this new way to teach and publish. And as an environment, "Faulkner" was full of temptations. When I learned about the existence of the actual magnetic tapes on which two earlier UVA English professors, Frederick Gwynn and Joseph Blotner, had recorded most of Faulkner's public sessions as the university's first Writer-in-Residence, I realized how much better it would be for my students to hear Faulkner himself relate how *The Sound and the Fury* began with "the picture of the little girl's muddy drawers, climbing that tree to look in the parlor window" (https://faulkner.lib.virginia.edu/display/wfaudio01_1.html#wfaudio01_1.5), than to listen to me reading that passage from *Faulkner in the University*. The Uncle Tom project—not to mention the many forms of earphones that students started sprouting—made it clear how well-suited electronic technology and audio files were to each other. All of these factors, along with a lot of work by several divisions of the UVA Library, combined to produce Faulkner at Virginia: An Audio Archive (https://faulkner.lib.virginia.edu), which seems to me to be the most successful and complete of the projects I've been involved in at deploying the technology as a mode of distribution.

On the other hand, more than once on the tapes Faulkner tells his audiences how much he values failure. Despite Adobe's decision, I'm grateful for what Flash taught me about the potentialities of digital display. The *Absalom* chronology was very imperfect—some of its technical features were awkward to use, and the compromises it made with the complexities of Faulkner's novel were troubling—but of these two Faulkner projects, it is the one that better represents the goal of using DH as a mode of discovery. By giving people the means electronically to search the transcripts of Faulkner's three dozen public sessions and to hear his voice as he answers over 1,400 questions about his own works and other matters, the audio archive does something that a print publication could not. But however imperfectly, the electronic chronology did something more: it offered people the means to reconceptualize *Absalom* and to study both its narrative structure and its thematic significance as a metanarrative—a story about storytelling—in radically new ways. From the beginning, Digital Yoknapatawpha (DY) was conceived as a means to that end: using DH to open up previously untrodden digital pathways into Faulkner's art.

Though I began with no clear ideas about how to do that, I did know that for this project I needed much more help than ever before, especially from the community of Faulkner scholars. In presentations to the Faulkner Society at MLA and the gathering of aficionados at the University of Mississippi's annual Faulkner and Yoknapatawpha Conference, we shared the earliest, Flash-based prototype of the project with this community. There was some understandable anxiety about the potentially negative effects of an online Faulkner, but as a group they overlooked the primitiveness of our prototype and my own status as an outsider to embrace the concept, and, as individuals, enough brave scholars signed up to collaborate on the project to allow it to move forward. It's now almost a decade later, and while a few of those original collaborators have moved on, other Faulknerians have signed on; the energy, expertise, and varied perspectives that this team continues to bring to the project have all been crucial, enabling us to maintain the highest standards of traditional scholarship in this new medium. Together we built the project's core databases, identifying and analyzing the locations, characters, and events in every one of the fourteen novels and fifty-four short stories that comprise the Yoknapatawpha fictions, translating the world Faulkner created in those texts into (so far) approximately half a million data points. A dedicated dozen of the collaborators are still at work on the events data, entering keywords for each of the over 8,000 events that will enable researchers to find, for example, every instance of domestic violence or Christian symbolism that appears in the cumulative saga of Faulkner's mythical county.

Although the keyword stage of the project is some years away from being even tentatively "finished"—one of the best and worst things about any digital project is that there's no place in virtual reality to write "The

End"—aggregating all the fictions that Faulkner wrote across the course of his career into one electronic resource has already provided scholars and students with new tools for studying his work. The potentially vast capacity of marking and storing textual data means, for example, that our character databases are much more complete than any of the many valuable print indexes to Faulkner's characters that have already been published. Our work relies heavily on the accomplishments of those previous scholars, who have to be included among the many inhabitants of the village that our DH work depends on, but the non-virtual constraints under which they worked means, for example, that most of the 2,732 "unnamed" men and women in his fictions whom we can include never appear in the published indexes; since a great many of these figures are black, their previous invisibility inadvertently made the population of the world Faulkner created seem much whiter than it is. And the capacity of the technology to interrogate and retrieve information makes it possible, for example, to search the 4,978 characters in our database for "mixed-race" characters. Since the "Search Characters by Text" function in DY sorts results by individual texts that are organized chronologically in the order of their publication, such a search reveals in broad terms one dimension of Faulkner's ongoing representation of race as a major issue. Mixed-race characters are very rare in his first Yoknapatawpha fictions (only two of the 282 characters in *Flags in the Dust,* for instance, are "mulatto"), which suggests that initially Faulkner accepted the stark two-term system—"white" or "colored"—that came with the segregationist culture of his South. By the middle of his career, however, such "mixed" characters play a much larger role in the story he's telling (this shift peaks in 1942 with *Go Down, Moses,* with 22 of 268 characters); the existence of such nonbinary figures in his fiction poses a challenge to the ideological status quo of his culture. After that, the number of such characters drops off dramatically (only three of the fifteen texts he published after *Moses* have any identified biracial characters at all). This kind of quantifiable search result, of course, can only serve as a starting point for critical interpretation—it can't tell us what the turn away from racially mixed characters might *mean*—but an analysis of Faulkner's evolving imaginative and moral engagement with race could do worse than to start with this kind of data point.

To me, however, the most promising way to use our data is as a base from which to launch new ways of conceiving and displaying Faulkner's fictions. In a sense, I'm still working out the implications of that first lesson the Twain class taught me: that virtual reality is preeminently a visual realm. Our first visualization experiment was mapping the texts. Faulkner himself, of course, drew the first two maps of Yoknapatawpha, and without their authority it's unlikely our project could even have begun. Faulkner's two maps capture "Yoknapatawpha" at two different fixed moments in his career; our 68 maps attempt to re-present "Yoknapatawpha" as it appears in each different text, reflecting the creative ferment that led Faulkner to re-create his county each time he returned to it imaginatively. The first of Faulkner's maps, drawn in 1936 for *Absalom*, plots over a dozen events from ten novels and stories; by playing the animations attached to our maps, users can display all the events in a text, and watch as Faulkner's imagination moves the story around in space—including into the larger world outside Yoknapatawpha. The original idea behind our design was inspired by the medical PET scans that indicate which parts of a human brain are activated as a result of certain stimuli: I wanted to see how different parts of the county became active for different texts and at different times in Faulkner's career, when for example he moved the center of a narrative to Frenchman's Bend, and what such shiftings might reveal about his evolving aesthetic and thematic project. Probably our most speculative venture in this respect is our decision to locate the wanderings of Joe Christmas in *Light in August* after he kills Joanna Burden in the one part of the county that Faulkner's fictions otherwise never inhabit: the southwest quadrant. As reconceptualizations, our maps require us to assign each event spatial and temporal coordinates. Throughout the project, we do our best to acknowledge the extent to which our data and our displays are the result of interpretive interventions or extrapolations: in this case, for instance, the "Mapping the Text" section of our note on the novel provides the textual evidence on which we based our decision to locate Joe's journey in what otherwise is Yoknapatawpha's no-man's land. At the very least this map can serve as a provocation. To the extent that our plotting is valid, however, it may provide a visual means to appreciate Joe's extreme existential alienation as a man who cannot know his racial identity in a culture where race is so determinant. It might even be a way to measure how pervasively spatial Faulkner's imagination is, how re-creating his "Yoknapatawpha" each time he returned to it served his project as an artist.

In addition, our maps include timelines that display the narratives in time as well as space. As part of a text's animation sequence, this added temporal dimension reveals one of Faulkner's most characteristic artistic signatures, the way his stories so often move backward as well as forward, continually returning to the "past"—earlier events in the characters' lives or the region's history. Such repeated temporal recursions are a very effective way to dramatize how the present is saturated by the past, how as Faulkner memorably puts it, "The past is never dead." On the timelines, for example, it's possible to see how often most of the events in a Faulkner story have already occurred by the time the story "begins." Deploying an algorithm, we can use the data to generate cumulative temporal heatmaps, allowing us to see *which* "past"—what part of a narrative's chronological span—seems most central to each story. The results of our efforts to reconceive the texts visually have often surprised me. Looking at 68 temporal heatmaps, I was startled to notice how, although Faulkner's narratives frequently visit "the past," the majority of them (39) center themselves chronologically on more or less the time in which Faulkner is writing them (http://faulkner.iath.virginia.edu/family/heat maps/temporal_heatmaps-all_texts.php). I should have read that famous quote more carefully. It is not really about "the past," but rather about its presence. This emphasis in Faulkner's work is one element of its timeless human significance, but I think his ultimate preoccupation with the present is especially meaningful for Americans trying to move beyond our history, to get past our past.

If our maps, even including the synchronized timelines, reconceive the fictions in ways that Faulkner himself could have anticipated—though I won't say "would necessarily have approved"—they are only two of the ways in which the technology allows us to display our textual data. With the help of our collaborating technologists, we have been experimenting with types of information graphics that I never imagined might be useful to a student of Faulkner—well, to be honest, that I had never imagined at all! Bipartite graphs, for instance, take the character and location entries that the scholars created and display them as a pair of parallel lists; using individually color-coded lines, an algorithm then connects each character to each location with which he or she is associated. When all 282 characters in *Flags in the Dust* are thus linked to all 77 of the novel's locations, the result can look something like a plate of psychedelic spaghetti. The first time Worthy Martin and Robbie Bingler, the project's lead technologists, showed me bipartite graphing on the screen in our IATH meeting room, I'm sure they saw a face as blank as any I ever saw on a student. It was by no means obvious to me what scholars or teachers could gain from such a transformation. The moment was a reminder that just as important as the virtual—and virtually unlimited—possibilities of the new technology are the real expectations, needs and even limitations of the people for whom we were building the project. Digital technology is a very powerful way to convey information, but digital *humanities* should aim to do more: to design its re-presentations as occasions for critical thinking and reflection. We had been diligently working to make our databases richer, denser, more complex; now it was time to design and implement ways to simplify, simplify, simplify, as that technophobe Thoreau would say—to allow users to curate the information to suit their own research or pedagogic goals. This realization has affected every aspect of the project, from providing options for the way locations and events can be plotted on the existing maps and timelines to creating a new "MapIt" feature that allows users to explore the results of their searches on maps and animations built around their own criteria. For the more visually and conceptually unfamiliar functions like bipartite graphing, this has meant providing users with filters so they can reduce the perceptual clutter that can make it difficult to see what such technological transformations of Faulkner's prose might reveal.

Even so, it took some time before I could begin to appreciate what a bipartite graph of *Flags in the Dust* might be good for. The process started with the realization that this particular type of display called the eye's attention not just to where characters were seen or mentioned in a story, but also to the locations where they weren't. Absence of course is a particularly Faulknerian trope. In this first Yoknapatawpha novel, for example, the Sartoris mansion is haunted not so much by the ghosts of Colonel John or brother Johnny as by the way they're *not* there. Faulkner's second Yoknapatawpha novel, *The Sound and the Fury*, is even more poignantly haunted by the absence of Caddy Compson, the lost daughter of another aristocratic southern family. You can use the filters to generate graphs that distinguish the places where a character is "Present" from the places where a character *isn't*, or is only "Mentioned." But I had even better interpretive luck when I asked for a graph to show where the Snopes family appears in *Flags*. I knew Faulkner had set aside his earliest attempt to create Yoknapatawpha, the unfinished "Father Abraham" manuscript which focuses on how Flem and his "poor white" relations invade Jefferson, to write *Flags in the Dust*, where the focus is instead on the social displacement of the upper-class families like the Sartorises. In view of this change, what might the data reveal about the places that he assigned "Snopeses" in the novel he ended up writing? The bipartite graph of the *Flags* data filtered by "Family=Snopes" showed ten places with which the narrative's nine Snopeses are linked. Most of the graph's lines connect to places one expects to find Snopeses: Turpin's Farm and Varner's Store in Frenchman's Bend, the section of the county they're from; and the Beard Hotel, I.O.'s House, the Power Plant in Jefferson, the places where they live and work after moving into town. But I confess it came as a surprise to see the lines linking two Snopeses—Montgomery Ward and Byron—with the Benbow House, the elegant antebellum home of the novel's other old family. Did this imply that Faulkner's imagination allowed the two extremes of Yoknapatawpha's white population—the traditional aristocracy and the parvenu lower class—to meet on common ground? But then I realized I was looking at places where the Snopeses are both present and mentioned. So I cleared the search form and searched again, this time just for the events in which Snopeses are physically "Present" in a setting.

The change was slight, but significant: Montgomery Ward Snopes disappeared from the Benbow House. Yet the line linking Byron with that location remained. Following that line led me to recall that there is one time in the narrative when Byron does get inside that house: when he breaks into Narcissa's bedroom in the dark to steal from her underwear drawer. This "crossing over" is literally a "trespass," a violation of the law. And that made me realize that the other upper-class location he is associated with—the Sartoris Bank where he works for much of the novel—also becomes the scene of a crime that same night when he breaks in there to steal from the vault. Ultimately, in other words, Faulkner *criminalizes* Byron's presence in these places, which is a very dramatic way to police the line that separates the Old South, as embodied by Sartorises and Benbows and their spaces, from the New, dramatically embodied by the way Snopeses violate those spaces. I'm not exaggerating to say that this gave me a new way to appreciate what "Yoknapatawpha" gave Faulkner. He could not change the new reality that modernity was forcing on the world he lived in, but in the world he created he could resist and even try to control those kinds of social disruptions, just as Byron's "presence" at the Benbows' and the Bank in the end results in his having to run back to Frenchman's Bend before exiting the novel, and its spaces, entirely. ("Leaving Yoknapatawpha," by the way, is the event keyword for a trope that recurs in many of the fictions. For more on using and interpreting bipartite graphs, see http://faulkner.iath.virginia.edu/characters-bipart.html.)

I don't offer my epiphany as a major moment in Faulkner criticism, but as an example of the kinds of heuristic analyses that the digital effort to capture and display the fictions might lead to. We have only started to explore these potentialities. The distinction that the event entries make between whether characters are "Present" or "Mentioned" has turned out to provide a very powerful vantage point from which to examine major thematic elements in the world Faulkner created, like the persistence of the past and the portentousness of absence. Another of the project's more radical techniques for re-envisioning the fictions are the force-directed graphs, which array texts visually employing a metric based on number and length of events and an algorithm that assigns values of attraction and repulsion to each character and location. If you use the Character-Character Force-Directed graph, for instance, to display all the members of the McCaslin family in *Go Down, Moses*, Old Carothers McCaslin, the founding patriarch of the family's racially diverse branches, occupies a spot near the center of the display, radiating lines to two dozen other characters. But if you filter the same McCaslin family data to show only the linkages between characters who are "Present" together in the events, Old Carothers's icon moves to the circumference and is now linked only to two other characters. Being able to visualize these differences provides a visceral way to appreciate how absence and the past can create the gravitational force around which the present continues to revolve, how a character who is hardly "there" in the narrative can largely determine the story. (For more on this function, see http://faulkner.iath.virginia.edu/char-char-force.html.)

Behind such moments of discovery are countless hours of work by that DH village: the scholars who identified and entered the 551 events in *Go Down, Moses* and who tabulated which of the book's 268 characters were "Present" or "Mentioned" in each, as well as the technologists who created the programs that integrate and refashion all that data into the project's various visualizations. All of this work, of course, can be second-guessed. How did we define such key categories as "Location," "Character," and "Event"? What was the scholarly or analytical process by which the data fields for each category—Present versus Mentioned, say—were constructed? Given the duration of the project, the number of collaborators, and the multiple choices involved in each data field, how well has consistency been maintained? We owe our users the clearest possible explanation about our methodology. Then, in addition to all the questions about what we have done, there are the questions we ask ourselves about what we haven't, or haven't yet. Is there, for example, a way to quantify relative degrees of "presence" or "absence"? At the end of that day in April 1928 when Benjy goes into the darkness of the night and the void of sleep on the last page of his section in *The Sound and the Fury*, he remembers the time thirty years earlier when his seven-year-old sister Caddy, lying next to him in bed, promised their father that she would always "take good care" of him. This is almost two decades after Caddy left the family, and yet in this mnemonic event she is surely "there" in a way that neither absent, present, or mentioned can capture.

Ten years into the project, I find myself asking a lot of questions like that. When we started designing the data entry pages back in 2011, one of the first fields we came up with asked scholars to divide each character's "Rank" into categories like "Major" and "Secondary." Looking back, I can see how the extant print catalogs of "Faulkner's characters" influenced that decision. There were no similar precedents for the location and event entries we set out to create. As the list of locations grew longer, we realized the value of distinguishing locations that were settings for events from places that were only mentioned, and so introduced that basic way of distinguishing among the entries. As yet, however, all our events are created equal. What if we went back through all 8,257 "Events" in the database and weighted them according to degree of significance? On what basis could the options be constructed?—Most Important? Most Traumatic?—and whose judgment would decide among them? Would counting the number of words in each event result in a more reliable way to weight them? In that case we could ask the technology to do the ranking. Either method could provide skeptics with a new hook on which to hang misgivings about the legitimacy of our attempt to pull Faulkner's extremely difficult and ambiguous prose through the starkly categorical terms of binary data. But at the same time I can't help thinking how useful—to students and perhaps even scholars—such hierarchical rankings might be.

As the project continues to evolve, we keep finding new occasions to recognize lacunae and oversimplifications in our protocols. But at least at this point in the journey, I don't feel a need to find or assert definitive answers to any of the questions. During my time in virtual reality, I have always seen my DH projects as exploratory in nature, as experiments in how the new technology might help us in our classrooms and our research. The results of that experiment aren't in yet. I've always believed that Faulkner's art would reveal as much about digital humanities as DH would reveal about Faulkner's art. In time we hope to produce a body of interpretive commentaries using the project in as many ways as we can imagine to move the conversation about Faulkner forward and to test the potential of using electronic technology to enhance the larger project of humanities research. This collection of essays is a good down payment on that, as are the "Commentaries" already available in the online project (for an example, see "Faulkner & Maps," http://faulkner.iath.virginia.edu/media/resources/DISPLAYS/FaulknerMapsHP.html).

User response offers another way of measuring the project's value. My own experience with this has mainly been limited to the students in my Faulkner classes. I have used the timelines of events in Faulkner's work to show them, for instance, how in each of his first three Yoknapatawpha fictions—*Flags, The Sound and the Fury, As I Lay Dying*—"the past" occupies more and less narrative time and gets redefined alternately as either the historical or the personal past. Seeing those differences makes it easier for them to appreciate how, paradoxically, Faulkner is continually determined as a modernist artist to follow Pound's dictum to "make it new" even as he keeps exploring the inescapability of the past. DY is a useful pedagogical resource—that is, at least from my own limited perspective at the front of the classroom. A less subjective measurement of the experiment's value for teachers is probably the work students have used it to produce. I was unwilling to assign "using the project" to students until the project itself had achieved a kind of critical mass of data and display for them to use, so I only have written evidence from one class, in the Spring term 2019. Halfway through that semester I asked the thirty-four students in ENAM 3214 to start with something that interested or perplexed them—a question of their own about any or all the Faulkner works we had read—and then see what kind of help the project could give them in answering it. I provided some examples to demystify the assignment, but stressed that they could ask any kind of question and use any aspect of the project. As I waited to see their responses, I'll confess I had none of the naïve confidence I'd had two decades earlier, when I gave the students in that Twain seminar my very first DH assignment. It turned out that several students had asked good questions that were nonetheless not well suited to the kinds of research the project can help with; these usually focused on individual characters. On principle I was glad to have their help seeing where critical inquisitiveness bumps up against the limits of the project, but there was nothing theoretical about my pleasure in reading most of the (illustrated!) assignments that the other students submitted. Their ability to navigate the project and to make it respond to their own interpretive queries about issues like race and gender or narrative technique well exceeded my expectations. In 2020 we began to create the pedagogy section we had long envisioned for DY; under this new "Teaching & Learning" heading you can see eight examples of the reports they wrote (https://faulkner.drupal.shanti.virginia.edu/content/swhomepage). I have to admit, however, that this test lacked one of the basic elements of any well-designed experiment: a control group. I can't tell you whether in the end the time and effort students invested in learning to use DY would have been spent just as if not more valuably in conducting more conventional forms of research—in reading secondary sources, or in rereading Faulkner.

The project is still very much a work in progress. One of the directions in which we are most anxious to take it is toward the classroom. We have already been trying to provide teachers and students with suggestions about how they might use DY to enrich the experience of reading and studying Faulkner, through annual presentations at the Faulkner and Yoknapatawpha Conference and at other venues, and in essays in the *Teaching Faulkner Newsletter* published by the Center for Faulkner Studies (https://semo.edu/cfs/teaching/index.html). While we have sought to make every function of the project as intuitive to use as possible, we recognize that even as classroom spaces become technologically more sophisticated and digital resources proliferate online, teachers have no more time than before. We owe them as much guidance as possible about efficient and appropriate ways they can use the project as a means toward their own pedagogic goals. On the other hand, it's likely that their students will find the challenges of navigating DY less daunting than the demands of Faulkner's fiction. Twenty-first-century students have certainly had a lot more practice with electronic technology than with modern literature. That was probably the aspect of DH that appealed to me most strongly when I started: the opportunity it affords to meet students where they already are so much of the time, online and in front of a screen rather than a book. For me, however, DH is always a means rather than an end; books remain the destination. This is central to the project too: from the first we have worked diligently to make sure that DY could never serve as a substitute for reading Faulkner—or as we put it in our unwritten mission statement, could never enable a student who hadn't done the reading to pass a reading quiz. Although we all know the many alarms that have been raised about the deleterious effects of the new technology on the next generation, to me the new technology is more promising than threatening. Beyond just grabbing our students' attention, it might be a way to engage their curiosity and intelligence. It might be a way to lead them back to the experience of reading, with an enhanced ability to explore and appreciate what they will find when they open the books we believe in as fundamental parts of their education and our evolving culture. If I knew that was happening, I'd have the result of our experiment. In the meanwhile, we'll keep working on it.

Acknowledgments

These are the Credits pages for the DH projects discussed in the essay:

http://twain.lib.virginia.edu/about/acknowl.html
http://utc.iath.virginia.edu/credits.html
http://twain.lib.virginia.edu/absalom/creditshp.html
https://faulkner.lib.virginia.edu/page%3Fid=about&section=credits.html
http://faulkner.iath.virginia.edu/family/credits.php

CONTRIBUTORS

JOHANNES BURGERS is an Assistant Professor of English and Digital Humanities at Ashoka University and Associate Director of Digital Yoknapatawpha. His research focuses on the intersections between transnational modernism, racial theories, sexology, and aesthetics. More recently, he has been writing on "fuzzy" data visualization and the spatialization of modernist narratives using GIS systems and techniques. His work for the project includes creating visualizations that provide new views into Faulkner's world. He has a series of forthcoming essays on the implications of these visualizations for Faulkner studies and the digital humanities more generally.

JOHN MICHAEL CORRIGAN is an Associate Professor at National Chengchi University in Taiwan. His books include *American Metempsychosis* (Fordham, 2012) and *Romantic Legacies* (Routledge, 2019), and he is a Senior Collaborating Editor for Digital Yoknapatawpha.

REN DENTON is the Director of the Center for Excellence in Teaching and Learning and an Associate Professor of English at East Georgia State College. A Collaborating Editor for Digital Yoknapatawpha, she has published articles on narrative aesthetics, Faulkner, and African American literature. Her research focuses on the power dynamics that play out in African American literature and southern literature. She also serves as an Executive Committee Member for the South Atlantic Modern Language Association, and she has completed a book-length project about voodoo aesthetics for McFarland Publishers.

JENNIE JOINER, a Senior Collaborating Editor for Digital Yoknapatawpha, is Professor of English at Keuka College in upstate New York, where she teaches American literature courses grounded in studies of place and geography. Her publications include articles on Faulkner in the *Faulkner Journal*, *Mississippi Quarterly*, and the *Flannery O'Connor Review*.

ERIN PENNER is an Associate Professor of English at Asbury University. Her first book, *Character and Mourning: Woolf, Faulkner, and the Novel Elegy of the First World War*, was recently published by the University of Virginia Press.

She has written on Faulkner for *Studies in the Novel, African American Review,* and *Mississippi Quarterly.* She is a Senior Collaborating Editor for Digital Yoknapatawpha.

STEPHEN RAILTON is Emeritus Professor of English at the University of Virginia and creator of Digital Yoknapatawpha. In addition to publishing widely on American literature, he has been at the forefront of developing digital humanities initiatives since the mid-1990s. His web projects include Mark Twain in His Times, *Uncle Tom's Cabin* & American Culture, and two other Faulkner projects: *Absalom, Absalom!* An Electronic Chronology and Faulkner at Virginia: An Audio Archive.

CHRISTOPHER RIEGER, a Senior Collaborating Editor for Digital Yoknapatawpha, is Professor of English at Southeast Missouri State University, where he directs the Center for Faulkner Studies. He is the author of *Clear-Cutting Eden: Ecology and the Pastoral in Southern Literature* (University of Alabama Press, 2009) and the coeditor of the Southeast Missouri State University Press essay collections *Faulkner and Chopin* (2010), *Faulkner and Morrison* (2013), *Faulkner and Warren* (2015), *Faulkner and Hurston* (2016), and *Faulkner and Hemingway* (2018). He has also published essays and presented conference papers on Ernest Gaines, Daniel Woodrell, Larry Brown, Mo Yan, and Karen Russell.

BEN ROBBINS, a Senior Collaborating Editor for Digital Yoknapatawpha, is an Assistant Professor in the Department for American Studies at the University of Innsbruck (Austria). His work on Faulkner, modernism, popular culture, and gender studies has appeared in the *Journal of Screenwriting,* the *Faulkner Journal,* and *Genre.* His piece on Faulkner and the digital humanities, which was published in *Studies in American Culture,* received the Jerome Stern Award for the best article in the journal in 2016. He has been a Visiting Fellow at both the University of Virginia and l'École des Hautes Études en Sciences Sociales in Paris.

MELANIE BENSON TAYLOR is Professor of Native American Studies at Dartmouth College. She is the author of *Disturbing Calculations: The Economics of Identity in Postcolonial Southern Literature, 1912–2002* (University of Georgia Press, 2008), *Reconstructing the Native South: American Indian Literature and the Lost Cause* (University of Georgia Press, 2012), and *The Indian in American Southern Literature* (Cambridge University Press, 2020). She also edited

The Cambridge History of Native American Literature (Cambridge University Press, 2020) and a Norton Critical Edition of Faulkner's *Light in August* (forthcoming, 2022). She currently serves as Executive Editor of *Native South*.

THERESA M. TOWNER is the Ashbel Smith Professor of Literary Studies at the University of Texas at Dallas and Associate Director of Digital Yoknapatawpha. She is former coeditor of the *Faulkner Journal*. Her publications include *Faulkner on the Color Line: The Later Novels* (University Press of Mississippi, 2000), *Reading Faulkner: Collected Stories* (with James B. Carothers; University Press of Mississippi, 2006), and *The Cambridge Introduction to William Faulkner* (Cambridge University Press, 2008).

LORIE WATKINS is Professor of English at William Carey University and a Senior Collaborating Editor for Digital Yoknapatawpha. Her publications include *A Literary History of Mississippi* (University Press of Mississippi, 2017) and *William Faulkner, Gavin Stevens, and the Cavalier Tradition* (Peter Lang, 2011).

INDEX

Absalom, Absalom!, 2, 5–6, 35, 160, 200
"Ad Astra," 36, 60
Allen, Chadwick, 154
"All the Dead Pilots," 36
Alvarado, Rafael, 126–27, 147
American Mercury, 176
"Appendix Compson 1699–1945," 4, 157
As I Lay Dying, 35, 43–47, 160, 178, 179

"Barn Burning," 15, 179, 183–84
Barnes, Djuna, 100
Beckert, Sven, 162–63
Bellanca, James, 174
Berlin, James, 182
Best, Stephen, 98–99
"Beyond," 70
Bhabha, Homi, 167n9
Bjork, Olin, 172
Blotner, Joseph, 201
Brandt, Ron, 174
Brooks, Cleanth, 52
Bryan, Victoria, 182
Burgers, Johannes, 81, 113
Burton, Stacy, 112
Byars-Nichols, Keely, 156
Byrd, Jodi, 164

Carson, James Taylor, 155
Caruth, Cathy, 95
Cassity, Maxwell, 65
"Centaur in Brass," 74
Chomsky, Aviva, 152
civil rights, 186
class, 16–17, 19, 20–25, 179
Cobb, James, 184
Colvin, Christina, 144
Connolly, Thomas, 53
Corrigan, John Michael, 39–40, 41–42

Cowley, Malcolm, 4, 104–6, 111
Cresswell, Tim, 37–38, 43

Dabney, Lewis, 157
D'Alessandro, Michael, 158–59
Davis, Barbara Gross, 175
Davis, Thadious, 107, 184
"Death Drag," 21
demographics, 25–29
Desan, Christine, 162–63
Dilworth, Thomas, 76
Dore, Florence W., 94
Doyle, Don, 157, 158
Drucker, Johanna, 100
"Dry September," 17–18, 185–86
Duck, Leigh Ann, 154

Eliot, T. S., 141–42, 146–47

Falkner, Murry, 167n11
Fargnoli, A. Nicholas, 53
Faulkner, William: audio, 201–2; cartography, 2, 14, 15, 21, 34–36, 43–44, 54, 73–74, 79, 204; manuscripts, 78, 179–80
Fink, L. Dee, 177–78, 178–79, 185
Flags in the Dust, 86, 91–92, 206–8
Fludernik, Monika, 86
Forbes, Jack, 156
Ford, Margaret Patricia, 52

Galloway, Patricia, 157–58
gender, 22–25, 57, 58–60, 88–90, 101n3
Gidley, Ben, 155
Gidley, Mick, 155
Giroux, Henry, 171
Go Down, Moses, 13, 15, 47–48, 114, 133, 157, 158, 208

Golay, Michael, 53
Gordon, Caroline, 155
Grace, Meghan, 177, 184–85
Graeber, David, 162
Great Migration, 121
Green, Michael, 155
Greeson, Jennifer, 154
Gwynn, Frederick, 201

Hagood, Taylor, 72
Hamblin, Robert W., 52, 53
Hamlet, The, 4, 13, 15, 28, 36, 48, 133
Handy, W. C., 176
Hannon, Charles, 131
Herman, David, 92–93
Hirsch, Brett, 171
Holland, Sharon, 156
Hönnighausen, Lothar, 157
Horsford, Howard, 157
Howe, Irving, 93–94
Howell, Elmo, 158

I'll Take My Stand, 156
Innocents Abroad, The (Twain), 194–95
Intruder in the Dust, 74, 120–21, 186
Isherwood, Christopher, 100

Jackson, Shona, 156
Johnson, Willard, 156
Joiner, Jennie, 15
Joyce, James, 100

Kacee, Cynthia, 153
Katz, William Loren, 156
keywords, 73
Kincaid, Suzanne, 52
Kinney, Arthur, 157
Kirk, Robert W., 52–53
Knight's Gambit, 71, 72, 78

Lalande, Aude, 160
Lang, James, 178
Lester, Cheryl, 105, 106, 110

Light in August, 22, 71, 85–86, 116–17, 165, 204

Mansion, The, 25, 145
Marcus, Susan, 98–99
Matthews, John T., 94, 116, 159–60, 167n14
McAdams, Janet, 153–54
Meriwether, James B., 107
Michaels, Walter Benn, 158
Miles, Tiya, 156
Minges, Patrick, 156
"Mississippi," 157, 159
Mississippi, University of, 48–49
Momaday, N. Scott, 153
Moore, MariJo, 153
Moretti, Franco, 97, 148
Morgan, Patrick Carroll, 164
Morrison, Spencer, 167n14
Morrison, Toni, 20
"Mule in the Yard," 51

narratology, 85–87, 93–99, 101n3
Native South, 153
Noble, Safiya, 172–73

O'Brien, Jean, 152
Oxford, Mississippi, 48–49, 117

Parker, Robert Dale, 157, 158
Pederson, Joshua, 95
Peek, Charles A., 52
Penner, Erin, 70
Perdue, Theda, 155
Portable Faulkner, The, 4, 104–6, 107
Porter, Carolyn, 145
Powhatan, Rose, 154–55

race, 17–18, 19, 21–25, 27–28, 54–57, 58–60, 114, 152–53, 156, 165, 173–74
Railton, Stephen, 35, 46, 48, 70, 71, 73, 77, 78, 79, 110, 112
"Red Leaves," 158
Reivers, The, 21, 23

Requiem for a Nun, 157, 160–62, 163
Rieger, Christopher, 35, 48
Robbins, Ben, 123n8
Roberts, Diane, 89
Romine, Scott, 154
"Rose for Emily, A," 36, 76, 179, 181–82
Runyan, Harry, 52

Sanctuary, 3, 17, 36, 160
Sciuto, Jenna Grace, 75
Seemiller, Corey, 177, 184–85
segregation, 17–18, 203
Sexton, Jared, 155
Simon, Roger, 171
Smith, Hal, 200
Snyder, Christina, 156
Sontag, Susan, 98
Sound and the Fury, The, 12–13, 18, 35, 36, 62–63, 72, 76–77, 107–9, 157, 209
Squint, Kirstin, 164
Stowe, Harriet Beecher, 196
systems theory, 128–30

Tallbear, Kim, 156
"Tall Men, The," 72, 80–81
Tate, Allen, 155
Tayac, Gabrielle, 156
"That Evening Sun," 173–75, 176, 177

Thompson, Shirley Elizabeth, 154
Town, The, 1, 15, 25, 28, 48, 70, 74, 145, 159–60
Towner, Theresa M., 70, 81, 94
trauma theory, 94–95, 99
Trefzer, Annette, 158
Twain, Mark, 194–96
"Two Soldiers," 78–79

Uncle Tom's Cabin (Stowe), 196–99
University of Mississippi, 48–49
Unvanquished, The, 38–43, 48, 56, 116
Urgo, Joseph R., 106

Volpe, Edmond L., 3, 52

Wainwright, Michael, 71, 159
Warren, Wendy, 162
"Wash," 25, 179–81
Wasson, Ben, 167n11
Watkins, Lorie, 149
Welty, Eudora, 155
Wilson, Benjamin, 160
Winston, Jay, 158
Woloch, Alex, 148

Young, Stark, 155

www.ingramcontent.com/pod-product-compliance
Lightning Source LLC
Chambersburg PA
CBHW030621230426
43661CB00053B/2095